Sarah Shatz

Eyal Press is a freelance writer based in New York. His work has appeared in *The New York Times Magazine*, *The Atlantic*, *Mother Jones*, the *Los Angeles Times*, *The Boston Globe*, and numerous other publications. He is a contributing writer to *The Nation* and a former contributing editor at the award-winning magazine *Lingua Franca*. He was a finalist for the J. Anthony Lukas Work-in-Progress Award and has received numerous journalism prizes, including the Science in Society Journalism Award from the National Association of Science Writers and the James Aronson Award for Social Justice Journalism.

Additional Praise for *Absolute Convictions*

"Riveting . . . The great strength of this fine book is that it successfully presents twin narratives: a clear-eyed journalistic look at the evolution of a movement . . . and the story of a son coming into an adult's understanding of his father."
— *Forward*

"What Eyal Press does with his profiles of antiabortion leaders — and his portrayal of their movement as a whole — is something that many other journalists seem to have forgotten is not only possible, but necessary: He is both entirely fair *and* appropriately damning."
— *Salon.com*

"A gripping and elegantly written combination of memoir, history, and social commentary on one of the most divisive issues in America."
— *The American Prospect*

"A scrupulous reporter . . . Deftly integrating personal and social history, Press junior chronicles his father's path to accidental heroism. . . . An absorbing narrative."
— *The Village Voice*

"This is recent history at its most powerful and its most moving. Press follows the fortunes of his beloved hometown as it passes through good times and bad, through deindustrialization and blight, and, finally, as it descends into the angry futility of the movement to oppose abortion. The costs and casualties of our cultural civil war are nowhere rendered as starkly."
— Thomas Frank, author of
What's the Matter with Kansas?:
How Conservatives Won the Heart of America

"Press, a journalist with an impressive propensity for investigation, goes beyond simple memoir to search for the tipping point between moral rhetoric and cold-blooded murder."
— *Mother Jones*

"The functional lesson that can be taken from Press's extremely helpful and concise histories of both movements is a lesson in responsibility. It's a story of how those who should have known better stood aside while the reckless and heedless polluted a difficult civic discussion with the histrionic language of incitement." —*Los Angeles Times Book Review*

"Eyal Press's *Absolute Convictions* is an invaluable contribution to understanding the vast and persistent divide over abortion. Reporting from the ground up, Press incisively and compellingly examines why and how opponents of abortion turned toward violence—and why and how in the face of that violence individuals like his father have stood firm for what they believe." —Alex Kotlowitz, author of
*There Are No Children Here: The Story of Two Boys
Growing Up in The Other America*

"This compelling book offers a personal and multilayered perspective on all sides of the abortion debate." —*Booklist*

"*Absolute Convictions* provides a remarkable new view on a familiar and embattled topic. Eyal Press's description of the drama that engulfed his family and town is both vivid and compassionate, and it helps explain what it would take to resolve America's abortion wars."
—James Fallows, author of *Blind into Baghdad: America's War in Iraq*

ABSOLUTE
CONVICTIONS

My Father, a City,
and the Conflict
That Divided America

■

EYAL PRESS

Picador

Henry Holt and Company
New York

www.picadorusa.com

Picador® is a U.S. registered trademark and is used by Henry Holt and Company under license from Pan Books Limited.

For information on Picador Reading Group Guides, as well as ordering, please contact Picador.
Phone: 646-307-5629
Fax: 212-253-9627
E-mail: readinggroupguides@picadorusa.com

Designed by Victoria Hartman

Map by David Lindroth Inc.

Library of Congress-in-Publication Data

Press, Eyal.
    Absolute convictions : my father, a city, and the conflict that divided America / Eyal Press.
        p. cm.
    Includes bibliographical references and index.
    ISBN-13: 978-0-312-42657-6
    ISBN-10: 0-312-42657-7
    1. Abortion—United States.   2. Press, Shalom, 1940–   3. Physicians—United States—Attitudes.   4. Abortion services—New York—Buffalo.   5. Pro-life movement—United States.   6. Pro-choice movement—United States.   7. Political violence—New York—Buffalo.   8. Abortion—Social aspects—United States.   I. Title.

HQ767.5.U5P735 2006
363.4609747'97—dc22

                                                                                    2005034064

First published in the United States by Henry Holt and Company

First Picador Edition: March 2007

10 9 8 7 6 5 4 3 2 1

In memory of my grandparents
Rosa, Albert, Shoshanah, and Benjamin

Contents

Prologue

On October 23, 1998, at around eleven P.M., the phone rang at my parents' home. It was Linda Stadler, my father's office manager. Linda didn't normally call at that hour, but she'd just heard something startling. According to a report on the local news, roughly an hour earlier a shooting had taken place at 187 Roxbury Park Road, a quiet, tree-lined street in the Buffalo suburb of Amherst. That address belonged to Dr. Barnett Slepian, a colleague and longtime acquaintance of my father's. Like my father, Dr. Slepian was an obstetric gynecologist who devoted part of his practice to performing abortions.

My father thought Linda was joking at first. After hanging up the phone, he heard the doorbell ring. He ambled downstairs in his pajamas. It was a detective from the Amherst police department. The detective confirmed that a shooting had occurred, but that wasn't the main purpose of his visit. He'd come to make sure there had been only one attack that night, since the whereabouts of the assailant were unknown.

I found out about Dr. Slepian's murder the following morning, after having breakfast with an old friend from college. I was living in Brooklyn at the time. It was a beautiful fall morning, the sun shimmering off the roofs of the brownstones, the sky blue. When I heard the news, my heart stopped. I'd like to say the first thing I felt was anguish and sympathy for the Slepian family—a wife who had just lost her husband, four sons who'd watched their father bleed to death on their kitchen floor. But my initial reaction was more selfish. What I felt at first was fear: that the murder might upend my parents' lives; that the perpetrator was still on the loose and might repeat the act.

I went to a pay phone to call my parents. My mother answered. Her voice was muted, the way it often is when she has something somber to report. She told me she had spoken to Dr. Slepian only hours before his death. He had called our house the previous night because that weekend, as on every third weekend of the month, he was scheduled to cover deliveries for my father. Afterward, my mother set about preparing dinner while Dr. Slepian headed off to temple with his wife to attend a service commemorating the death of his father. When he got home, after he had emptied his keys, pager, and wallet from his pocket and put a bowl of soup in the microwave, a bullet struck him in the back. It was fired from a Russian-made SKS semiautomatic assault rifle, a full-metal jacketed slug that pierced a double-paned window, shattered Dr. Slepian's spine, tore through his chest cavity, and exited beneath his armpit. The bullet then struck a wall and ricocheted into the family room, just missing Dr. Slepian's fifteen-year-old son Andrew, who was watching an ice hockey game on television.

I called my sister, who was as stunned as I was. "It's scary; these people have a list!" she said. It would not be the last time I would hear this phrase. A few days after the murder, I flew back to Buffalo. Two days later, the phone rang again at my parents' home. Again my mother answered.

"Death threat?" I heard her say. "Death threat? . . . Excuse me, you'll have to speak with my son."

Her hand shook as she passed me the phone. It was a detective from the Amherst police, calling to inform us that a newspaper in Hamilton, Ontario, had just received an anonymous threat that my father was "next on the list."

"Our cousins in the U.S. have their list. We have ours," warned the caller.

The following morning, the story that another doctor had received a death threat was splashed across the headlines of *The Buffalo News*. By week's end, my parents were living under twenty-four-hour protection by federal marshals. Their two-story house in the suburbs was converted into a fortress: cameras on every corner, the shades drawn, an armed guard out front. The search for Dr. Slepian's assassin, which would lead to the arrest nearly three years later of a thin, red-haired man named James Charles Kopp, had begun.

THIS IS THE story of the abortion wars that racked the city of Buffalo, New York, for nearly two decades and culminated with a murder that left in its wake one local doctor who performed abortions at his office: my father. A murder that provoked a typically polarized set of reactions—some wept and attended candlelight vigils; others suggested that Dr. Slepian had gotten exactly what he deserved—and that in an eerie way symbolized where, a quarter century after *Roe v. Wade*, the struggle over abortion stood.

It is a peculiarly American story, for while many Western countries have legalized abortion in recent decades, only in the United States has the issue sparked turmoil and violence on such a scale. To outsiders, it may seem bizarre that such a fuss could be raised about what many people view simply as a medical procedure, and an extremely common one at that. Yet in the world of American politics, abortion has always been much more than this. It is a symbol: of liberation and empowerment to some, of spiritual and moral degeneration to others. It is also a prism through which debates about sex and gender, religion and politics, and (less overtly but no less unmistakably) race and class have long played out. How those debates unfolded on the streets of Buffalo can tell us a lot about the nature of American politics in recent decades: the passions that drive it, the contradictions that riddle it, the cultural divisions that cleave it as sharply as any economic or racial lines do. More than three decades after it was introduced, the right to choose enshrined in *Roe*—not a choice, but *murder*, to those who believe life begins at the moment of conception—remains as bitterly contested as ever. Whether it may one day in the near future be discarded remains of immense concern: to those who have fought for years to see this happen, to those who shudder at the thought, to several generations of women who have grown up taking the legality of abortion for granted.

The murder of Barnett Slepian was not the first time abortion thrust Buffalo into the nation's headlines. Six years earlier, in April 1992, the city was the site of the Spring of Life, a campaign of clinic blockades organized by what was then the nation's most powerful grassroots political organization, Operation Rescue. Like the Slepian murder and, later, the trial of James Kopp, the event would temporarily transform Buffalo into ground zero in the culture wars—and draw hordes of demonstrators and reporters to the low-slung medical building where my father worked. By this point, he'd grown accustomed to the attention. Beginning in the mid-1980s, pro-life activists began demonstrating outside his office and those of several other abortion providers in the Buffalo area. By 1988, the year Operation Rescue made its mark on the national stage, sit-ins and occupations had become regular occurrences in Buffalo, some outside the clinic where Dr. Slepian worked, others at my father's office. There were death threats and menacing phone calls. There were mock funerals. There were women who came into my father's office sobbing after being confronted by a protester, and others so furious they exploded in rage. The fact that only a small part of my father's practice was devoted to abortion—most of his work involved providing women with pre- and post-natal care; most of his trips to the hospital were to deliver babies—did little to quell the protesters' rage.

I was in high school when the turbulence began. Driving past my father's office on my way home from school, I saw the protesters huddled outside. I read articles in the paper about the demonstrations and saw reports on television. I don't recall feeling frightened at the time. But I must have internalized some sense of shame and embarrassment, for I never talked about the subject with my friends, even the closest ones. I didn't want them to ask questions, didn't want to draw attention to something that seemed so tense and polarizing.

Still, the turmoil intrigued me. In a nation where politics seemed disconnected from people's lives, here was something that excited genuine passion. Nobody paid the protesters to demonstrate, yet demonstrate they did, rain or shine, day after day, week after week. As alarming as their rhetoric was to me—in particular, the constant accusations that my father was a "murderer" growing rich off abortion (in fact, the unrest it caused placed his entire practice at risk)—their dedication was impressive. In a blue-collar Rust Belt city that watched a staggering number of jobs disappear during the 1970s, no other issue aroused such zeal. In this sense, Buffalo serves as a parable for late-twentieth-century America: a place where issues of morality and culture would come to supersede those of class.

I didn't realize at the time that what was happening in Buffalo closely mirrored national trends. Like most people, I assumed the protests could be chalked up to the fact that the city was heavily Catholic. Yet in western New York, as throughout the country, many of the most committed pro-life activists would turn out to be born-again Protestants. The radicalization of the abortion conflict coincided with the political reawakening of evangelicals and the growth of the Christian right, whose leaders framed abortion as part of a cosmic struggle for the soul of the world's most technologically advanced—but also one of its most religious—countries.

The protesters' embrace of civil disobedience didn't necessarily endear them to the citizens of a law-and-order city like Buffalo. On the eve of the Spring of Life, a poll found that just 6.8 percent of Buffalonians, and 5.5 percent of Catholics, unconditionally welcomed the demonstrators to town. That same poll revealed that 64.4 percent actually described themselves as pro-choice (meaning they believed "a woman should have the right to choose whether to have an abortion"), though many of these respondents also favored parental consent laws and restrictions on late-term abortion. Like the majority of Americans, they saw shades of gray in an issue that was portrayed in stark black-and-white polarities on the barricades.

My father's career has been defined by those polarities. Over its course, he has been called everything from a "baby killer" to a "Jew with a circumcised heart." He has also been told he is a hero. He insists he is none of these things but is simply a physician carrying out what he views as his professional responsibilities, albeit in a context that has forced him to grow accustomed to wearing bulletproof vests over his doctor's scrubs to work. Since 1977, there have been 41 bombings, 172 arson attacks, 655 anthrax threats, hundreds of bomb threats, and countless acts of vandalism directed at abortion clinics in America. There have also been seventeen attempted murders, shootings that, before Dr. Slepian's death, I largely dismissed as a fringe phenomenon.

This was, in retrospect, a form of denial, though I wasn't entirely wrong. The vast majority of Americans who consider themselves pro-life abhor violence. Most view James Kopp as a traitor to their cause. On the other hand, in a movement that defined abortion as murder, that for two decades fought with limited success to overturn *Roe v. Wade* while employing rhetoric that grew increasingly combative, the fact that some activists eventually came to view the shooting of physicians as justified is not so difficult to fathom. It is especially not difficult if viewed in the context of what the writer Andrew Sullivan has termed "our new wars of religion": wars "not of Islam versus Christianity and Judaism" but of "fundamentalism against faiths of all kinds that are at peace with freedom and modernity." In May 2003, nearly five years after Dr. Slepian's murder, I would sit in a packed courtroom in downtown Buffalo and listen to James Kopp, the man who shot him, justify his act on the basis of his Catholic faith. Across the aisle from me sat Lynne Slepian and three of her sons, Philip, Michael, and Brian. Kopp's words may have appalled many peace-loving, law-abiding Catholics, but he was speaking a familiar language—the language of militant fundamentalism, which not infrequently invokes faith as a rationale for violence.

That my father would hear this language surface in, of all places, western New York is highly ironic. He came to Buffalo from Israel, a country where militants who invoke the name of God to justify force have arguably produced more turmoil and bloodshed than anywhere else. How this milieu shaped him holds the key to understanding why the murder of his colleague did not weaken his determination to continue providing abortions but strengthened it. Since I, too, was born in Israel, but did not grow up there, my father's background serves as both a bond and a point of differentiation between us. Nothing more clearly marks me as his son, or more sharply underscores our differences, as when we spar at the dinner table about Israeli politics. Or in the aftermath of Dr. Slepian's murder, when like everyone else in our family I urged my father to put his safety first and stop providing abortions, knowing all the while he would do no such thing.

Between 1992 and 2005, a period when six doctors and clinic workers were shot and killed in the United States, more than 250 hospitals and more than 300 private practitioners stopped performing abortions. As this book goes to press, my father is nearing retirement. When he does so, abortion will remain legally available in Buffalo only because a handful of physicians fly in each week from out of state to staff the clinic where Dr. Slepian once worked.

Naturally, I've thought often about why my father has persisted in doing what so many other doctors in his line of work have given up. I've thought, as well, about what I would do in his shoes. "We spend most of our adulthoods trying to grasp the meaning of our parents' lives," writes Phillip Lopate in *Portrait of My Body*, "and how we shape and answer these questions largely turns us into who we are." My father insists that his decision to remain an abortion provider is not a political act but a function of his professional responsibilities. But are those responsibilities worth the risk to his life? Would I do the same thing in his place? Would he want me to? My father has often insisted that the political member of our family is not him but me: the son with a penchant for turning dinner conversations into heated discourses, the journalist drawn to stories about injustice (so it seems to him). I've happily accepted the label, though I now know better than to believe it. There is a vast difference between writing about divisive political issues and living them out. That is the gap that separates my father and me, and peering across it has made me rethink much that I thought I knew, not only about him but about myself.

To know that one's parents will not live forever—that they are mortal, like everyone else—is part of what it means to become an adult. To imagine they might be targeted by an assassin on account of a commitment to some abstract principle is quite another. Theoretically, such a thing ought to fill one with pride. But who among us would like to see a parent become a martyr? Or, for that matter, become one themselves? As no abstraction could, my father's experience has forced me to think hard about the tension between remaining true to one's convictions and the practical necessity of surviving in the world. This is something that has always fascinated me, perhaps because, as Dr. Slepian's murder would reveal, it touches on a rift within my family: between the defiant Israelis on one side, and those with a vivid memory of surviving the Holocaust on the other. There are strands of both histories in me, which is perhaps why I felt torn between conflicting impulses following Dr. Slepian's death.

I don't know that I'll ever stop being haunted by what happened on the night of October 23, 1998. I do know that, ever since, the compulsion to unravel the threads that coalesced to produce a murder in the city where I grew up has led me to explore questions I suppressed in the past. Doing so has not always been comfortable or easy. Yet it has been necessary to achieve at least a measure of understanding about why events turned out the way they did, and why my father has a place in this story. Being his son may disqualify me from serving as a neutral guide to the conflict at the heart of that story (but is anyone in America completely neutral on the subject of abortion?); it need not prevent me from exploring it in a way that recognizes the sincerity, passion, and fierce moral convictions on both sides. There is no other way to understand why the abortion conflict has assumed such a prominent place in American life for so long, I believe, and why so many people have come to feel deeply invested in it, not least my father himself.

THE STORY BEGINS in 1973, the year a woman named Norma Mc-Corvey won a Supreme Court case that would alter the course of American history, the year my father arrived alone in a city about which he knew virtually nothing.

PART 1

Seeds of
Discord

■

· 1 ·

Jet-lagged and slightly bewildered is how I imagine my father on the morning he first set foot in Buffalo. He arrived by plane from New York City, carrying with him a brown suitcase whose contents — shirts, slacks, socks, and sandals, but no hat, scarf, thermal underwear, or winter boots — betrayed his newness to the place. The suitcase had been packed in Haifa, the sun-drenched city on the coast of northern Israel where my family had been living for the past few years.

It was the second week of February 1973, a bright, cold winter morning, the temperature in the low teens, the streets and sidewalks dusted with snow, which was a novel sight to my father. I was two years old at the time. He was thirty-three, an Israeli emigrant on his first trip to America, his first trip anywhere outside the Middle East.

The photograph in the back of his passport shows a dark-featured man with curly black hair that rises above his forehead in a prominent widow's peak. The hair is thick, the way I remember it from my early childhood. He has his mother's full lips and slightly rounded jowls. The rest of his features—the long oval face, the high sloping forehead, the large ears that protrude slightly outward—are his father's. He's wearing thick black plastic-frame glasses, the kind that were fashionable among college students during the Kennedy era, and he's gazing at the camera with an earnest self-consciousness. There is a gentleness in his expression, a softness about the lips and mouth that hints at his shyness and emotional reserve. He is a native-born Israeli, a Sabra—tough on the outside, tender on the inside, like the popular Middle Eastern prickly pear from which the expression derives. Yet in the photo my pale-skinned father looks less Middle Eastern than East European, which is indeed where his family's roots can be traced. He is a soft-spoken man with a subdued, humble manner. Only his thick Israeli accent would have provided a clue to his background. That and his brown eyes, which are fixed and steady, and strain to look calmly on a world he has never known to be lacking in danger.

My father had come to Buffalo to begin a three-year residency in obstetrics and gynecology. Three weeks earlier, on January 22, 1973, the U.S. Supreme Court handed down a decision in a case pitting the district attorney of Dallas, Texas, Henry Wade, against a pregnant woman, Norma McCorvey (a.k.a. Jane Roe), seeking an abortion there. The 7–2 ruling, joined by the Court's only Catholic, Justice William J. Brennan, and written by a Nixon appointee, Harry A. Blackmun, overturned the Texas ban on abortion and legalized the procedure throughout the United States.

MY FATHER HAD never heard of *Roe v. Wade,* and if someone had warned him then that he might one day find himself enmeshed in a controversy that a court case would unleash, he would have found the idea preposterous. He was in Buffalo to complete his professional training, after all, not to advance a social cause. In coming to America, moreover, he assumed that he was temporarily leaving a war-torn, polarized environment, not entering one.

The oldest son of a Polish father and Ukrainian mother who met and married in Palestine, my father was born in January 1940 in Hadassah Hospital, on Mount Scopus, in Jerusalem. Israel did not exist in the year of his birth—the territory stretching between the Jordan River and the Mediterranean Sea was ruled by Great Britain—but his parents nevertheless gave him a Hebrew name: Shalom. This was the name of his maternal grandfather, the Hebrew word for "hello," "goodbye," and "peace."

"For a century, life in Palestine, then in Israel, swung between terrorism and war and war and terrorism," the historian Tom Segev has written. This is the world in which my father grew up. As a child, he played soccer on streets strewn with artillery shells, in the shadow of buildings pockmarked with bullet holes. On May 14, 1948, a few months past his eighth birthday, the State of Israel declared its independence. The next day, the regular armies of Syria, Iraq, Lebanon, Transjordan, and Egypt invaded the country. In Jerusalem, fierce battles broke out between the Israeli Haganah and the Arab Legion. At the time, my father was living with his parents and younger brother in an apartment building perched atop a hillside in Rehavia, a neighborhood in West Jerusalem. One night during the war, he awoke to the sound of explosions—*pop, pop, pop.* A sniper had just fired several bullets through an open window into my grandparents' apartment. The bullets sailed directly above the area where my father and his brother normally slept, one piercing a closet door, another tearing a thumb-sized hole through the breast pockets of my grandfather's dress shirts. The children had been moved into an adjoining room as a precaution.

The 1948 Independence War ended victoriously for Israel, but not before six thousand Israelis died, 1 percent of the Jewish population, and seven hundred thousand Palestinians were driven from their homes. (Palestinians would mark the 1948 war with a different name: al-Nakba, the Catastrophe.) There would be more wars—the 1956 Suez Crisis, the 1967 Six Day War—and between them the constant skirmishes born of the conflicting claims of two competing nationalist movements for the same narrow strip of land. The Israeli novelist Amos Oz, who was born one year before my father, told the journalist David Remnick that "for people in the West history is something that comes across the television screen," whereas in Israel, for his generation, it was experienced with a direct, palpable immediacy. Like Oz, my young father crossed paths with few people who didn't know someone who had either been killed or wounded in uniform. He woke up each morning to news of the latest "incident": a border clash here, a bombing there. The hills surrounding his parents' home in Jerusalem were, like much of Israel, not just places but battlefields, drenched in history and blood.

I imagine growing up in such a place and wanting desperately to flee. Yet if my father felt this impulse, he has never expressed it to me. What he has expressed is the thrill and excitement of having lived through an exhilarating, if precarious, time. All around him, a nation was being born, a Jewish state formed on the heels of the United Nations 1947 partition plan of Palestine. There was, of course, a pall of gloom hovering over Israel, and not just on account of its tense relations with its neighbors. Most of Israel's Russian and East European founders had lost relatives, sometimes their entire families, to the Holocaust. The sunken-faced survivors who streamed into Israel after its creation, among them the grandparents, great-aunts, and great-uncles on the other side of my family, came with deeply haunted memories. For my father, however, this collective trauma was overshadowed by a story of redemption. He belonged to the generation expected to fulfill the dreams of Israel's founding fathers, the *halutzim* (pioneers) who fled Europe so their children and grandchildren could grow up free and independent.

My father did not have to search hard for a role model who fit into this category. His own father, Benjamin Press, hailed from Bialystok, a city that was then nestled in the Russian Pale of Settlement but is today a part of Poland, and that, in 1905, the year he was born, was home to a sprawling Jewish community. The Bialystok of my grandfather's youth had an array of Jewish shops, businesses, and synagogues, and even a kindergarten where Hebrew was taught. But it was also, like much of turn-of-the-century Russia and Eastern Europe, awash in anti-Semitism. In 1906, a pogrom in Bialystok left seventy Jews dead. A decade later, in 1917, another wave of pogroms throughout Russia began. Everywhere a young man like my grandfather might have looked—the Balkans, Romania, Lithuania—discrimination against Jews was ubiquitous. A cousin of his did manage to escape, settling with his family in Paterson, New Jersey; they sent papers to Bialystok so my grandfather could join them. By the time the papers arrived, however, he had decided on another course, entering the socialist wing of the movement that had gained a growing following among the young Jews of Bialystok: Zionism.

My grandfather was a baker's son with thick dark hair, an iron constitution, and the nerve to say good-bye to his family and trek off to Palestine in 1927, alone. He arrived in a land of arid hills and olive groves where, soon, fierce tensions would erupt between the indigenous Palestinians and the incoming Jews. On the other hand, it beat staying in Bialystok, where, during the course of World War II, nearly 50,000 Jews, including my grandfather's brother, were killed or deported to concentration camps (where they met the same fate). While fascism swept across Europe, my grandfather found a job in a bakery in Jerusalem. When the workers there decided to form a union, they chose him as their representative. He soon became a leader in the Histadrut, the confederation of Zionist trade unions. After World War II broke out, he joined the Jewish Brigade, a unit of the British army, serving four years, two on the European front.

My father still remembers the day his father returned home from World War II, a stranger in a uniform greeting the dark-eyed son he'd barely seen since his birth. He grew up under the gaze of this man, whose force and attraction I would one day also feel. When I was growing up my grandfather was a Solomonic figure to me, a white-haired patriarch who would take me along on walks through the winding streets of Jerusalem during our summer visits to Israel. He must have been in his seventies by then, but he seemed indestructible, and nobody could have convinced me he wouldn't live forever. I was his *neched* (grandson), he would tell the stream of acquaintances who stopped to talk to him, and when they pointed out the resemblance between us, I'd feel my pride well up. My grandfather: a man of consequence, a former government official on personal terms with people like Yitzhak Rabin and Golda Meir, whom he'd gotten to know while working in the Israeli Department of Labor.

Actually my grandfather was not the towering public figure I imagined him to be. A success story in our family, he was an unassuming man who spent most of his career as a mid-level bureaucrat, shunning suggestions that he aspire to bigger things by running for office. Yet this did not diminish his stature in my eyes or the size of the shadow he cast over my father, who to this day tends to speak about his father less as a person than an ideal: a Labor Zionist who devoted his life to a noble cause. An arrow-straight civil servant who never drank or smoked, who continued representing workers in the Israeli labor movement long after he'd retired and who, at age eighty, was awarded a golden pin in honor of a lifetime of public service in Jerusalem. From him, my father would inherit the same brisk-paced walk, the same reserved demeanor, the same interest in politics, and the same combination of outward humility and inner pride.

My father's was a typical Israeli childhood, which is to say, not the kind western Jews often envision when imagining the open-shirted offspring of the Zionist revolution. "They love the land," Chaim Weizmann, Israel's first president, proclaimed in a letter to his wife of the young Jews settling Palestine. Maybe so, but like most Israelis he knew, my father grew up in a city, not on a *moshav* or a kibbutz. Most of his friends were Ashkenazi Jews whose parents were teachers, government workers, engineers, professors—the educated European elite who would dominate Israeli culture and politics for the nation's first three decades. These people were not hardy agrarian pioneers and their children, if my father is any measure, were more likely to be found bent over a book than on a tractor. As the son of parents who were both gainfully employed—my grandmother Shoshanah was a nurse—and who did not bear camp tattoos on their arms, my father was comparatively privileged, if hardly spoiled by American standards. The rooms in my grandparents' apartment on Balfour Street, in West Jerusalem, were plainly furnished, the laundry washed by hand and hung to dry on clotheslines, the kitchen a small cubicle where not even a crust of bread was wasted—a reflection of my grandparents' Spartan values and humble roots. To further imbue him with the egalitarian ideals of Labor Zionism, my father was sent to a youth group associated with the left-leaning United Labor Party. Each year he went to May Day parades saluting the virtues of Israel's workers. He would eventually come to argue with his father about the virtues of socialism, about which he was an early skeptic, but, as with many Jewish fathers and sons—including, one day, him and me—these occasionally heated tussles served mainly to deepen their bond.

It was an upbringing steeped in politics, in a society where the choices available to most young people were significantly narrower than those of the typical American. If the United States was the land of opportunity and self-invention, Israel was a land of duty—duty to family, to state, to the army. "In those days," recalls the Israeli writer Yaron Ezrahi in his book *Rubber Bullets*, "it was extraordinarily difficult and rare for a young Israeli to express ambivalence toward the demands for sacrifice in the struggle for security and independence which almost the entire society took for granted." As the stoic son of stoic parents who, like most Israelis, prided themselves on weathering life's challenges with steely resolve, my father would express no such ambivalence. A bomb went off in a nearby market? You shopped there the next day as though nothing had happened. War loomed on the horizon? You went about your business just the same. On walks with my grandfather, we'd often stop at the Supersol to buy groceries—olives, cucumbers, tomatoes, pita bread so fresh the plastic bags filled with steam—and invariably have our belongings searched, in case someone was planning to smuggle in a *ptsatsah*, a bomb, that day. Not infrequently during our summer visits, a nearby explosion would rattle my grandparents' walls. Each time, it startled me. My father? Never. This strong-willed Israeli mentality was drilled into him from an early age, and while I know that in theory he would have preferred never having to deal with such things, I can't help but wonder if a part of him didn't welcome the opportunity to face (and pass) a test of his resolve in a nation where, as Amos Elon has written, the burden of living dangerously was not merely a necessity but "almost a canon of existence."

Before me is a photograph of my father shortly after he entered the Israel Defense Forces. He is sitting on a terrace with the sun to his back, the light slanting in at a low angle. He's dressed in a dark green army uniform and a matching hat with Hebrew lettering. "Chael Reglayim" ("infantry") the lettering reads. He's smiling in a way that makes his eyes pinch half-shut (a trait I've inherited), a neatly trimmed mustache on his otherwise still-boyish face. He looks relaxed and comfortable, a glimmer of pride, even cockiness, in his gaze. It is a portrait from a more innocent time, before events such as the Lebanon war and the Palestinian Intifida would diminish the luster associated with that uniform. For my father's generation, the event that cast a shadow over military service was not the Intifida but the Holocaust. How could a self-respecting people have allowed six million Jews to die without even their dignity intact? *Never again*, young Israelis were taught, not because the world had become a less dangerous place but because Jews would no longer play the role of hapless victims. Serving in the army was not only obligatory in Israel. It was also a rite of passage on the road to embodying a new kind of Jew: the intrepid citizen-soldier, a gun slung over the shoulder, a pair of sunglasses perched on the bridge of the nose.

As a slender, five-foot-five-inch teenager, my father did not exactly fit the image. Yet the raw-boned kid in the army photo would go on to serve as a lieutenant and, in a story I would hear during my own upbringing, teach Paul Newman how to hold and fire a submachine gun during the filming of a scene in the movie *Exodus*. He would avoid seeing live combat, but only because no wars broke out during the time he was enlisted. Would he have continued serving had something akin to the Lebanon war erupted back then? I have no doubt that he would have. There is a part of me that can't help but see in this the imprisoning sense of duty that the writer Yaron Ezrahi has described, the collectivist ethos that made it nearly impossible for any one person to shake off the bonds of national solidarity. Yet there is another part of me that envies it, that sees in his soldier's gaze not the reflexive obedience of a conformist but the unbending determination of a young man more anchored in his beliefs than most people will ever be.

It is fitting, I suppose, that an incident in the army would play a role in placing my father on the path that would lead him, eventually, to Buffalo. One night during a routine training exercise, a soldier in his platoon was accidentally struck by friendly fire. (The incident would be investigated by a young Israeli colonel named Ariel Sharon.) My father rode in the ambulance with the wounded soldier, watching as a team of surgeons tried, in vain, to stop him from bleeding to death. He'd already been thinking about pursuing a career in medicine. After completing his service, he spent a summer pouring concrete for a construction company. Then, thinking of those surgeons trying to save that soldier's life, he took a set of exams and enrolled at Hebrew University Medical School.

TEN YEARS LATER, after medical school, after he'd met and married my mother, after they'd had two kids and settled down, everything about my father's life still seemed to point to a future in Israel. It was 1972, and my parents were living in Haifa, in a second-floor apartment facing the Mediterranean coast. They'd moved there the previous year, after my father was offered a position as a resident at Rothschild Hospital. He worked in the Department of Obstetrics and Gynecology, the field he'd chosen as his specialty under the tutelage of a popular instructor at Hebrew University who was a gynecologist. It was in many ways an ideal setup—an apartment near the beach, a position at an established hospital, a pleasant city in the northern part of the country. As the months passed, however, my father started to grow frustrated. Doctors in his residency program often weren't trained in basic surgical procedures. The system was rigid and hierarchical. One day, he bumped into a colleague who told him that, if he were smart, he would complete his medical training in the United States, where the standards were superior.

A decade earlier, few Israelis would have considered such a thing: leave the Promised Land for wretched exile? No Zionist worth his salt should have even entertained the thought. Yet in the aftermath of the Six Day War, the idea of a trip abroad, particularly to America, had begun to gather appeal. The United States was now Israel's closest ally, its leading financial and military backer, the bustling superpower with which Israelis increasingly identified. When my father came home that evening, he mentioned his colleague's idea to my mother. The thought of packing two kids and all their possessions onto an airplane didn't thrill her. It was met with even less enthusiasm by my grandfather, who feared that once his son grew comfortable in America, he would find it difficult to leave.

It must have been hard to hear this, but my father was undeterred. At most, he told himself, he would spend a couple of years in America, then return. Was there an element of denial in this? In retrospect, clearly so, but also, I believe, no lack of courage. To chart his own path, he had to be willing to risk disappointing the man he most admired, and to leave the country that he loved. In the fall of 1972, having convinced my mother that no harm could come from seeing what the possibilities were, my father sent off a dozen letters to residency programs in America. The following January, an envelope arrived at my parents' door postmarked Buffalo, New York. The city happened to be hard up for medical residents.

THE STREETS OF Buffalo were quiet on the morning when, a month or so after receiving that letter, my father showed up at Children's Hospital, a tan-brick building on the city's west side. Compared to Israel, where before year's end yet another round in the Arab-Israeli conflict, the 1973 Yom Kippur War, would break out, Buffalo was bound to seem like a model of tranquillity. People moved at a more relaxed pace and didn't follow the news with the same avid, anxious foreboding. There were no daily funerals for soldiers like the ones my mother remembers watching through the window of my parents' old apartment in Jerusalem, wiping away tears as she held my baby sister in her arms. In the halls of

Children's Hospital, my father overheard talk about Valentine's Day, not politics.

And yet, in that very building, something that would one day spark fierce unrest was taking place, and had been ever since July 1, 1970. On that day, nearly three years earlier, Children's and four other local hospitals had begun to perform abortions under a new state law, signed by Governor Nelson Rockefeller in April 1970, that permitted a woman to terminate her pregnancy up until the twenty-fourth week. The law's passage hadn't touched off violence, but neither had it gone over quietly. In the New York State Assembly, the bill to legalize abortion passed by a margin of one vote—this after Assemblyman George M. Michaels, a Democrat from Auburn, a heavily Catholic town in the state's Finger Lakes region, stood up during roll call to announce he would back the measure. Michaels had opposed it earlier, and his dramatic switch brought tears to the eyes of some of the bill's supporters. But not the contingent from Buffalo. Representatives from western New York voted 12–4 *against* legalization. In the Senate, five of the area's six members voted the same way, among them Earl W. Brydges, the majority leader, from Niagara Falls, just north of Buffalo. During the emotional five-hour debate that preceded the Senate vote, Brydges, a devout Catholic and the father of seven children, read from what he described as "The Diary of an Unborn Child." "Today, my parents killed me," he proclaimed, his voice cracking, tears welling in his eyes. Then he stopped. "I'm sorry, Mr. President . . . I cannot read it all." Joining Brydges in opposition was James D. Griffin, a Democrat representing South Buffalo. "I suppose I'm a square," Griffin told his Senate colleagues, "but I see these plans to liberalize abortion as another sign of the permissiveness, the decay of our society."

The sentiment would have resonated in many parts of Buffalo, a blue-collar city thick with bars, churches, factories, and union halls. But, like much of America, Buffalo was undergoing wrenching changes. The same spring that the legislature legalized abortion, the city's residents watched in astonishment as antiwar demonstrations spun out of control on the Main Street campus of the University of Buffalo—a jarring spectacle in a city known for its tight-knit, law-abiding neighborhoods, places where people knew one another by name, often because they worked at the same factories, drank at the same taverns, belonged to the same churches. Jimmy Griffin himself had grown up in the Old First Ward, a neighborhood of modest frame houses where Irish immigrants had first begun settling in the 1840s, back when Buffalo was America's largest inland port, a commercial entrepôt perched at the juncture of Lake Erie and the Erie Canal. In those days, the Irish came mostly to work along the docks, a hard life that required the comfort of a drink and the solace of prayer. In 1848, Pope Pius IX appointed John Timon, an Irishman from Pennsylvania, to head the newly formed Diocese of Western New York. In the decades to come, as new groups of immigrants arrived and settled, they invariably built their own churches, institutions that were as much a part of the landscape as the factories, bars, and snow.

Of course, by the 1970s, much had changed since those first immigrant communities formed. By the time my father arrived in Buffalo, the Catholics who'd once been outsiders constituted the majority. Many had moved out of the old, ethnically bound neighborhoods to places like Hamburg, Cheektowaga, and West Seneca—suburbs that, with the help of federally subsidized highway construction and housing loans, had boomed since World War II. Their children were growing up in a society more open, secular, and socially permissive than Americans who'd come of age during the 1950s could ever have imagined: the America not of Dwight Eisenhower and the Man in the Gray Flannel Suit but of Jimi Hendrix and Janis Joplin. Culturally, it was a nation that had changed more drastically over the past ten years than any time in memory. Was this a good thing? Yes, to many young people; no, to traditionalists like Jimmy Griffin, to many parents, and to the city's Catholic leaders, who for years had watched church attendance in many parishes decline while the city's social problems deepened. Those problems were, to be sure, rooted in more than just falling church attendance. Young people in Buffalo were entering the labor force of a city where, over the past fifteen years, the number of retail and manufacturing establishments had fallen by 30 percent, a city where landing a job in a factory, which had once seemed easy, was by no means assured, and where in some neighborhoods the only growth industry in the years to come would be the drug trade. A dark cloud hovered over the steel mills, auto plants, and machine tool shops that for decades had formed the backbone of Buffalo's economy.

None of which made the city unique, of course. Though inflected by its own peculiar history, the challenges facing Buffalo in the early seventies appeared symptomatic: of the Rust Belt, of the Northeast, of America in the aftermath of the Vietnam War and, with it, the end of an era of unprecedented prosperity. What's more, as my father would soon discover, there was far more to Buffalo than problems. There were beautiful parks in the city. There were buildings designed by Louis Sullivan and Frank Lloyd Wright. There were blocks that hummed with street life. If this was a place deserving of pity, that would have been news to my father, whose first impressions were uniformly positive. He'd never seen houses like the ones lining some of the streets near Children's Hospital, which bordered the Delaware District, an area of elegant mansions and curving parkways that had long been home to Buffalo's elite. Like everything in America, the city's hospitals seemed modern and efficient. The people my father met didn't seem ashamed of where they lived; they seemed proud. They also seemed refreshingly down-to-earth and friendly, smiling when they sensed he didn't understand something (which was often). It was cold in Buffalo, just as people warned, but nobody seemed to fret much about the weather, an attitude my father would learn to adopt.

For the next two months, he lived alone in the city, meeting his medical colleagues, living out of a suitcase, slowly learning to read the street signs. On the advice of a colleague, he scanned the papers one day and spotted an ad for a used-car dealership. He called the number, went out, and purchased a mango-colored Ford Maverick. A few weeks later, he found an apartment to rent, in a suburban housing complex called Williamsburg Square. (Before that, he'd slept in the rooms made available to newly arriving residents in the hospitals.)

Shortly thereafter, at the end of March 1973, my mother, my sister, and I boarded a plane to join him.

By this time, it had been nearly three years since Governor Rockefeller had signed the law liberalizing access to abortion in New York, a law to which many people in Buffalo remained no more reconciled than Jimmy Griffin had been in 1970. The people unhappy about this no longer had their representatives in Albany or their governor to blame, however, but instead the nation's highest court.

· 2 ·

N ation Is Shocked," declared the January 22, 1973, *New York Times*. Next to the headline appeared a portrait of America's thirty-sixth president, Lyndon Baines Johnson, his brow furrowed, his eyes weary with a look that had become difficult not to associate with the Vietnam War. The architect of the Great Society programs, the southerner who oversaw the passage of the 1964 Civil Rights Act and the Gulf of Tonkin Resolution, had died the previous day of a heart attack at the age of sixty-four.

The same day, in the left-hand column of the same front page, a story appeared about what the *Times* described as "a historic resolution of a fiercely controversial issue": the Supreme Court's 7–2 decision legalizing abortion in *Roe v. Wade*.

In Buffalo, at least in certain quarters, there was little ambiguity about what the day's most startling news was. "Shocking and appalling are words too weak to describe the ruling of these Supreme Court judges who placed a mother's right to privacy over the right of the unborn child to life itself," declared the executive council of Buffalo's

Catholic Physicians Guild in reaction to *Roe*. "Tragic," announced Bishop Edward D. Head, the newly appointed leader of the eight-county Diocese of Buffalo.

No Supreme Court ruling in history would stir more controversy or more firmly divide liberals and conservatives. For the latter, *Roe* would become a textbook example of judicial overreach: of ideology masquerading as reason (where exactly did the Constitution delineate a right to privacy, much less to abortion?) to advance the "rights revolution" begun during the Chief Justiceship of Earl Warren. For liberals, it would stand as a fundamental affirmation of personal liberty. The irony is that, far from bolstering the liberal drive to augment government power, *Roe* did just the opposite, circumscribing the state's authority to intervene in what the Court deemed was a citizen's private life. This was a conservative rather than a liberal notion, a point not lost on commentators at the time. "The present Supreme Court, in a test between the rights of the individual and the power of the state, comes down in a truly decisive fashion on the side of the individual," wrote the columnist Joseph Kraft in *The Washington Post*. "Such a choice is, of course, completely true to the principles of conservatism in this country."

But if the principle underlying *Roe* was conservative, its implications were radical. Just like that, the Supreme Court had demoted what millions of Americans took to be incontrovertible—that human life begins at conception—to the status of an opinion no more valid than any other. With the ruling, women throughout America were granted virtually unfettered access to a procedure many states had banned for decades, even if some of the initial press coverage made the consequences seem more limited. "Supreme Court Allows Early-Stage Abortions," read the headline in *The Washington Post*; the reporter noted that states could continue to regulate abortion during the second trimester of pregnancy and ban it outright during the third. The second-trimester regulations, however, were limited to those that protected maternal health, and even during the third trimester abortion was theoretically permissible if a woman's life or health was threatened. Six weeks after the decision, both of New York State's senators, Jacob K. Javits and James L. Buckley, reported receiving more correspondence in February from opponents of abortion than on any other topic.

The firestorm had only begun.

ROE V. WADE would send a wave of shock and anger rippling across the American political landscape. It would turn tens of thousands of Americans, some of them housewives, others previously disengaged evangelical Christians, into full-fledged crusaders. It would bring more protesters onto the streets of Buffalo than any event since the Vietnam War—in fact, it sparked more protest than Vietnam, about which the rumblings in western New York took place mainly within the confines of the University District (home to the University of Buffalo). With *Roe*, rage would spill across neighborhood lines, class boundaries, eventually even religious denominations, leading to countless protests, thousands of arrests, sit-ins, building takeovers, mock funerals. It would clog the city's court system, land Buffalo in the national spotlight on several occasions, and inspire a murder. Through much of this, my family would find itself at the center of the turmoil. I have, perhaps inevitably, often wondered what course events might have taken had the Court reached a different conclusion.

Yet in the hospitals where my father started working only weeks after the ruling was announced, *Roe*'s effect was curiously muted. Far from creating a sudden glut of patients seeking abortions, as was true in many other parts of the country, the decision initially *reduced* demand in western New York. This apparent anomaly is explained by the fact that, for nearly three years, abortion had already been legal in New York but almost nowhere else, a situation that brought thousands of women from other states to Buffalo. In 1971, 262,807 abortions were performed in New York, 60 percent of them (159,969) on out-of-state women.

Had my father been around during these years, he might have realized that becoming an abortion provider would complicate his life. For no sooner had abortion in New York been legalized than grassroots Catholic activists, ecclesiastical leaders, and elected officials like State

Senator Jimmy Griffin began pushing to ban it. In 1972, two years after the state legislature decriminalized it, these forces actually succeeded in passing a bill that once again made abortion a crime in New York, only to see Governor Nelson Rockefeller veto it.

Throughout this period, however, the focus of debate rested in the legislature, not on the streets, and it remained this way for some time. When, during the first year of my father's medical residency, the head of the ob-gyn program at Erie County Medical Center brought him into a room to observe a first-trimester abortion, there were no protesters huddled outside. Nobody warned my father that physicians who performed abortions risked isolating themselves from their colleagues. Nobody so much as hinted that doing so might actually be dangerous for the doctor.

A more seasoned observer of American politics might have seen a political storm looming on the horizon. But perhaps not. There were, after all, plenty of other seemingly more vexing problems at the time—Vietnam, Watergate. Among mainstream commentators, moreover, *Roe* appeared to mark the end rather than the beginning of controversy. "The Court's verdict on abortions provides a sound foundation for final and reasonable resolution of a debate that has divided America too long," wrote *The New York Times* in a January 24, 1973, editorial on *Roe*. The editors at *The Buffalo News* expected the decision "to quiet a bitter moral controversy that could have gone on in perpetuity." In a column published around the same time, Anthony Lewis warned of "painful tests of liberty ahead"—preserving the constitutional balance of powers against "a determined executive branch," for example. But abortion was not such a test, Lewis argued, since it was "a problem on which—for all the controversy—opinion was moving toward a new consensus, so that nineteenth-century state anti-abortion statutes were already being worn away by changed attitudes."

IT IS EASY, in hindsight, to marvel at this naïve optimism. Yet in some ways the optimism was understandable, for public attitudes and laws governing abortion *had* just undergone a dramatic shift.

Not long ago I visited the archives at *The Buffalo News* to collect articles the paper had run during the 1940s and 1950s on abortion. I came away with a sheaf of news clips, none of which actually mentions the word "abortion." Instead, I found several dozen brief notices indicating that someone in Buffalo had been arrested for performing an "illegal operation," usually after a woman had died or been injured. An article on July 5, 1955, "Man Is Charged in Girl's Death," for example, described the death of a fifteen-year-old following an "illegal operation" (the person under investigation, Jack E. Burke, made his living as a furnace operator). Another reported the death of a school teacher, mentioning that Buffalo police were seeking to question a steelplant technician who was involved in the criminal operation.

Aside from the names and ages of the victims, the stories reveal little; in a few cases, records have survived from the trials that spun out of these arrests. They are bound in dusty volumes at the Erie County Clerk's Office, where I went not long ago in search of them. Among the trial transcripts I found was *The People of the State of New York v. Juanita Davis et al.*, a case heard on November 15, 1950 in the State Supreme Court in Buffalo.* The lead witness in the case was Marion A. Evans, a twenty-one-year-old waitress who worked at the Buffalo Club. In halting, fearful words, Evans told her story on the witness stand. One night in June 1949, she and her boyfriend, a musician who performed at various local clubs and worked by day as a tool designer for the American Optical Company, went to see a play called *Stage Door*. Afterward, they were intimate. Not long after this, Evans discovered she was pregnant. Her boyfriend didn't want to get married. He wanted her to get an abortion, and he was willing to pay for it, provided Evans kept everything secret. "He would kill me if I told anyone about it," Evans told the court. Terrified and depressed, Evans said she attempted suicide by taking iodine — "I didn't want to live anymore." The attempt failed. In September, she went to an office on Delaware Avenue where a sign hung on the door: "Hours By Appointment." A man there told her to go to 588 Broadway, where she could get her problem taken care of. She remembered

---

*In New York State, the trial-level court is called the Supreme Court. The state's highest court is the Court of Appeals.

seeing three other girls there and meeting a woman named Ruth, who administered "the solution"—a douche inserted through a tube that Evans was told would terminate her pregnancy. Instead, Evans started bleeding and writhing in pain. When the bleeding didn't stop, she made her way to the emergency room of Meyer Memorial Hospital. "I was too afraid to tell the truth," she testified, but the physicians figured it out, diagnosing her as suffering from an "incomplete abortion." It was after this that the police were called in.

Evans's testimony resulted in the conviction of "Ruth," whose real name was Clara Krause, and Juanita Davis, her partner, to two to four years at the Westfield State Farm prison in Bedford Hills, New York.

How many women in Buffalo underwent such experiences is unknown, for the world Marion Evans described was hidden. Like sex itself, abortion was not something respectable people talked about during the 1950s. The trial transcripts evoke a world of shame and secrecy, in which women were coerced into testifying against people they had gone to see voluntarily. Yet, in a sense, they tell stories of comparative fortune. Women like Marion Evans survived their ordeals, after all. Others—the fifteen-year-old girl treated by Jack Burke, the school teacher—didn't. In New York City, the number of abortion-related deaths nearly doubled between 1951 and 1962, a decade when restrictions tightened and the procedure became harder to obtain; the victims were four times as likely to be black or Hispanic as white. Cities such as Los Angeles and Philadelphia had to devote whole wards of public hospitals to treat women recovering from illegal and self-induced operations. Chicago's Cook County Hospital reported treating nearly 5,000 women for abortion-related complications (shock, infection, injury) in 1962, four times as many as two decades earlier.

I found no statistics to indicate how widespread such problems might have been in Buffalo. What I did find, scrolling through reels of microfilm at the Buffalo public library, was a fifteen-part series on abortion published in *The Buffalo News* in April 1967. It was the first in-depth examination of illegal abortion in the Buffalo press, and it began bluntly. "An estimated three out of every ten pregnancies in the United States end in abortion," wrote the reporter, Mildred Spencer; the vast majority of abortions were performed "by the pregnant women themselves or a variety of illegal practitioners." In the days that followed, in addition to opinion columns arguing for and against changing the law, the paper published harrowing accounts of women in Buffalo who had punctured their uteruses, sterilized themselves, or nearly bled to death following self-induced or illegal abortions. "I was determined to go through with it, even at the risk of my life," one woman said. Another woman described going to a hotel to get an abortion that was performed with no anesthetic by someone who was clearly unskilled; she developed an infection and, after going to the hospital, was told she would likely never be able to bear children. A third woman explained the torment of discovering that her daughter had been raped by a relative ("It was like the end of the world to her father and me"). Should she be forced to bear the child? According to what the family's faith taught, yes. Yet the mother arranged for her daughter to get an abortion, an option that, as the *News* pointed out, was far more likely to be available to women of privileged backgrounds. The only way to get a safe abortion in New York prior to 1970 was to convince two psychiatrists that one's life would otherwise be at risk. Each had to be paid $75 for the consultation, beyond which there was the cost of the procedure itself. A study performed in two Buffalo teaching hospitals found that, between 1943 and 1964, 482 hospital-approved therapeutic abortions were performed on private patients, just 22 on poorer clinic patients. The class division overlapped with a racial one. "So many Negroes do not realize that there is any possibility of abortion within the law," a black woman told the *News*. "In desperation they turn to all sorts of quack practitioners."

THE *BUFFALO NEWS* series did not arise out of a vacuum. By the time it appeared, the climate of local opinion had begun to change, thanks to two events that had taken place five years earlier. In 1962, the prestigious American Law Institute (ALI) endorsed a model legal code permitting abortion in cases of rape, incest, severe fetal abnormalities, or when the mother's physical or mental health was in danger. A moderate proposal by today's standards, it seemed anything but that at a time when every state in the country allowed abortion only if the mother's life was at risk. The ALI model code soon inspired a wave of reform. Around the same time, an attractive Phoenix television hostess named Sherri Chessen Finkbine became a media sensation after traveling all the way to Sweden to get an abortion, which her doctor had recommended but a judge in Arizona forbade. While pregnant with her fifth child, Finkbine had taken a tranquilizer, thalidomide, that she didn't know caused severe birth defects. Babies born to women who'd taken the drug in Europe often lacked limbs; few survived more than a few months. Finkbine's decision prompted hate mail and death threats. But it also put a pretty, all-American face—her story was featured on the cover of the August 10, 1962, issue of *Life*—on an issue that had previously been invisible. A Gallup poll taken afterward found that 50 percent of Americans supported her decision.

Soon, surveys started showing that a majority of Americans actually favored abortion law reform. It was still unusual for women to speak openly about the issue—none of those interviewed in the *Buffalo News* series allowed their full names to be used—but this, too, was beginning to change, thanks to the emergence of the modern women's movement. In 1966, a former housewife named Betty Friedan, author of the 1963 best-seller *The Feminine Mystique*, met in a hotel room in Washington, D.C., with a group of like-minded activists and launched the National Organization for Women (NOW). The next year, NOW adopted a "Bill of Rights" that championed an array of measures, including an end to sex discrimination in the workplace; equal job training and educational opportunities; and the right to a safe, legal abortion.

It was a bold agenda. Yet as feminism caught fire among a younger generation of women, it soon seemed almost tame. While leaders like Friedan couched their objectives in the language of equality, by 1969 thousands of young women were talking about empowerment and liberation. Frustrated by the attitude of their supposedly enlightened male counterparts in the "movement" ("The only position for women in SNCC is prone," Stokely Carmichael of the Student Nonviolent Coordinating Committee had famously joked), feminists started to form organizations of their own. They began to see gender as a category distinct

TV hostess Sherri Finkbine packs her suitcase for Sweden to get an abortion. This photograph appeared in the August 10, 1962, issue of *Life*.

from, and no less important than, race and class. They gathered at speak-outs and for the first time traded stories about what the historian Ruth Rosen terms "the hidden injuries of sex": rape, spousal abuse, sexual harassment, and the terror of getting an illegal abortion, which feminists recast not as a crime but as a prerequisite to sexual autonomy. As an activist in the Society for Humane Abortion, a California-based group, put it, "When we talk about women's rights, we can get all the rights in the world—the right to vote, the right to go to school—and none of them means a doggone thing if we don't own the flesh we stand in . . . if the whole course of our lives can be changed by somebody else that can get us pregnant by accident, or by deceit, or by force."

There were signs that not everyone in America thrilled to such talk. In state after state where feminists pushed to expand access to abortion, right-to-life organizations began forming to defend the status quo. Speak-outs on abortion often took place on the lush greens of the nation's college campuses, not in the nation's churches, where so many other efforts to win new rights began. The drive to legalize abortion did not, however, meet with universal hostility in religious quarters. In Buffalo as elsewhere, clergymen in fact played arguably the most important role in removing the public stigma from abortion in the years prior to *Roe*. In 1969, a Unitarian minister named Blaine Hartford met with a group of fellow ministers in western New York. He soon founded an organization whose purpose was to help pregnant women seeking abortions find physicians willing to perform them. The group modeled itself on a similar organization that had formed two years earlier in New York City, part of a nationwide network that emerged to help women circumvent laws many were coming to view as archaic and cruel. In Buffalo, the network began with four members, Hartford told me in an interview, but quickly mushroomed into "twenty or thirty," all of whom had heard horrifying stories of women rushed to emergency rooms following botched abortions. Since their actions were illegal, the ministers in Buffalo printed no literature and spread the news of their existence mostly by word of mouth, which did not prevent them from being flooded with calls. Some women traveled as far as England to get a safe abortion, according to Hartford. "What we discovered is that women would go absolutely anywhere so long as they could afford it," he said. "There was an absolute avalanche of need."

This network of ministers, not Operation Rescue, was the first campaign of civil disobedience in America related to abortion, and its impact was dramatic. By 1972, thirteen states had enacted ALI-style reforms; four more—New York, Washington, Alaska, and Hawaii—had repealed virtually all restrictions on abortion. As a result, the number of legal abortions performed in America leaped from an estimated 8,000 in 1966 to 500,000 in 1972. As the political landscape changed, so did the climate of opinion. A poll conducted in 1970 found that 50 percent of Americans agreed that the decision to have an abortion should be left to the woman, up from 15 percent four years earlier. In 1972, 64 percent endorsed this view. That same year, the U.S. Congress passed the Equal Rights Amendment. *Ms.* magazine was launched. The Equal Employment Opportunity Act was enacted to prohibit sex discrimination in employment. Women's studies programs were forming at universities throughout the country, including the University of Buffalo, where a branch of NOW was also established. Its founder, a tall, red-haired woman named Mary Schwartz, recalls the early 1970s as a period of dizzying excitement. Women in Buffalo were getting together to question "everything," she says. Careers that had been put on hold for decades were being pursued. Barriers to women at work were shattering. "It was so wonderful," says Schwartz. "I was a woman in her thirties with two kids, happily married, a social worker, and suddenly it occurred to me, well, maybe I should pursue something better." Schwartz soon enrolled in a Ph.D. program, on her way to becoming a professor.

THAT MY FATHER would one day find himself portrayed as an ally of the movement that transformed the lives of women like Mary Schwartz seems almost comical to me. For while in the 1970s the women's movement was spreading across campuses and altering attitudes, his views remained stuck in a time warp. Although the word "feminism" would mean plenty to his daughter one day (and to most of the women I would date in college), it meant nothing to my father in 1973, a year he associated not with *Roe* but with the outbreak of the Yom Kippur War. When it came to the women's movement, he was about as advanced in his consciousness as most Israeli men of his generation: that is, not very. Although his own mother had worked for years outside the home, the household in which he grew up was a traditional one, with my grandmother performing all the duties (cooking, cleaning, washing the clothes) it was assumed women carried out. That "the personal is political" is not something my father had ever heard. Nor, despite having gone to medical school, was abortion something he had ever thought much about in political terms. The truth is, few Israelis of his generation did, even though, until 1977, the procedure was illegal there. As the political scientist Yael Yishai has shown, this had less to do with morality than with demography: in a nation struggling to expand its population, bearing as many children as possible was framed as a national responsibility. "Every Jewish mother can and must understand that the unique situation of the Jewish people . . . imposed on her a sacred duty to do her utmost for the nation's rapid growth," wrote David Ben-Gurion. For this reason, Israel retained a law dating back to the British Mandate that made abortion illegal.

That my father did not spend a lot of time contemplating the hardship this imposed on women owes much to another factor—the fact that, as he discovered while working at Rothschild Hospital in Haifa, the law was widely ignored. Despite formal restrictions, it was an open secret that many Israeli doctors performed abortions in their private offices, and that women routinely made appointments to see them. Nobody protested this, nor were doctors prosecuted for what was, technically speaking, a crime. The relative lack of civil unrest may reflect the fact that Israelis had other things to worry about. It also likely reflected the more tolerant view of abortion embedded in Jewish law and, in turn, Jewish culture. There is, on the one hand, a general bias in favor of life in Judaism, and some Orthodox Jews oppose abortion in all circumstances. On the other hand, the Talmudic Sages view the process of gestation developmentally—the zygote is understood to be "simply water" during the first forty days after conception—and not only permit but *require* abortion in cases when the mother's life is threatened. Like surveys of American Jews, polls of Israelis found that an overwhelming majority of citizens believed the decision about an abortion should be left to the woman and her doctor.

This was my father's view. Abortion was not a vehicle of empowerment in his eyes. But neither was it murder. It was, he believed, a last resort for women who felt they could not go through with an unplanned pregnancy. Not in all cases: as he would soon discover, he did not feel comfortable performing abortions in the later stages of pregnancy. There was a point, in his mind—the point at which the developing human embryo could survive on its own—where another life was at stake. But it made sense to him that, prior to this point, the decision should be left in the hands of the woman carrying the child and her physician, not a government bureaucrat.

It was less a theory than a gut instinct, one that did not make my father terribly unique among his medical colleagues. In the spring of 1973, a survey of 33,000 U.S. doctors revealed that nearly two thirds agreed with the Supreme Court's ruling in *Roe*. Among those under thirty-five, the figure was 75 percent. According to my father, of the dozen or so residents who began training with him in Buffalo, only one voiced any objections to learning how to perform an abortion.

This tolerant attitude is perhaps not surprising: it was, after all, doctors who had manned the emergency rooms where the victims of botched abortions showed up before *Roe*. As they watched women suffer, some physicians began speaking out. Others secretly began "stretching, twisting and torturing the law," as *The New York Times* reported in 1967, to circumvent the restrictions. Buffalo was no exception. "I can think of at least four doctors, and there were probably more, who, well before abortion was legalized, were doing many therapeutic abortions here," Dr. Ronald Foote, an obstetrician who arrived in Buffalo in 1965, told me. He said the number steadily increased as physicians who had seen the results of illegal abortion green-lighted more and more cases. Foote himself did not perform abortions, but he did witness the realities of the pre-*Roe* era. "I have seen people die in the ER from a botched abortion," he told me. "I have taken a uterus out of a sixteen-year-old girl following a botched abortion." Dr. Jack Lippes, a Buffalo obstetrician best known for inventing a popular intrauterine birth control device (the "Lippes loop"), echoed this. "Lots of doctors were doing abortions in Buffalo before it was legal, and nobody raised an eyebrow," he told me.

There is a rich irony to this. A century earlier, it was not the Catholic church that had spearheaded the drive to ban abortion in the first place. It was the professional organization my father would soon proudly join.

"Let us glance for a moment at the moral wrong of criminal abortion," thundered an editorial in September 1858. "It is murder . . . and few there are who do not know of such occurrences, even in the highest walks of society." The editorial appeared not in a church newsletter but in the *Buffalo Medical Journal*, house organ of the local branch of the American Medical Association, which had just launched a campaign to put abortionists throughout the country out of business. Up until this point, abortion prior to "quickening" (the moment when a woman can feel the fetus moving inside her womb, between the fourth and fifth month of gestation) had not been a crime anywhere in the United States, and by all accounts was widely practiced. As the historian James Mohr has shown, physicians set about to change this as much for professional reasons as for moral ones. Doctors in the newly formed AMA wanted states to impose sanctions on "irregulars" (midwives, unlicensed healers) who engaged in a lucrative practice that robbed physicians of the status and authority they craved. There was a strain of anti-Catholic nativism to the crusade. During the nineteenth century, the birthrate among U.S.-born women declined by nearly 50 percent while the immigrant population soared, a trend that fueled widespread anxiety that native-born Protestants might soon become a minority. It did not go unnoticed that, in cities like Boston and Buffalo, middle-class women were having smaller families, while the ranks of Catholic immigrants were skyrocketing. "Now we have ladies, yes, *educated and refined ladies*, who patronize those persons who advertise to prevent an undue increase of family!" complained the *Buffalo Medical Journal*, whose founding editor, the Harvard-educated Austin Flint, was, like most of the city's physicians, a blue-blooded Yankee.

The physicians' crusade was nothing if not successful. Between 1860 and 1880, states across the country passed tough new laws banning abortion at any stage of pregnancy. The legislation coincided with a wave of anti-obscenity laws culminating in the 1873 Comstock Act, which made it a federal crime to mail, advertise, or sell any information on birth control or abortion. A combination of Victorian-era morality and lobbying by physicians succeeded in driving the topic of sex out of the public sphere for nearly a century.

But the AMA's campaign did not stop abortions from being performed. Although no national surveys are available, late-nineteenth-century observers estimated the ratio of abortions to live births as one to four, sometimes one to six, sometimes one to two—rates close to those in the United States today. A survey of almost 1,000 women who visited a Bronx birth control clinic in 1931 and 1932 found that 35 percent of Catholic, Protestant, and Jewish women had had at least one abortion. Banning the practice did not eliminate it but merely drove it underground, sometimes into the hands of physicians who acted secretively, other times to dangerous quacks. In 1936, *The Buffalo News* reported that a special committee on maternal mortality found that "illegal operations" accounted for "one-fourth of all maternal deaths" in Erie County.

IF MY FATHER arrived in Buffalo with no knowledge of this history, why did he feel compelled to get involved in the controversy?

The truth is that, like another local physician who would wander unknowingly into it, he didn't. In 1993, five years before Barnett Slepian's murder, *The Buffalo News* asked him whether he would have begun performing abortions had he known how much pressure he would subsequently face.

"I don't like to admit it, but probably not," Slepian replied.

I asked my father the same question recently. We were seated at home for dinner, the shades in the kitchen drawn—an added measure of protection taken after Dr. Slepian's murder. He'd driven past protesters that very day. "I don't know," he told me, pausing. "I guess, probably, I would do what most physicians do now and not get involved. I mean, I was new to the country. Why get involved in something controversial . . ."

His voice trailed off.

But my father did not have a crystal ball. He did not have the prescience of Supreme Court Justice Harry A. Blackmun, who, the fall before *Roe* became law, scrawled a note to himself: "not a happy assignment—will be excoriated." In the decision that would forever be associated with his name, Blackmun proceeded to frame abortion as a matter of freedom from government interference in certain "zones of privacy," the same line of reasoning invoked in the 1965 *Griswold v. Connecticut* ruling, which struck down a state law barring the use of contraceptives, and by appeals courts in Georgia and Texas in abortion cases. Just as the government should not determine what couples did in their bedrooms, Blackmun reasoned, neither should it dictate whether a pregnant woman should bear a child, arguably the most personal decision she would ever make. In framing the issue this way, Blackmun drew on one of the most cherished principles in American life: "the right," in the words of Justice Louis Brandeis, "to be let alone—the most comprehensive of rights and the right most valued by civilized men." The emphasis on individual sovereignty would resonate with more than just liberals in the years to come. "For me, abortion is a personal issue—between mother, father and doctor," a first lady would write in a memoir several decades down the road. Her name was not Hillary Clinton but Barbara Bush, and by the time her husband was president polls would show that a solid majority of Americans agreed when the issue was framed this way.

What Blackmun's ruling failed to explain is why a "right to privacy," which had earlier been invoked to overturn barely enforced laws banning contraception, should so thoroughly trump a competing interest: protecting fetal life. The Court did acknowledge the state's "legitimate interest in protecting the potentiality of human life." But this very wording ("potentiality") contained within it a value judgment that to prolifers seemed both arbitrary and abhorrent. The trimester formula *Roe* proposed—permitting some regulation of abortion during the middle third of pregnancy, allowing states to proscribe it during the final third—made sense to physicians and biologists who, like my father, drew the line at viability. It made no sense to people who believed life begins at conception, those who felt that the fate of another person—the unborn child—was at stake. The outrage among such people would only deepen as they read the opinion and discovered that the Court had evaded the question at the heart of the debate. "We need not resolve the difficult question of when life begins," *Roe* stated. If this was not resolved, on what grounds did seven men sitting on a bench presume to tell states throughout the country what to do?

"Raw Judicial Power" read the headline of a scathing essay that would soon appear in the conservative *National Review*, a phrase taken directly from the dissent of Justice Byron R. White. Without realizing it, Harry Blackmun had just handed a generation of conservatives a powerful club with which to beat liberals for decades to come: a Supreme Court ruling that seemed to epitomize the scenario of robed elitists overriding the popular will to impose their values on everyone else. The fact that the opinion's author was a Republican who grew up in Dayton's Bluff, a working-class neighborhood in St. Paul, and whose record had been vetted approvingly by William Rehnquist, then an assistant attorney general in the Nixon administration, which had appointed Blackmun to the Supreme Court, would largely be forgotten. So would the fact that, as strange as it might seem in retrospect, Blackmun was more likely *responding* to popular opinion than attempting to subvert it. Among the news clips the reporter Linda Greenhouse found in his files while researching her book *Becoming Justice Blackmun* was an August 1972 article in *The Washington Post* reporting the latest Gallup survey on abortion. "Two out of three Americans think abortion should be a matter for decision solely between a woman and her physician," it found. Fifty-six percent of Catholics in the survey agreed with this view, as did 68 *percent* of Republicans. In later years, even some feminists would come to regard *Roe* as an example of the dangers that arise when courts leapfrog public opinion on volatile social issues. This concern is understandable, but it's worth noting that the legal landscape prior to *Roe* (abortion banned in thirty-three of the fifty states) was arguably as out of synch with public opinion as the decision itself.

None of this prevents a part of me from wishing that Harry Blackmun had issued a less sweeping ruling, one that would have enabled the issue to continue playing out in the states, as some of *Roe*'s critics subsequently argued should have happened. I say this not because such a course would have proven less messy or divisive. Those nostalgic for some pre-*Roe* day when abortion did not poison American politics would do well to recall how bitterly it divided state legislatures like New York's in the late 1960s and early 1970s. They might ponder what it was like when people like Emma K. Herrod, director of Erie County's Maternal and Infant Health Service, wondered aloud whether "motel abortoriums" would open in Buffalo because so many women from other states were coming to the city to have their pregnancies terminated. Straightening out the messy patchwork of state laws and removing the issue from the vicissitudes of the legislative process is partly what impelled the Supreme Court to intervene.

In doing so, however, the Court did not settle the abortion conflict but rather escalated it, and helped to shift the battle from the legislature, where compromise was at least conceivable, to the streets: from the steps of state capitols to the offices of physicians like my father. If few people foresaw this at the time, perhaps it's because they failed to anticipate how abruptly the momentum in the conflict would shift, thanks in no small part to *Roe* itself. Far from energizing the women's movement, the Supreme Court's decision drained its momentum, as many feminists understandably assumed one front in their struggle for equal rights was over. It would have the opposite effect on the pro-life movement, for which *Roe* served, in the words of the writer Cynthia Gorney, as a "massive recruiting call."

The scale of the backlash would become clear only later. In the meantime, my family and I settled into our lives in Buffalo, a city that appeared to have other, bigger problems: of race, of class, and above all, of economic decline.

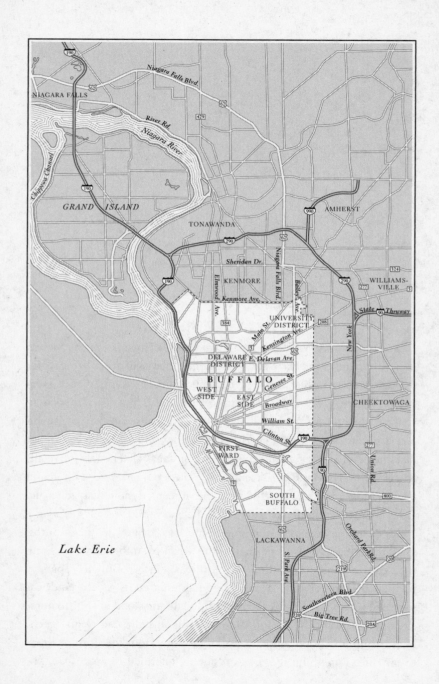

· 3 ·

Number 58A Williamsburg Square is firmly etched in my memory. I remember the black-and-white Zenith television in our living room, through which my sister and I received our first infusions of American pop culture. There was a courtyard out front, surrounded by a dozen or so identical two-story brown-brick buildings, each of which was subdivided into a pair of duplexes that rented out, in 1973, for $185 a month. Our apartment had three small bedrooms and a bathroom upstairs, a kitchen, living room, and washroom below. It wasn't fancy—the kitchen floors were of linoleum, the walls plain and bare—but to my father it seemed more than adequate. *Three* bedrooms? *Two* floors? Few Israelis he knew lived in such splendor.

As its name suggests, our new home was located in the suburbs: Williamsville, which was nestled in the Town of Amherst, a fifty-three-square-mile expanse abutting the northeast side of Buffalo. Sparsely populated before World War II, the area boomed as vacant land was parceled up and paved over to accommodate the flood of suburbanites streaming in. Like the rest of Amherst, Williamsville had clean streets, quality public schools, and a sense of distance from the gritty realities of city life, something the area's residents intended to keep that way.

When, in 1970, William E. Keller, then superintendent of the Williamsville Central School District, proposed busing 110 black schoolchildren from Buffalo into the area, with an equal number of suburban youths bused out, local residents launched a campaign to block his plan. Proponents of busing were subjected to threats and harassment. A group of antibusing candidates was elected to the School Board. In a privately sponsored poll, residents voted 7,256 to 238 against the initiative.

By the standards of the surrounding area, the inhabitants of Williamsburg Square were interlopers—not colored folks from the inner city, mind you, but not middle-class suburbanites, either. Most of our neighbors survived by stretching weekly paychecks down to the last penny and purchasing discounted items at the supermarket, which was, for the next four years, exactly how we would live. Both my parents worked during this period, my mother as a lab technician in the virology department at the University of Buffalo, my father as a medical resident. Between them, they earned just enough to pay the rent and cover our monthly expenses.

But it wasn't money that most distinguished the people we knew from the broader community in which we lived. It was culture and identity. When my father moved into Williamsburg Square, he did so in part because another Israeli family, the Flemingers, already lived there. Within two years, half a dozen Israeli families moved in. The result was to turn the Square into a cross between suburban Buffalo and Tel Aviv— "an Israeli colony," my mother joked—and to reinforce our sense that we were different. We spoke Hebrew at home. Our refrigerator was stocked with pickles, olives, puréed eggplant, and other staples of a Middle Eastern diet (and not enough fresh cucumbers and tomatoes like the ones grown in Israel, my parents often complained). Football to us was a game played with a round ball and two nets, not a pigskin and goalposts. We didn't celebrate Thanksgiving or the Fourth of July. The truth is, we didn't really know what these holidays were yet.

It never occurred to my family that, however strange this all seemed, our experience was hardly unique—that virtually every immigrant group that had settled in Buffalo through the years had likewise gathered in a

Corner store in Buffalo (photograph by Milton Rogovin)

cloistered community of some kind, eating strange foods and peering out nervously at the world around them. The polyglot nature of the city was reflected in the names of the families that peopled its neighborhoods: Chlebowy, Wojtowicz, and Janowski on the Polish East Side, which serves as the backdrop to Verlyn Klinkenborg's book about a working-class bar on Sycamore Street, *The Last Fine Time*; Sullivan, Fitzpatrick, and O'Hara in Irish South Buffalo, where Tim Russert's memoir about his father, *Big Russ and Me*, is set. These neighborhoods were their own separate worlds, and, as one after another formed, they gradually transformed a city of genteel WASPs into a blue-collar, predominantly Catholic one. Buffalo worked hard and drank hard—a local observer counted up 1,467 taverns the year we arrived—and combined a taste for contact sports (football, hockey) with a proud aversion to snobbery. The City of Good Neighbors, Buffalo's boosters liked to call it, though, if you looked closely enough, what you found was a social landscape no less cleaved by race and class divisions than any other place in America, and a good deal more diverse than outsiders typically imagined. By the early 1970s, large stretches of the East Side were black, owing to the great postwar migration that had brought tens of thousands of African-Americans to Buffalo and other northern cities. The formerly Italian lower West Side was home to a growing Puerto Rican community, as well as to a sprinkling of Native American, Asian, and working-class white families. The West Side's diversity is captured in a series of arresting portraits that the photographer Milton Rogovin began taking around this time, pictures of housewives, street hustlers, cops, senior citizens, auto mechanics, steelworkers, barflies, the ordinary Buffalonians whom Rogovin affectionately referred to as "the forgotten ones." One photo shows a shirtless Puerto Rican man, his muscle-bound torso covered in tattoos, smiling in a way that makes him look not mean and defiant—another badass from the 'hood—but tender and sweet. In another, two black men shuffle exuberantly by the jukebox in a bar. There are photos of what looks to be the Old World—a couple of elderly Italians passing the day on a bench—alongside a more recently transplanted one—two dark-skinned Asian women in elaborately embroidered Indian dresses on a couch. We see the West Side's graffiti-strewn walls, its bodegas, its churches, storefronts, porches, and street scenes: three men playing dominoes, a derelict sitting alone.

In the decades to come, new immigrants from India, Pakistan, Korea, and the Philippines would set up communities of their own; like their predecessors, they would wake up one day to find that their children had assimilated. What made the experience of these recent immigrants different is that, like my parents, many came with skills and education that enabled them to bypass the traditional occupational destiny of new arrivals to the city: factory work. For several generations, the road to assimilation in Buffalo had led through the gates of steel mills and auto plants, places that served as a source of mass employment and, with the help of a union, a stepping-stone into the middle class.

MY PARENTS WERE lucky an alternative path was available to them. Just as they arrived, the gates of Buffalo's factories began to slam shut. American Standard, Remington Rand, Kimberly-Clark, Hewitt-Robbins, Continental Can, Morrison Steel, Western Electric, Central Foundry, Wurlitzer: no fewer than thirty-eight large manufacturing firms closed up shop in the Buffalo metropolitan area between 1971 and 1976 alone. As the United States withdrew from Vietnam, the military contracts that had fueled the local defense industry likewise dried up. The plant closings rippled through the economy, emptying bars of regular patrons, draining the city of tax revenue, and upending the narrative of progress to which its residents for decades clung. "Down and Out in America" blared the somber headline of a photo spread in the February 9, 1975, issue of *The New York Times* magazine. Below the caption were the despondent faces of Buffalo's unemployed, a suddenly ballooning lot. In 1974, unemployment in Buffalo soared to 12 percent, nearly double the national average. The next year, the jobless rate fluctuated from a *low* of 13.2 percent to a high of 16.1 percent.

The exodus of jobs, not abortion, was the issue that dominated the headlines in Buffalo during the 1970s. My family and I had arrived in a city on the losing side of the great economic transformation that unfolded during the Nixon, Ford, and Carter years, as declining productivity, foreign imports, and oil shocks combined to bring an era of American industrial hegemony to an end. Factories paying high wages to unionized workers in places like Pittsburgh and Buffalo no longer seemed invincible: they seemed obsolete. Many companies started to relocate—to the Sun Belt, where tax abatements and union-free environments offered an appealing contrast to the Northeast; or overseas, where you could pay your workers even less. "The most repetitive complaint that crops up when talking to industrialists is labor costs," James Jordan, executive director of the Erie County Industrial Development Agency, told *The Buffalo News*.

All of which, more than three decades later, has a familiar, inevitable ring to it. Buffalo in financial trouble? What could surprise anybody *less*? Aside from snowstorms, arguably nothing about the city is more firmly etched in the popular imagination than its financial woes. Say Buffalo, and you think Rust Belt: Flint, Youngstown, all those hollowed-out manufacturing towns from which the jobs long ago vanished.

To those who lived through it, though, the story was anything but familiar. Only a decade earlier, in 1966, the New York State Department of Labor had counted 184,300 factory jobs in the greater Buffalo area. Unemployment was a mere 3.5 percent. Purchasing power was expanding. "The Niagara Frontier area's 'guns and butter' economy is closing out 1966 at a record pace," *The Buffalo News* reported that year, "and moving into 1967 with no appreciable letup in sight." This was not just wishful thinking. It was what any reasonable person would have surmised. Both the Republic and Bethlehem steel companies had just completed record-shattering years. The mood was similarly upbeat in the automobile industry, and at companies such as Textron's Bell Aerosystems, one of dozens of military contractors in the area. The Vietnam War had yet to trigger runaway inflation. For the time being, it was simply good for business. "Buffalo's Year to Shine," proclaimed an editorial in *The Buffalo News* a year later. The city was "roaring into 1968 on all fronts," the paper reported, with 95 percent of area businessmen forecasting a "booming" outlook ahead.

This was, granted, no ordinary period in American history. It was the tail end of the great postwar boom, an era that David Halberstam would rightly term "the highwater mark of the American century, when the country was rich, the dollar strong, and inflation low." It was the era of the Ford Mustang and of a level of material abundance unlike anything previously seen. It had been different in Buffalo back in the 1930s, when the city distributed food vouchers to the growing ranks of the unemployed and advised families to stock up on cabbage, potatoes, rice, and lard. Even so, although it was no stranger to adversity, the most recent postwar boom was by no means the first time fortune had smiled on the city where my parents now lived.

· · ·

IN 1800, A land surveyor named Joseph Ellicott mounted a horse and traveled through the mud-strewn woodlands of western New York. "One huge Forest" is how Ellicott characterized the territory of the Holland Land Company, for which he served as resident agent. Within a few years, he had laid out a street plan for the town then known as New Amsterdam, a radial grid modeled on a similar one that he and his brothers had helped develop for Washington, D.C.

Things did not start out terribly well. In 1813, eight months after the Village of Buffalo was officially incorporated and more than a year into the War of 1812, marauding British soldiers burned it to the ground. Eighteen years later, when Alexis de Tocqueville paid a visit, he found a town teeming with Seneca Indians seeking payment for their land, much of which they had ceded in the Treaty of Big Tree, signed in 1797, for a mere $100,000, a swindle that a local chronicler would later deem "incredible." Like many future visitors, Tocqueville was less taken with Buffalo than with the spectacle to its north, Niagara Falls. "The whole river formed a crystal arch," the Frenchman observed. When Charles Dickens visited in 1842, he, too, rhapsodized about the falls ("What voices spoke from out the thundering water") but dismissed Buffalo ("chilly and raw; a damp mist falling; and the trees in that northern region quite bare").

Yet if Buffalo's exposure to Lake Erie made it susceptible to storms and inclement weather, it also signaled opportunity. Under the leadership of a judge and future mayor named Samuel Wilkeson, a group of residents dredged the Buffalo Creek, paving the way for the city's selection as the western terminus of the Erie Canal, which opened for business in 1825. In the decades to follow, gray-skied Buffalo would blossom into the nation's largest inland port. It was the gateway between the rolling farmland of the Midwest, to which the city was connected by the Great Lakes, and the Eastern Seaboard, to which it was linked via the canal. Ships stuffed with grain, livestock, and other goods soon crowded into Buffalo's harbor to unload their cargo. Hotels, banks, and insurance firms opened. In 1842, a Buffalo merchant named Joseph Dart built the world's first steam-powered grain elevator along the city's riverbanks. By 1867, there were twenty-seven grain elevators in the city;

three fourths of the nation's grain and half its rolling freight changed hands there. Visiting Buffalo around this time, Anthony Trollope wrote, "I went down to the granaries and climbed into the elevator and saw the wheat running in rivers from one vessel into another. . . . I began to know what it was for a country to overflow with milk and honey, to burst with its own fruits and be smothered with its own riches."

Buffalo was a city of merchants, eight of whom served as mayor between 1832 and 1860, and of scoopers, dredgers, and other working-class immigrants who toiled on the docks. While the merchants lived in elegant houses on tree-shaded boulevards, the mostly Irish dockworkers crowded into jerry-built flats along the waterfront, a rough-hewn area awash in saloons and gambling dens that earned Buffalo a reputation as a "dirty, mean-looking, trunk-stealing . . . sort of town," as a correspondent for the *Detroit Tribune* wrote. Prostitutes and hucksters roamed the streets. Bodies turned up frequently in the canal. To the local elite, the waterfront was simply "the infected district"—contaminated not only by poverty and crime but by labor unrest. As the historian David Gerber documents in his book *The Making of an American Pluralism*, work along the docks paid little and was often dangerous, prompting sporadic protests. During the 1858 "Work or Bread" demonstrations, hundreds of dockworkers staged rallies and marched to the mayor's office to demand that the city feed them or create more jobs. Mayor Timothy Lockwood responded by hiring guards to shield municipal offices.

The crisis passed and, by the turn of the century, Buffalo began to assume the trappings of a modern city. In 1896, one of the world's first modern skyscrapers, Louis Sullivan's Guaranty Building, a majestic metallic-framed structure with a terra-cotta façade and ornate marble interior, was built downtown. A network of parks and public spaces had been created to lend the city a pastoral elegance, many of them designed by Frederick Law Olmsted, who judged Buffalo "the best planned city, as to its streets, public places and grounds, in the United States." The "Queen City of the Lakes," as it came to be known, had its own circle of influential power brokers (the Rumseys, the Milburns) who dined at the Buffalo Club and cut lucrative business deals in smoke-filled rooms—but also its share of poverty. In 1901, a correspondent for *The Atlantic* described Buffalo as a "noble city" but admitted it was actually two cities: the West Side, where men in top hats rode in fancy carriages to the theater; and the East, which teemed with working-class immigrants and "hordes of drifting men."

That same year, Buffalo caught what seemed to be its biggest break yet by playing host to the Pan-American Exposition, an event that was supposed to showcase the nation's glory in the aftermath of the 1898 Spanish-American War. A fountain court and esplanade were laid out. Thousands of visitors streamed into town. On September 4, no less a dignitary than President William McKinley arrived. Two days later, inside the Temple of Music, an auditorium on the exposition's grounds, McKinley stood before a procession of admirers eager to shake his hand. He was in good spirits, having just visited Niagara Falls. Among the spectators was Leon Czolgosz, a handsome blacksmith's assistant from Cleveland. Czolgosz had come to Buffalo a week earlier. A disturbed loner and anarchist, he approached McKinley with a handkerchief draped over his hand, concealing an Iver Johnson .32-caliber pistol, which he fired twice.

"The Foulest Crime of the New Century" howled the press about the assassination.* So began the McKinley Curse, some maintain, the century-long hex that has hovered over Buffalo ever since. The truth is, the city's fortunes *were* changing, though larger forces than McKinley's death were at work. With the frontier settled and the nation crisscrossed by railroads, Buffalo could no longer coast to prosperity on commerce alone. America had entered the industrial age and Buffalo, a city built on trade, was lagging behind.

But not all hope was lost. For Buffalo had two commodities suited to the changing times: electrical power, courtesy of nearby Niagara Falls, and an abundance of cheap labor, courtesy of the waves of immigrants—Irish, Poles, Italians, Slavs—that had settled on its shores. In 1899, a group of businessmen led by John Milburn, an attorney from one of

---

*It was certainly among the most politically consequential, foiling the plan of Mark A. Hanna, the Karl Rove of his day, to pursue a plan of creating "a Republican machine that would go on forever," in the words of the historian Sean Wilentz. Instead, Theodore Roosevelt became president and pursued progressive policies. As Wilentz notes, "What followed shifted the Republican Party in a direction it had not planned to go, and created the groundwork for 1912 and eventually the New Deal. . . . One can't imagine what American history might have looked like had McKinley continued to the end of his second term."

those power-broking families, lured the Lackawanna Iron and Steel Company from Pennsylvania to western New York by highlighting these advantages. "This wonderful plant is rising in our midst, stupendous, massive!" a local paper exclaimed. By 1914, there were more than 2,000 manufacturing establishments in the city. "One never-ending factory" is how *Business Week* would describe Buffalo five decades later, in 1955. *Fortune* magazine published a gleaming twelve-page photo spread around the same time, depicting a city of billowing smokestacks whose factories churned out everything from airplane parts to jukeboxes.

As always, progress came at a cost. As industry boomed, so did the number of plants belching out pollutants. During the 1940s, the Hooker Chemical and Plastics Corporation began dumping thousands of gallons of toxic chemicals into nearby Love Canal, which decades later would prompt the federal government to evacuate hundreds of families from the area. Yet few people at the time complained about the drawbacks. Buffalo had stumbled on the formula that seemed to guarantee prosperity in the decades after World War II: a mixed economy powered by heavy industry that rewarded labor and capital alike. In 1955, statistics showed that Buffalo's factory workers were the highest-paid in New York State. "More than 200,000 workers in the immediate Buffalo region are union members," the Buffalo *Courier Express* reported that year, and the remarkable thing was that the corporations didn't seem to mind. In exchange for recognizing unions they got stability. Profits soared. Wages rose. For the time being, it went unnoticed that the people who owned Buffalo's factories didn't actually live in the city, or that an array of federal outlays helped keep the city's economy afloat.

WATCHING THE FORMULA unravel in the mid-1970s, my father could not help but be taken aback. Here he was in America, the land of progress, the wealthiest nation on earth—in a city where, every day, another company seemed to be announcing its departure. What surprised him even more than the steady drumbeat of announcements was the fact that nobody seemed to be doing much about it. He was not, generally speaking, a militant, let's-storm-the-barricades type. But he had grown up in a country where protests of a certain kind—labor strikes—

had been an integral part of life, and where the dignity of manual labor was simply assumed. At his father's knee, he'd heard stories about what working in a bakery had been like before the employees there formed a union: shifts that began in the morning and lasted through the night. Exhausting, repetitive work. (I heard such stories myself: when he and his coworkers first went on strike, my grandfather told me one time, their initial demand was that nobody be forced to work more than a *seventy*-hour week.) My father had gotten a taste of this when, after finishing his army service, he spent a summer working in the construction industry, mixing concrete beneath the broiling Israeli sun. It was the hardest work he had ever done, and it left him with a deep respect for people who made their living with their hands.

As the factory jobs disappeared from Buffalo during the 1970s, my father couldn't help but wonder why nobody was kicking up more of a fuss. Where were the city's supposedly powerful unions? Why was nobody out on the streets?

It's a question that apparently left many people in Buffalo equally befuddled. "Theoretically, if a union was a union and really worked as a fighting body representing the working people, it would fight back against this," a steelworker complained to researchers who interviewed eighty laid-off and unemployed Buffalonians in 1975. "But the United Steel Workers of America, the only response we've drawn from them is that you've got to look at the company's side of things. And with the no-strike clause we have right now, it's an illegal wildcat if we try to pull people off from inside ourselves." Reading these interviews thirty years later, what is most striking is not the anger expressed but the sense of powerlessness conveyed, an early glimmer of the harsh reality that, in the age of globalization, blue-collar workers throughout the country would come to face. Companies "get in, they make a buck, they get out," one worker complained. Another spoke of labor leaders co-opted by being handed plum management jobs before cutbacks were announced. Yet another, just back from Vietnam, railed at the indifference of elected officials: "the government don't give a damn about its people. Like in Vietnam, I sold myself to them, and when I got out, that was it. Goodbye. Nothing."

. . .

A DECADE LATER, the plight of the unborn would spark the sort of street demonstrations the plight of factory workers did not, a contrast that says something about the increasing potency of social issues—teen pregnancy, crime, abortion—in American politics and the declining significance of class. What my father saw in Buffalo during the 1970s—or rather, *didn't* see—naturally led him to conclude that America was, if not quite a classless society, a place where the kind of politics that marked his own father's world had simply never taken hold.

He was partly right about this: between its faith in free enterprise and its cult of individualism, America had been a difficult place for unions to take root. The country had no Labor party and scarcely any laws protecting workers prior to the New Deal, providing part of the answer to the old question sociologists posed, "Why no socialism in the United States?" And yet, for the better part of five decades, class struggle had hardly been absent from the Niagara Frontier. A half-century before my parents and I arrived, thousands of workers at the Lackawanna Steel plant joined the great steelworkers' strike of 1919. Their demands included union recognition and an end to the twelve-hour day, enough to inspire most of the press to side with the company, even as Lackawanna Steel imported black strikebreakers from the South and resorted to another familiar weapon in corporate America's assault against unions: violence. On September 25, 1919, company police fired into a crowd of workers amassed at the factory gate, injuring three and killing one. Afterward, 7,000 mourners paraded the victim, Casimir Mazurek, a Pole, through the streets, his coffin wrapped in an American flag.

The steel strike of 1919 would go down to defeat, but, two decades later, members of the newly formed CIO went plant to plant in Buffalo to organize factories. "CIO, CIO, we're all members of the CIO!" chanted workers in the coke ovens at Bethlehem Steel (the former Lackawanna Steel, bought by Bethlehem in 1922). Once again, workers were beaten up and bloodied. But times had changed. The New Deal brought with it the Wagner Act, the landmark 1935 law establishing the right to collective bargaining. One by one Bethlehem Steel, Republic Steel, Ford, and other local firms were forced to recognize independent

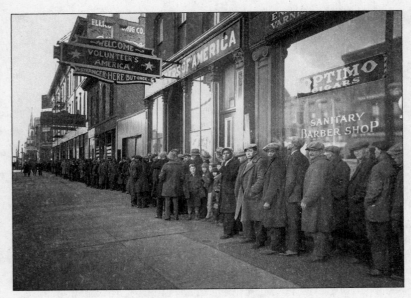

Thanksgiving Day, 1931: Buffalonians line up for food during the Great Depression.

unions, until by 1943 only four unorganized plants with more than 500 employees remained in the Buffalo area. "Solid Unionism is Solid Americanism," it was said in 1919, and for several decades the slogan would ring true, elevating tens of thousands of blue-collar workers into the ranks of the middle class. Working in a factory in Buffalo might not make you rich. It could still get you injured or killed—in 1969, the health clinic in Lackawanna fielded a staggering 58,956 emergency visits by injured steelworkers. But for at least a generation or two, it offered a measure of stability: a steady paycheck, a modest house, maybe even an opportunity to send your kids to college one day.

All this changed during the 1970s and, as it did so, it would have made sense for organized labor to rise up as my father expected it to. By the early 1970s, however, union leaders in America were no longer accustomed to calling for street protests. They were more comfortable sitting at the bargaining table. The energy that was once poured into organizing now went into hammering out the details of contracts, and, in exchange for a seat at the table, unions ceded control over investment decisions to management. It was sit-down strikes and direct action that had spurred the rise of organized labor during the Great Depression. Two decades later, in 1953, the president of the United Steelworkers came to Buffalo to call strikers back to work when a wildcat strike began. It was a dangerous time to be branded a radical and, as the historian Alex Blair has shown, union leaders in Buffalo generally cooperated with the McCarthyite purges of the 1950s, which stripped shop floors not only of Communists but of dozens of effective organizers.

The result was that, by the early 1970s, what had once been a movement had withered into something very different: an interest group. "When I joined the CIO [during the 1930s]," Joseph Molony, a veteran labor organizer in Buffalo, would recall, "it was like joining a church. It was both a religion and an emotional outlet and it gave me a sense of being important, that I meant something in the scheme of things." In the decades to come, fewer and fewer people in Buffalo would find this in the movement that, for Joseph Molony and many others, had once served as the functional equivalent of a church. Perhaps it's no surprise that, in a city where people had good reason to want to believe some higher force was looking after them, more and more would gravitate from the brotherhood of labor to another kind of fraternity: the fellowship of Christ.

LIKE THAT OF many newcomers to the city, my father's experience of the hard times that befell Buffalo in the 1970s was mostly secondhand. He didn't know many people who worked in the steel mills and the auto plants. The professional association he eventually joined was the American Medical Association, not the AFL-CIO. Although he crossed paths with plenty of poor people in the city's hospitals, and although we ourselves were hardly living a lavish existence at the time, the fear and insecurity that hovered over many families in the city did not lurk over us.

Even so, it was impossible to be in Buffalo at the time and not feel that something was profoundly awry, that something in the American

Dream, which was supposed to guarantee opportunity to anybody who worked hard and strived to get ahead, had soured. As it turns out, the factory workers in Buffalo who started to view this dream as a mirage were not alone. The year my parents and I arrived in America, 1973, marked the beginning of what the economists Bennett Harrison and Barry Bluestone later termed the Great U-Turn. In the decades to come, several million manufacturing jobs disappeared from the United States, wages fell, the middle class shrank, and the U.S. economy more and more closely resembled an hourglass, with inequality rising and more and more people concentrated at either the bottom or the top. The jobs vanishing from Buffalo would eventually return but, as throughout the country, many of the new jobs would be part-time and lower paid. A new category, the working poor, would arise, and the era when a family supported by one breadwinner was a realistic vision for most Americans drew to a close. These were national as well as local trends. With or without feminism, they would help to render the traditional nuclear family (Mom tidying up the house, Dad at work, the kids in school) obsolete.

It was the perfect recipe, in theory, for a resurgence of the sort of class politics that had crystallized during earlier periods of economic duress. The Great Depression had prepared the way for the rise of organized labor and Franklin Roosevelt's New Deal. Forty years earlier, during the 1890s, the plight of small farmers and mounting anger at big business had sparked the rise of the populist movement. "We have millionaires by the thousands and mendicants by the millions," Eugene Debs declared on a visit to Buffalo in 1896, just as the movement was gathering force. "A land where wealth accumulates and men decay." A quarter century later, in the 1920 presidential election, one in ten Buffalonians cast their ballot for Debs, the jailed socialist candidate.

There would be a resurgence of populism at the end of the twentieth century as well, only this time it would take radically different form. As the chasm between rich and poor widened, conservative activists would hone a language that linked the insecurity many Americans felt to the depredations of an immoral elite: not the economic elite nineteenth-century populists had inveighed against but a cultural elite. Not to financiers and robber barons but liberals, homosexuals, and feminists. Not the people who had moved Buffalo's factories to the Sun Belt and decimated its unions, but the ones who supported abortion rights and could be blamed for the nation's moral and spiritual decline.

· 4 ·

I have an image of my father from our days in Williamsburg Square. He's dressed in a pale blue scrub shirt, gray slacks, brown shoes. It is early morning, frost coating the windshields of the cars outside, and he is rushing out the door. His face is clean shaven, the sideburns grown out a bit in seventies style. The lunch my mother has packed for him is sitting on the kitchen counter. He's late, as usual, not because he overslept but because, if this is a normal morning, something trivial has distracted him. I see him open the door to the mango-colored Maverick, toss his things inside, and slowly pull away into the slate-gray Buffalo morning. I wonder when I'll see him next.

During the early years of my childhood, my father was more or less a stranger to me, the man who drove off every morning and returned home late, often after my sister and I had been put to bed. I had a vague notion of where he was going: to the *beit-cholim*, the hospital. Only after the photographs began appearing on our refrigerator—my father standing alongside a woman reclining on a hospital bed with a doll-sized, wrinkly-faced figure wrapped in a blanket in her arms—did I start to figure out what he did there. The babies weren't cute like the ones on TV commercials, and the women tended to look more exhausted than elated. Most of the time, though, they were smiling and so was my father, the sheepish grin he wears when something both pleases and slightly embarrasses him. Often a thank-you note was attached to the photographs. It was by reading those notes and studying the photos that I came to know what my father did for a living (even if I remained clueless as to how the biological process actually worked): he delivered babies.

I did not know that, in 1976, my father started doing something else as well. That year, he finished his residency, which according to the original plan meant we would be returning to Israel. Instead, my father stayed on at E. J. Meyer, where he was offered a half-time position overseeing the residency program he'd just completed. He ignored my mother's suggestions that we begin thinking about leaving Williamsburg Square and placing a down payment on a house somewhere. Settling permanently in America was not something he could contemplate yet; but another year in Buffalo evidently suited him fine.

On the days he wasn't slated to work at E. J. Meyer, my father filled in at various gynecological clinics run by the Erie County Health Department. By this point he had gotten to know a fair number of local physicians. One of them was an ob-gyn named Kenny Kushner, who had recently opened an office in one of those new commercial buildings that were sprouting up like weeds in the suburbs. Since he had his hands full running his office, Dr. Kushner asked my father whether he might be willing to cover for him on certain days at the hospitals. He also asked my father to substitute for him on Saturday afternoons at a place called the Erie Medical Center.

Located on the fifth floor of a brown concrete building at 50 High Street, half a block east of Main near downtown Buffalo, the center sat among a cluster of medical facilities that included Buffalo General Hospital and the Roswell Park Cancer Institute. From the outside, it looked no different than the other buildings surrounding it. But the Erie Medical Center was not just another reproductive health facility: it was an abortion clinic, the first of its kind in western New York and among the first to open in the country.

Health officials in Erie County had officially approved its formation

in June 1972, half a year before my father arrived in Buffalo, two years after New York became one of the first states to legalize abortion. As
would soon be true elsewhere, the shift in the law left unclear where exactly abortions should be performed now that the back alley was being
phased out. One possibility was hospitals. But many hospital administrators feared that a flood of patients would leave them overwhelmed. In
June 1970, Emma K. Herrod of the Erie County Maternal and Infant
Health Service warned that hospitals throughout western New York
were already booked through mid-August. Long waiting lists and a glut
of patients would mean limited access and more late-term abortions.
Hospitals were also expensive, charging an average of $450–$500 for an
abortion, which might exclude poor women.

Freestanding clinics seemed like the ideal remedy, which is why reproductive rights advocates spearheaded the call for their creation. In
his 1973 book, *Abortion II: Making the Revolution*, Lawrence Lader, one
of the founders of the National Association for Repeal of Abortion Laws
(NARAL), argued that because hospitals charged too much and had
limited space, "the only rational solution was a network of freestanding,
ambulatory clinics." When New York State health officials proposed restricting abortion to hospitals (or hospital-affiliated clinics) shortly after
the procedure was decriminalized, feminists who favored independent
clinics picketed with signs that read, "Raped by Medical Bureaucracy."

Few advocates anticipated that, in establishing clinics, they would
unwittingly be creating a nationwide network of *targets*—and isolating
abortion from the rest of mainstream medicine. Suppose a woman went
to a hospital for an abortion. How would anybody on the outside know?
There was no such ambiguity about the patients who showed up at 50
High Street. Later, when the protests would begin to escalate, hospitals
wishing to avoid the controversy would simply refer patients to clinics.
In the years immediately after *Roe*, more than half of all abortions in
America were performed in those hospitals. By the late 1980s, 86 percent were performed in clinics. In western New York, two thirds of
women who had abortions in 1975 went to hospitals; by 1995, just 7 percent did.

Not clinics but abortion *mills*—so opponents of abortion took to characterizing places like the Erie Medical Center: bloody, for-profit enterprises whose owners fattened their pockets by preying on desperate, ill-informed women. In fact, nobody forced women to go to the clinics, whose emergence reflected the enormous demand for the service they provided. But the opponents' claim that financial motives played a part in fueling the clinics' rise is not entirely unfounded. They were not, after all, charitable organizations. The founders of the Erie Medical Center, Moshe Hachamovitch and Gerald Grossman, were out-of-town physicians from, respectively, New Rochelle, New York, and Greenwich, Connecticut. "They believed in it, but their motivations were monetary," says Marilynn Buckham, who began working at the Erie Medical Center in 1972 as a receptionist. (A decade later, Buckham would cofound a clinic of her own, the one where Barnett Slepian eventually worked.)

Eileen Alt, a nurse, says that among the female staff at 50 High Street a sense of a larger social mission was not uncommon. "We were feminists," she says. "We were all politically motivated and knew that we were treading new ground, that *Roe v. Wade* represented a momentous step for women." Of the physicians, though, Alt says, "I have no doubt they saw this as an important service, and I remember one nurse who said she was there because she had seen women die of illegal abortions. But my sense is that many of the doctors were doing this to make money while their practices were growing. This was a check they knew they were going to get." One of the first physicians to begin performing abortions in Buffalo after New York State legalized the procedure, a doctor from Michigan named Jesse Ketchum, wound up being expelled from the Erie County Medical Society—and serving time in jail—after a woman in his care died. An investigation subsequently revealed numerous cases of alleged malpractice in his past.

KETCHUM'S CRIMINAL NEGLIGENCE was unusual. But the pragmatic outlook Alt described was not. When I asked my father recently what swayed him to begin working at the Erie Medical Center, he flashed me a look that suggested he'd never really thought about it before. "It was work," he finally replied.

There's a reason that photographs of women who came to 50 High Street did not adorn our refrigerator at home. Feminists spoke of abortion in terms of empowerment, but the experience of actually having one was rarely pleasant. Every day at the Erie Medical Center, women arrived pregnant and, a few hours later, returned home having decided *not* to become mothers. As my father would come to appreciate, few did so without some internal conflict. Some cried afterward. Others were deeply shaken. Many years later, after spending a day in my father's office on a day abortions were performed and coming home emotionally drained, I wondered whether this ever gave him pause. There were few smiles on the faces of the women I saw that day. There was, on the other hand, a palpable sense of loss and sadness. Did this ever make my father question whether perhaps the protesters had a point: that these women might be making a decision they would come to regret? And what sort of gratitude could my father possibly extract from what looked like such a thankless job?

When I worked up the nerve to ask him, he admitted that sometimes women did seem unsure afterward whether they'd made the right decision—and less than genial in their feelings toward the staff. On one occasion, he told me, a patient was so distraught after her abortion that she started screaming at him, "How can you do this?" He was unsettled. More often, though, he said what patients expressed was a sense of relief. Though few left with smiles, many did say thank you. "You know you do a delivery and you see a child born and you feel it's so nice," he explained. "When you do an abortion, you don't see that result—it's not a joyous event, like a birth. But what you can see many times is a patient who you've helped and who is grateful for that." When he started working at the Erie Medical Center, he added, he understood that most of the women in the waiting room would have preferred not to be there. But what struck him was that they *were* there—not because somebody had forced them but because, for reasons only they could ultimately explain, this was the choice they had decided to make.

Had the women showing up at 50 High Street been radical free-love advocates for whom abortion seemed merely a matter of convenience, I suspect my father's sympathy for them would have been limited. But his patients were nothing of the sort. They looked instead like a cross section of Buffalo: black, white, middle-class, poor, single, married, Jewish, Protestant, and, yes, Catholic. There were older women who were married, with children. There were adolescent girls. There were women who knew virtually nothing about birth control, and others who had been using it for years but had let it slide just once. Some were there because of a mistake, others because of a misplaced hope, others still because of something they didn't want to talk about. As I would later learn by speaking to some of my father's patients, generalizations on this score were dangerous, as were assumptions about a patient's political and religious background. Of the first 1,064 abortions performed in the Buffalo area after New York's law was changed in 1970, the most common self-description the patient offered was not "feminist." It was "housewife."

My father recalls sitting in on board meetings of the Erie Medical Center's medical advisory board at the time. Numerous physicians, including some of the best-known obstetricians in Buffalo, were members back then. "The atmosphere in the medical community was very pro-choice," he says. "We discussed things like what to do in the case of a complication. There was no mention of protests."

THE FIRST ACT of civil disobedience in the abortion conflict had, in fact, already occurred. On August 2, 1975, six demonstrators were arrested at a peaceful sit-in at Sigma Reproductive Health Services, an abortion clinic in Rockville, Maryland. Two years later, a bright, bespectacled, intensely pious Harvard graduate named John O'Keefe began organizing sit-ins outside clinics in Norwich, Connecticut, and several other East Coast cities. O'Keefe was a devotee of Thomas Merton, the monk and best-selling philosopher whose embrace of Gandhian civil disobedience had struck a chord in the 1960s among liberal Catholics. After a spell alone in the New Mexico desert, during which he ruminated about a conversation he'd had with a woman who had an abortion, O'Keefe returned to the East Coast, shaved his head in the style of a monk, and set about applying Merton's teachings to his new preoccupation: the plight of the unborn. In 1978, he published "A Peaceful Presence," a recruiting pamphlet that called on pro-life activists to engage in nonviolent civil disobedience against abortion. The message slowly began spreading among small pockets of mostly Catholic activists, including a group of seminarians at St. Louis University, a Jesuit institution, who would soon launch the first sustained campaign of pro-life sit-ins. For the time being, most activists heeded O'Keefe's emphasis on nonviolence, though not all. In March 1976, a Planned Parenthood clinic in Eugene, Oregon, was set ablaze. A year later another clinic, in St. Paul, Minnesota, was torched.

Yet in Buffalo, as in most cities, there were neither arsons nor sit-ins during this period. This was not because the city lacked opponents of abortion but because the most outspoken of them preferred to get their message across through other means. The public face of the pro-life community in western New York during the 1970s belonged to Bishop Edward Head, leader of the Catholic Diocese of Buffalo, and to a former substitute schoolteacher named Helen Greene.

An image exists today in the liberal imagination of the typical pro-life activist: a Bible-thumping white man for whom equality of the sexes ranks somewhere near communism on the list of desirable social experiments. At the protests I would later witness in the 1980s, the loudest voices always did seem to belong to angry white men—men whom I had a hard time imagining accepting the idea of having a woman tell them what to do in *their* personal lives.

Yet in the decade after *Roe v. Wade*, the pro-life movement was led by women like Helen Greene. The mother of four children, Greene lived in Hamburg, a suburb south of Buffalo. During the 1960s, she had joined a branch of the National Council of Catholic Women, a church-based civic group. One day, Greene heard that legislators in Albany were planning to introduce legislation liberalizing access to abortion. A devout Catholic who'd suffered four miscarriages, each of which she'd grieved as though she'd lost a full-term child, Greene was shocked that any woman would *voluntarily* terminate a pregnancy. She began working with a coalition of like-minded church members to defeat the abortion bill.

Greene soon found herself working the phones at night from her kitchen, delivering talks, traveling to Albany to lobby legislators. "It became a full-time job," she says. Like many pro-life activists, she sought to spread her belief that abortion involved the taking of an innocent human life by displaying pictures of unborn and aborted babies that a couple from Cincinnati, John and Barbara Willke, had begun passing around to fellow activists conducting outreach. The photos—of an eighteen-week embryo sucking its thumb, taken from a famous series that originally appeared in *Life* magazine in 1965; of an aborted baby in a bucket, arranged by a physician who was opposed to the procedure—were the movement's answer to the image of a coat hanger. They offered a visual refutation of the familiar charge that what motivated pro-lifers was the desire to punish women for the unforeseen consequences of sex and to impose their religious beliefs on others. Not so, the photos said: the goal was to save lives.

Through pictures like these, the upper hand was gained in the war of images. Once people saw a baby floating peacefully in the womb, or looked at its perfectly formed hands and toes, pro-lifers believed, they would be moved to recognize the humanity they shared. The images were indeed powerful, as I discovered by examining some. The magnified image of an embryo at twenty-two weeks, with its identifiable facial features and limbs, really does look a lot like a premature baby. Nobody looking at it can fail to register what he or she is seeing as recognizably human. An embryo at six weeks, on the other hand, looks nothing like an actual baby. It is perhaps for this reason that, although the two stages are morally equivalent from a pro-life point of view, the Willkes advised against brandishing images from such early pregnancy ("the audience may change their minds from their conviction that this is human life").

Helen Greene would become the first woman to chair the New York State Right to Life Committee, and she was not alone. Across the country during the 1970s, middle-aged women like her joined the burgeoning pro-life movement. It was the feminism of the antifeminists, a clash of worldviews that revolved around much more than just abortion. In her seminal 1984 study, *Abortion and the Politics of Motherhood*, the sociologist Kristin Luker drew on extensive interviews with pro-choice and pro-life women to show that the debate about abortion was also "a referendum on the place and meaning of motherhood." To pro-choice women, it seemed self-evident that equality would never come if they had to drop everything and become mothers whenever they got pregnant. To their pro-life counterparts, it seemed equally clear that such an attitude toward motherhood (and, implicitly, toward sex) threatened to undermine the natural division of male and female spheres as well as the sanctity of the family. Women in the first group tended to work in the paid labor force, to be well educated and *not* particularly religious. Those in the latter camp tended to be married and religiously observant, and to view abortion as part of a broader cultural breakdown—rising divorce rates, growing promiscuity, the blurring of gender roles. To Helen Greene, a straight line connected *Roe v. Wade* to the loosening of attitudes during the 1960s, what she described as "women's lib—the very radical do-it-my-way atmosphere."

"Women of my generation didn't just fall into bed with anyone," she explained. "I was watching my kids grow up and I thought, I don't want them living in this free style. . . . The promiscuity, the freedom that you started having in the sixties—this was very much against my values."

FAST-FORWARD A DECADE to the 1980s, when language such as this would define the culture wars. The speaker would be a Republican. The opposition to abortion would come packaged with similar sentiments about homosexuality, pornography, and secular humanism. The rhetoric would yield, in due time, to talk of a "new abortion"—gay marriage, which in the eyes of the religious right would come to symbolize a threat to traditional values every bit as grave.

But in the 1970s, none of this was clear yet. It was a Republican, Governor Nelson Rockefeller, who had signed New York State's liberal abortion bill in 1970, and another Republican, a matronly assembly-woman named Constance Cook, who had cosponsored the legislation. In 1972, Edward Golden, the director of the New York State Right to Life Committee, told *The New York Times* that his organization didn't care whether a politician was "a Democrat, Republican or independent, or how he voted on any other issues." All that mattered was his or her position on abortion. This nonpartisan, single-issue approach made sense in a world where many self-proclaimed conservatives—particularly the business Republicans of the so-called eastern establishment—held liberal views on social issues, a position rooted in opposition to government intervention in all forms. "I had supposed it to be a fundamental principle of conservatism to challenge *every* doubtful intrusion of the state upon the freedom of the individual," the conservative columnist James Kilpatrick wrote in explaining why he did not oppose *Roe v. Wade*. "The more serious the intrusion, the more it must be resisted." In fact, one poll showed that more Republicans (by a margin of 62 to 36) than Democrats (54 to 43) supported a woman's right to choose during the first trimester of pregnancy.

Yet to certain conservative strategists, such polls represented not a problem but an opportunity. It was during the 1970s that some Republicans started to realize that adopting a more conservative stance on social issues could potentially unravel the majority that had enabled Democrats to dominate American politics for nearly a quarter century. In 1970, Pat Buchanan, then an aide to Richard Nixon, handed his boss a book called *The Real Majority*. Written by the political strategists Richard M. Scammon and Ben J. Wattenberg, the book conjured up an imaginary voter, the "forty-seven-year-old housewife from the outskirts of Dayton, Ohio whose husband is a machinist." This voter and her husband had traditionally voted Democrat on the basis of their pocketbook, but they were increasingly dismayed by what Scammon and Wattenberg termed "the Social Issue"—crime, racial tension, riots, protests, disaffected youth, drugs. "That the Democrats have held the allegiance of most of the 'plain people' has been the critical fact in American presidential politics for more than a third of a century," Scammon and Wattenberg observed. "Now, upon the shoals of the Social Issue, there seems to be the possibility of a rupture in that pattern."

Richard Nixon loved the book, and was soon telling his aides, "Preempt the Social Issue in order to get the Democrats on the defensive. We should aim our strategy primarily at disaffected Democrats, at blue-collar workers, and at working-class white ethnics. We should set out to capture the vote of the forty-seven-year-old Dayton housewife." This was the next logical step in the drive to forge a Silent Majority, the broad coalition of "middle Americans" who emerged from the sixties craving not revolution but a reassertion of traditional values. Democrats for Nixon,

Reagan Democrats: a political realignment was taking shape that would soon leave liberals scratching their heads over why their message wasn't getting across to their traditional constituents.

Buffalo was just the kind of place where it stood to reason that Scammon and Wattenberg's imagined scenario might play out. On the surface, everything about the city—its blue-collar workforce, its unions, its growing minority population, its patronage-wielding Democratic machine—made it a political wasteland for Republicans. In 1934, two years into Franklin Roosevelt's tenure, the city registered a Democratic majority for the first time since the Civil War. By the 1970s Democrats outnumbered Republicans in the city by nearly 3 to 1. For decades they'd held a virtual monopoly on power, racking up wide majorities on the city council while the Democratic machine placed one mayoral candidate after another in city hall.

Many Democrats in Buffalo, however, were not liberals in the conventional sense of the term. They were more like that forty-seven-year-old Dayton housewife: Polish-, Irish-, and Italian-American "white ethnics" who went to church on Sunday, worked hard, loved their country. They voted Democratic because everyone in the old neighborhood had, or because everyone in the local did, but they didn't necessarily sympathize with antiwar protesters or feminists or Black Power activists. Many no longer lived in their old neighborhood, and those who did were often afraid to walk the streets at night. They had been lifelong Democrats, yet what had that gotten them? Being a Democrat didn't stop the good jobs from leaving their city. In fact, weren't high taxes and affirmative action policies responsible for *taking away* some of those jobs? And weren't Democrats the ones trying to forcibly integrate their schools? As the historian Mark Goldman shows in his fine book *City on the Lake*, the debate over busing, though not quite as incendiary as in Boston, roiled Buffalo throughout the late 1960s and early 1970s, pitting blacks and liberals against working-class whites. In a sign of the growing backlash, a Polish woman named Alfreda Slominski ran for councilwoman-at-large in 1967, as the champion of "neighborhood schools." That summer, race riots erupted for several days on the predominantly black East Side, accelerating the flight of its white residents to the suburbs. A few months later, Slominski was elected in a landslide, carrying every neighborhood in the city except the predominantly black Ellicott and Masten Districts and the "silk stocking" Delaware District, where, not coincidentally, many parents could afford to send their kids to private school.

David Gerber, a historian at the University of Buffalo who served as director of George McGovern's 1972 presidential campaign in Buffalo's University District, a middle-class precinct lined with modest wood-frame houses and postage-stamp-sized lawns, recalls the mood among the voters he canvassed:

> Most of these voters were supposed to be Democrats but their party loyalty had grown tenuous. . . . They felt disaffected from the mainline liberalism of the party establishment, which they blamed for the disorders and derangements around them—a war they did not understand that challenged their patriotism and took away their sons, the demands of angry black people, the seeming collapse of order and rise of crime, and the growing evidence of economic decline in their own city. Not ideological liberals, they had been Democrats because that had long been the party that had been protecting the little guy, but by 1972 they were unsure exactly what their party stood for.

What the liberal, McGovernite wing of the Democratic party stood for, Republicans informed voters in 1972, was "acid, amnesty [for Vietnam draft evaders], and abortion." Though the latter issue had yet to emerge as a major factor in presidential politics, it would not go unnoticed. Before the 1972 election, Richard Nixon sent Cardinal Terence J. Cooke a letter, drafted by none other than Pat Buchanan, praising the Catholic church's efforts to overturn New York's liberal abortion law. At the time, even some of Nixon's supporters criticized the move as ham-handed. "Nixon Bungled Abortion Issue," complained the columnists Rowland Evans and Robert Novak, noting that the law the Catholic church was trying to overturn in New York had been signed by Nelson Rockefeller, a key Republican ally who was Nixon's reelection campaign chairman in the state and who might perceive the move as a slap.

But Nixon was pioneering a strategy that Republicans would skillfully refine in the decades to come: safeguarding what would come to be known as "family values" in order to convert disgruntled Democrats into their friends. Although the letter was not enough to help him win Buffalo in 1972, the narrow margin of Nixon's defeat—in a city where registered Democratic voters outnumbered Republicans by 60,000, he lost by only 21,500 votes, less than half the margin of his loss in 1968—signaled his success at reaching across party lines. Nixon *did* win normally Democratic (and heavily Catholic) New York State, as well as a majority of the nationwide Catholic vote, according to postelection surveys. Four years later, the Catholic vote would go (narrowly) to Jimmy Carter, but in the four presidential elections after that, no Democrat would command a Catholic majority. Just as when the South had fallen to Barry Goldwater in 1964, a key cog in the historic coalition forged during the New Deal had come unglued.

JANUARY 28, 1977, began as a fairly ordinary day in Buffalo. It was cold outside, as it had been for months. The forecast called for snow, but it had been snowing virtually nonstop since late November, a whopping 151 inches in what had begun to seem like a daily (hence unremarkable) occurrence. My parents had grown accustomed to the snowstorms by this point. Like most people, they went to work that day unfazed by warnings of "near blizzard conditions" forecast for the afternoon.

The forecast proved an understatement. By noon, the snow in Buffalo was falling in fists. More ominously, the temperature dropped to zero and the lake-effect winds kicked up a notch. Several notches, in fact. Gusts of up to sixty miles per hour started whistling across the frozen surface of Lake Erie, sending the snow that had accumulated there for months swirling through the air and cascading onto the city. Drivers peered through their windshields at a white blur. The wind-chill factor plummeted to −60, cold enough to freeze exposed flesh in one minute.

Most people who'd gone to work that morning, including my mother, did the sensible thing: they stayed overnight at their offices to avoid the roads. Not my father. With his usual bullheaded determination, he got in his car and drove home along Main Street, a fifteen-minute trip that took six hours. What was a little snow on the ground, he figured? Actually, it was enough to leave twenty-nine people dead, many from hypothermia or carbon monoxide poisoning in stranded cars. Whole blocks were encased in snowcrete, a cementlike substance that had to be busted apart by bulldozers. At the Buffalo Zoo, the drifts enabled three reindeer to waltz across the fences to freedom.

For kids, the Blizzard of '77 was mostly fun—a couple of days off school and the best sledding of our lives. But it wasn't much fun for Buffalo. "This city is fighting for its life," Mayor Stanley M. Makowski told Jimmy Carter, who declared Buffalo a federal disaster area. The blizzard cost $300 million to clean up. It also sealed Buffalo's reputation as the blizzard capital of the United States, a place whose residents might as well live in igloos and tromp to work in snowshoes. It didn't matter that many other cities saw more annual snowfall and colder temperatures, or that Buffalo managed to survive the blizzard with its sense of humor intact. "I Survived the Blizzard of '77" T-shirts became a local fad. In the years to come, comedians would prefer to laugh at, not with, the people who wore them.

MAYBE IT WAS the blizzard, maybe the city's dire financial shape, or maybe Buffalo's mayor was just ready to move on. Whatever the case, a few months after the worst snowstorm in local history, Stanley Makowski, the incumbent and the preferred choice of Erie County party chairman Joseph Crangle, who headed Buffalo's Democratic machine, announced he would not be running for reelection.

Into this political vacuum stepped a candidate who, had the 1960s gone the way supporters of the civil rights movement hoped, would have been an ideal replacement, an African-American assemblyman named Arthur Eve. Tall and articulate, Eve represented the mostly black 143rd District, which stretched across Michigan, Jefferson, and Fillmore Avenues on the East Side. He'd first come to Buffalo in the 1950s, a decade during which the city's African-American population nearly doubled, to more than 70,000. These were Buffalo's golden years, when *Fortune* magazine was showcasing the city in photo spreads, but it was never quite so simple if you were black. Although, by virtue of its proximity to Canada, Buffalo had once been an important stop on the underground railroad, blacks there, as everywhere in America, encountered discrimination in forms both subtle and blunt. In the city's factories, they were often confined to the worst-paid, least desirable jobs. In the public housing market, they were steered into all-black projects, sometimes after residents in white neighborhoods protested alternative plans. Among the places where my father had worked as a resident in the early seventies was E. J. Meyer, a county hospital on the East Side around which, in the preceding years, one block after another—Kensington, Fillmore, Leroy—had undergone racial turnover, whites fleeing, blacks moving in. One of the first things my father was told was to avoid walking there at night.

Eve was first elected to the State Assembly in 1966. In his ten years there, he had distinguished himself as an outspoken civil rights advocate unafraid to buck the Democratic machine. During the 1971 uprising at Attica prison, Eve had stood in the trenches at D-yard, then called for Governor Rockefeller to be impeached for allowing so many inmates to be shot. He supported busing and had been one of the few local politicians who had gone to meet Martin Luther King, Jr., when the great civil rights leader had come to town. Could such a man be elected mayor of Buffalo? Not a chance, most observers would have said at the time, but in 1977, Eve rallied support within the black and Hispanic communities, portrayed himself as the candidate of the people rather than the bosses (i.e., Crangle), and confounded the skeptics by winning the Democratic primary, which usually cleared an unobstructed path to city hall.

In 1977, however, an obstacle stood in that path: Jimmy Griffin, the state senator from South Buffalo, the man who, seven years earlier, had denounced legal abortion as one more sign of permissiveness run amok. Griffin was bald and irascible, and his manner reflected his working-class background and Irish Catholic roots: tough, no-frills, politically incorrect, he was a former grain scooper who knocked back his share of beers and rarely minced words. "I'm just like one of you," he would tell his supporters, and you didn't have to ask what color skin (white), religion (Catholic), or ethnicity (Irish) this implied. Griffin's love for the city was genuine, and he was a deft politician who knew how to strike a populist chord, once denouncing bankers for having "hearts like caraway seeds." But, though a Democrat, he was no liberal. Unlike Arthur Eve, Jimmy Griffin didn't support busing. He didn't champion welfare or prisoners' rights. He was adamantly opposed to abortion. When *The*

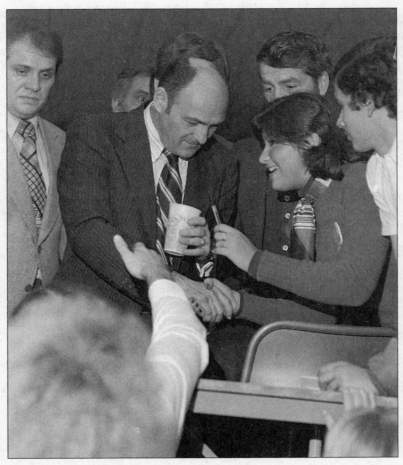

James D. "Jimmy" Griffin

Buffalo News ran a 1974 article headlined "Buffalo Democrats Appall NYC Liberals," highlighting the contrast between what it meant to be a Democrat on Manhattan's Upper West Side and in a place like South Buffalo, Griffin was Exhibit A.

He decided to challenge Eve on the Conservative Party ticket. Eve versus Griffin: two mavericks, two distinct social types, the one a reform-oriented black politician whose politics bore the stamp of the sixties, the other a brass-knuckle Irish Catholic who did nothing to hide his Right to Life views. The two had been able to coexist within the broad tent of the Democratic Party for decades, but by the late seventies they didn't have much in common anymore. During the campaign, racial tensions simmered just beneath the surface, with Griffin portraying his opponent as soft on welfare and crime. His supporters stenciled "EVE" beneath stop signs in white neighborhoods.

On November 8, 1977, the voters flocked to the polls in what proved to be a record turnout. Eve swept the black neighborhoods. But Griffin won the election, in which Republicans captured control of the Erie County Legislature for the first time in six years. The Democratic establishment had been toppled, not from the left but from the right.

My father paid close attention to an election of his own that year, not in Buffalo but in Israel. That same year, the Labor Party—for which my grandfather tirelessly campaigned—lost its grip on power for the first time since 1948, as Menachem Begin, the mannered Polish Jew who led the right-wing Likud Party, was elected prime minister. Like Jimmy Griffin, Begin rode to victory on the strength of a disgruntled populist insurgency, in his case Sephardic Jews fed up with the Labor Party–Ashkenazi elite that people like my grandfather represented. My father didn't notice the parallel at the time. One day soon, he would know full well who Buffalo's mayor was, and where he stood on social issues.

· 5 ·

J ews go home!" read the message scrawled in big block letters on the
side of my mother's station wagon. The handwriting and the
method of delivering the message, white chalk, led my mother to suspect this was the work of some bored teenagers. She washed it off without thinking too much of it.

The next morning, it reappeared. Not everyone in Williamsburg
Square evidently thrilled to overhearing neighborhood kids speak Hebrew in 1976.

That my father wasn't flummoxed by this incident doesn't surprise me—he'd heard and seen far worse, after all, and anyway prided himself on being an unflappable Israeli. That my mother took it all in stride is more notable, for she had good reason to be thin-skinned about such things.

Growing up, I had only the haziest notion of my mother's origins. I knew that my maternal grandparents spoke Yiddish and German, and that they were originally from somewhere in Romania. I also knew that they were Holocaust survivors. How exactly I learned this I can't really say, since it was not a subject I recall my mother speaking about. The word *lager* (German for "camp") came up occasionally in conversation between relatives on my mother's side of the family, but explicit talk about the Holocaust, at least in my presence, did not. Perhaps there was too much pain associated with it. The sole memento in our home that hinted at my mother's past was a framed black-and-white photograph of a young girl with flowing black hair pulled back in a braid. The girl had pale skin and a round, pretty face, and something in her features made me think she was a relative. One day, I asked my mother who this was. It was Anna, she told me, her older sister, a sister she had never met. Anna, I understood, hadn't made it through whatever ordeals my grandparents had endured.

Through interviews with my mother and my aunt, Talma, I later learned the full story. My mother was born in the fall of 1942 in Yampol, a deportation work camp run by the Nazis. Yampol was in Transnistria, a muddied stretch of land north of Odessa to which approximately 200,000 Jews were deported in October 1941.* In his book *The Seventh Million*, the historian Tom Segev reports that within a few months, two out of every three of the deportees had either died or been murdered: "About 70,000 were left alive." My grandparents, Albert and Rosa Herbst, were among them, but their daughter Anna—Anika—was not: she had died of typhoid shortly after they arrived. My grandmother also lost a brother, Leopold (whose own three children were killed), and her

---

*Transnistria is today part of Moldova, the poorest nation in Europe and the first former Soviet republic to elect a Communist president.

father, Zelig, who like many older people—what good would they be at
a work camp?—was taken to the Bug river and shot.

The grandparents I knew bore the scars of this history. My grandfather Albert, a rail-thin chain-smoker with a soft voice and hazel eyes that
formed milky-brown pools, was an exceptionally handsome young man,
I'm told, with high cheekbones and sharp, chiseled features. I have seen
faded black-and-white photographs suggesting as much, but by the time
I knew him the ravages of a brutal life were etched into his bearing. I remember his gaunt, weathered face and his long bony fingers moving the
pieces as we played chess together in the corner of my grandparents'
apartment in Holon, a suburb of Tel Aviv. I remember the feel of his ribs
against my body when we hugged. My grandmother Rosa would lay out
a tray of cakes for our visits, then ask my mother why I was so skinny as
she pinched my cheeks—my *yingalah*—and urged me to eat. Food was
her obsession, particularly for the grandchildren, which later made for
comic lunches at which my cousins and I would gather to be plumped
up. In the middle of a sweltering summer day, with the temperature
near 100, Grandma Rosa would feed us piece after piece of her freshly
baked chicken, which we joked was as hot and dry as the surrounding
desert. Eat one, and two more pieces would instantly appear on your
plate.

My grandparents never spoke to me about their youth. Years later, by
which time they had both died, I heard the historian Eric Hobsbawm
deliver a lecture in which he made passing reference to the city of
Czernowitz, where both my grandparents were from. Once part of the
Austro-Hungarian Empire, Czernowitz had been a beautiful, cosmopolitan city, Hobsbawm explained, teeming with artists and intellectuals. It
was indeed a city of "beautiful people," my mother remembers my
grandmother telling her, with an opera house, theaters, cafés, and parks.
My grandparents did not belong to the intelligentsia but neither were
they destitute; they lived in their own elegantly furnished home, the
ground floor of which was a millinery shop that my grandfather ran. He
had "golden hands," it was said, embroidering stylish hats and fabrics
that were so popular he envisioned retiring at forty. Once he made a hat

for the king of Romania, a story that became the pride of the family. He had considerable musical talent and, on days off, played the mandolin. When the Jews were rounded up and transferred to a ghetto—the prelude to deportation—my grandfather took the instrument with him. An officer saw it, grabbed it from him, and smashed it to pieces. "We'll make you forget how to play!" he snapped. Albert apparently never played again.

Many years later, my mother would hear protesters in Buffalo compare the genocide her parents survived with the "American Holocaust" of abortion. Needless to say, the comparison carried a personal sting, not only because of what her parents had endured but because she was a survivor herself. After Anna's death, my grandmother was so depressed that she openly contemplated suicide. My grandfather used to follow her around everywhere, standing outside the door when she went to the bathroom to make sure she didn't take her own life. A doctor at the camp advised him that the only thing that would revive her will to live was to have another child. Although she cried throughout the pregnancy for the memory of Anna, a year or so after arriving in Yampol my grandmother bore a second child, a tiny four-pound baby named Carla, the gentile version of the Hebrew name Chaya, which means life. This is how my mother came into the world.

She was the first child born there, blessed by a rabbi in the camps who predicted that, despite the circumstances, she would live long and be prosperous. How she survived the next few years remains something of a mystery, for she was an extra mouth to feed in a place of desperate hunger. During the first few months, my grandmother received help from a local peasant who took pity on her and passed milk and food through a fence barricading the camp. One day, a Nazi soldier caught them in the act and warned them that if he ever witnessed this again, he'd shoot them both. After that, the burden fell on my grandfather, who would sneak into the countryside at night in search of peasants with extra food. He, too, was eventually caught one night, beaten, and tossed into the woods by a soldier who assumed he was dead. My great-uncle Milo, the husband of my grandmother's sister, Loti, found him and dragged him back in a wheelbarrow to the squalid shack they shared, where he somehow recovered. Another time, Milo told me, the guards at Yampol lined up a group of men by a river. "Who can't swim?" they barked. A few hands shot up. Those men were promptly pushed into the water. Then there were nights when the guards rounded up the camp's inhabitants and randomly selected a few to be shot. My mother saw all of this through an infant's eyes—dark sparkling eyes that, along with her temporarily blond hair (it would later turn jet-black), made for a striking combination. Her beauty would prove fortunate. According to my grandmother, the guards would point to my mother during the lineups and whisper approvingly to her, "Sie ist keine judine—sie soll lange leben" ("She's not Jewish—may she have a long life").

In 1944, the Red Army liberated Transnistria. Free at last, my grand-parents traveled by train and on foot back to Romania with my mother on their back. My grandmother had just given birth to a third child, my aunt Talma. It was the dead of winter and, one night, the temperature dropped so low their limbs went numb. In desperation, they knocked on the door of a peasant's house. A woman opened it, welcomed them inside, and cleared the space above her oven so they could sleep there. She then set about baking bread and fed them the fresh, hot loaves at dawn. For the rest of their lives, my grandparents would swear the aroma of that bread was the greatest thing they'd ever smelled.

My mother and her parents made it to Bucharest, and for the next fif-teen years lived under a Communist dictatorship. Prewar Czernowitz it was not. During winter the entire family slept in one room, which was all they could afford to heat. They ate dinners of bread fried in chicken fat and lived in constant fear of the absolute power of the government. My mother remembers going to sleep at night fearing she would never again see her father, since on occasion he tuned in to Radio Free Eu-rope (which, of course, was banned). Like most Jews, they applied to go to Israel, but year after year they were turned down.

Finally, in 1960, their application was approved. My mother was eighteen now, a pretty dark-haired girl with her father's high cheekbones. She didn't speak a word of Hebrew but, after Yampol and communism, resolved never to complain about the basics of survival again. In Israel she enrolled in an *ulpan* (intensive language school) and after that in a school for lab technicians at Hadassah Hospital. She learned Hebrew and started meeting people. One day, a friend of hers, Yardena, who often helped her with her written assignments in school, invited her to a party, saying a medical student she knew would be there to whom she wanted to introduce her. That medical student was my father. He and my mother talked at the party, danced a bit, and soon started to date.

What did my mother see in him? Not, it appears, a smooth-talking lady's man. Shy, polite, serious—this is how my mother remembers him in the early stages of their courtship. Theirs was a meeting of two worlds, the native-born Israeli and the Holocaust survivor, though she was the olive-skinned, Middle Eastern–looking one. He, the Sabra, was reticent; she, the survivor, quick with a snap judgment. And yet she sensed in him—it was part of the attraction—an underlying certitude. His soft brown eyes exuded kindness but also a quiet confidence, a sureness of purpose that must have been immensely appealing to a young woman whose own parents were, quite understandably, prone to worrying and to assuming the worst, as she herself often was.

They exchanged vows in 1966, in Jerusalem. It would turn out to be a suitable match, although I wonder how well they actually knew each other. They were both, in their own ways, guarded. In the wedding photographs, my mother appears in a plain white dress, white gloves, and white shoes. Her jaw is clenched, her eyebrows arched, her bearing rigid. She looks aloof and hard-edged, like someone who is either naturally cold or emotionally withholding. She is neither of those—beneath the hard pose I can sense her pride in this moment and the immense love she feels for my father—but the circumstances of her upbringing have taught her to keep her emotions under wraps. I can see from the photographs why it is her reprimanding gaze, not my father's, that I will most come to fear as a child, and why her approval will seem hardest to win. She is a woman who has learned to navigate through life by dividing things into rigid categories, adopting a cold-eyed pragmatism. You make a decision—you stick with it. You reach a judgment—that's all there is to say. You prioritize things and live your life accordingly. At the top of her list of priorities, not surprisingly, was making sure that the people closest to her—husband, children, family—were safe.

HAVING FINALLY INTEGRATED into Israeli society, my mother was less than elated to pack up her belongings and move, yet again, to an unknown city in another foreign land. Yet she followed my father to Buffalo without complaining—no feminist instincts prompted her to voice misgivings—and was pleasantly surprised by what she found. On the plane ride over she'd envisioned living in a squalid tenement building. Instead there was the spacious duplex in Williamsburg Square. Accustomed to city life, she found the suburban environment strange at first, but gradually warmed to it. She even landed a job as a lab technician, at the University of Buffalo, where years earlier the head of the virology department happened to have met her on a visit to Israel.

The incident of car vandalism notwithstanding, she and my father felt comfortable in Buffalo. It was a Catholic city, they'd been told, but there were synagogues as well as churches, families named Stein and Cohen. There was a bakery, Kaufman's, that sold authentic Jewish rye bread, and a luncheonette, Ralph's, that served New York–style pastrami and corned-beef sandwiches.

My parents didn't know it, but at one point there had even been plans to turn western New York into a Jewish homeland. Back in 1825, a playwright, judge, and diplomat named Mordecai Manuel Noah donned a robe and, at a ceremony in St. Paul's Episcopal Church in Buffalo, announced that he was forming a Jewish state in Grand Island, a wooded strip of land located across the Niagara River from Buffalo. Noah formulated his plan after becoming convinced that he'd been removed from a diplomatic mission in Tunis because he was a Jew. No exclusionist, he invited not only Jews but also American Indians, who he was convinced were among the lost tribes of Israel, to live in the new Jewish state. "I have deemed it expedient to reorganize the nation under the direction of the Judges," the portly visionary proclaimed beneath a sandstone monument transported to Buffalo from Cleveland and inscribed with the words "ARARAT: A City of Refuge for the Jews." Shortly after delivering his peroration, however, America's first Zionist split for New York City, leaving his dream unfulfilled.

Even without their own Ararat, Jews slowly began trickling into Buffalo. In 1847, a small group of German Jews gathered in a roughly furnished room in the Western Hotel, on the corner of Pearl and The Terrace, and founded Beth El, the city's first synagogue. By 1920, there were eight synagogues on the East Side alone, which was now home to the William Street ghetto, a Jewish enclave teeming with Russian immigrants. As in most cities, the older, more established German Jews tended to look down on the newcomers, who crowded into a neighborhood that, like New York's Lower East Side, soon boasted a Yiddish theater, pawnshops, rag peddlers, kosher delis, and bakeries that sold pumpernickel and challah bread. Local branches of the Zionist movement sprang up—in 1915, the fraternal order of Labor Zionism held its national convention in Buffalo—along with an array of leftist political groups. Had my grandfather rather than my father been the one to journey to Buffalo, he might have frequented the Socialist Library on the corner of William and Monroe, and attended lectures such as "Why the Jew Should Be an Internationalist" and "Socialism as Messiah." The William Street ghetto abutted a small black community and the Polish Broadway-Fillmore area. Emmanuel Fried, an actor and union organizer whose father was the treasurer of one of the local synagogues, told me he recalls sitting out in front of a record shop on William Street and listening to jazz music blaring out. "It was Jews, blacks, and Poles all mixed together," he said.

Not everyone welcomed the "Russian Hebrews" to town. "Many of them are indolent and unclean in their habits, dissatisfied with what they get, and frequently insubordinate," a local correspondent complained. For the most part, though, in a city overflowing with Poles, Italians, Slavs, and Hungarians, Buffalo's Jews managed to blend in. The fact that most of their fellow immigrants were Catholic was a blessing, since the xenophobia of the WASP establishment fell on the more conspicuous—and multitudinous—faith. As in many American cities, it was Catholics, not Jews, who bore the brunt of religious discrimination in Buffalo. "The pretended miracles and lying wonders of Paganism and Popery have not a single feature in common with the miracles of Christ as revealed in the Bible," warned Buffalo's preeminent nineteenth-century theologian, John Church Lord. "Let the citizens of the Republic see to it that the swarm of locusts are stayed in their course." In 1856, Buffalo's own Millard Fillmore ran on the ticket of the virulently anti-Catholic Know-Nothing Party, whose local branch championed "Eternal Enmity to all who attempt to carry out the principles of the foreign church." Catholic children in the public school system were forced to read the Protestant (King James) Bible. At the turn of the century, as foreign-born workers began to organize in the steel and rail industries, hostility to Catholics and immigrants melded with fears of radicalism. Workers in the Buffalo area were subjected to intense Americanization campaigns—English-language classes, flag-raising ceremonies—geared to molding them into loyal citizens.

The WASP establishment could have spared itself the trouble. As elsewhere in America, the vast majority of immigrants who arrived in Buffalo, Jews and Catholics alike, would prove only too happy to adapt and assimilate. Like my parents and their friends, most eventually fell in love with a nation where, in the course of a generation or two, it was possible to go from being a faceless member of the great unwashed to a respectable member of the middle class. As they scaled the social ladder—and with it, the walls that had once barred entry into professions such as law, medicine, and banking—Jews in Buffalo abandoned their dreams of turning America into a socialist republic. They became proud capitalists instead. They also began leaving the William Street ghetto, first for more upscale neighborhoods such as North Park, a middle-class enclave abutting the Delaware District, then for the suburbs, where by the 1950s sprawling brick temples were being built. Jews still weren't welcomed in places like the Buffalo Club, home to what remained of the WASP elite, but they'd opened a club of their own, the Westwood, replete with tennis courts, swimming pools, and a nine-hole golf course.

By the time my parents arrived in Buffalo, Jews, like Catholics, had shed their status as outsiders, blending into what the sociologist Will Herberg termed the "triple melting pot" of American life. "To be a Protestant, a Catholic, or a Jew are today the alternative ways of being an American," wrote Herberg in his 1955 book, *Protestant, Catholic, Jew.* The reason these different faiths could coexist so easily, Herberg argued, was that the vast majority of Americans practiced religion "in a secularist framework." Americans were simply too pragmatic and materialistic to pray in any other manner, which is why although a majority told pollsters they viewed the Bible as the "revealed word of God," a majority also couldn't name any of the first four books of the New Testament. The nation's unofficial faith was a "secularized Puritanism," Herberg insisted, grounded in a set of values (individualism, free enterprise) that transcended denominational lines.

WILL HERBERG'S MODERNIST, pluralist vision of America is one into which my parents and I easily fit. Yes, we had come to Buffalo from a Jewish state. But like most Israelis of his generation, my father had been raised in a secular household where few religious holidays were observed. (You didn't have to observe holidays in Israel in order to feel your Jewishness.) Eventually, my parents would join a temple in Buffalo and, like many American Jews, begin to show up on the High Holidays as a way to affirm their identity. Even so, we neither lit candles on the Sabbath nor kept a kosher kitchen at home.

Having arrived in a country as modern and dizzyingly commercialized as any on earth, my family assumed all of these contradictions made us, well, normal. Buffalo a Catholic city? Perhaps, but the city didn't have an official church. The stores didn't close on Sundays, the way they did on Saturdays (at the behest of the Orthodox community) in Israel. There were no neighborhoods in Buffalo like Jerusalem's Mea Shearim, home to the quasi-medieval world of the black-hatted *haredim.* This was the image of fundamentalism for my parents and, later, for me: a throng of men with side curls clustered in the back of an

El-Al flight, bobbing their heads in prayer while everyone else watched *Fiddler on the Roof.* These people didn't watch television, didn't allow boys and girls to swim in coed pools. Some didn't even recognize Israel, since in their eyes a Jewish state could be built only after the Messiah appeared, although insistence on the latter point had begun to soften after the 1967 Six Day War, which another wing of Orthodox Judaism interpreted as a sign from God that the time had come to reclaim the land accorded to Jews in the Bible. Soon, yarmulke-clad settlers fresh out of yeshivas were roaming the West Bank, embracing Zionism with messianic fervor.

It never occurred to my parents that, just as fundamentalism was surging in the country they'd left, the same was true of the nation where they'd arrived. In 1976, the year I entered the first grade at North Forest Elementary School and began reciting the Pledge of Allegiance each morning ("one nation, under God . . ."), America elected Jimmy Carter, a Bible-quoting Baptist, as president. George Gallup, Jr., declared it "the year of the evangelical" after polls showed that one in three Americans said they had been "born again" and 44 percent that religion was "increasing its influence on American life," up from 14 percent in 1970. The latter figure, against the backdrop of the cultural upheaval of the 1960s, had once prompted many observers to conclude that religion had ceased to be a major influence on American life. "What religious institutions are encountering," observed *U.S. News & World Report* in a 1970 report, "Why Churches Are Worried," "is . . . massive indifference in a world increasingly enveloped by material values and worries."

By 1976, it was clear the media had been looking at the wrong churches. Membership in mainline Protestant denominations—Episcopalian, Presbyterian, Congregationalist, Lutheran—had indeed declined sharply. Among Catholics, the proportion that reported attending church "practically never" or "not at all" doubled between 1966 and 1975. During this same period, however, the ranks of Southern Baptists grew by 18 percent, of Seventh-Day Adventists by 34 percent, of Pentecostals by 37 percent. The denominations in particular trouble were those that practiced religion the way Will Herberg had described—in a secularist framework, with services reduced to a civic function. The ones that were growing stressed the inerrancy of Scripture and an emotional, sometimes even ecstatic, style of worship. In western New York, while the Catholic church struggled to keep urban parishes alive, *The Buffalo News* reported that fifty-two new prayer groups had registered as part of the growing Charismatic movement, a Catholic version of Pentecostalism that embraced faith healing and speaking in tongues. Nearly one in five Americans would describe themselves as Pentecostal or Charismatic by 1979.

That more traditional forms of Christianity were thriving in a decade widely remembered for its vapid consumer culture—the era of disco, designer jeans, and polyester—is perhaps no accident. What these denominations offered their members was a clear alternative to the soulless materialism of the secular world, whose spiritual shortcomings had been clear enough to the generation of the 1960s. In some respects, the Jesus People flocking to Bible colleges and charismatic churches could be viewed as spiritual cousins to the hippies who'd made their way to communes and folk revivals a decade earlier, even if it is true that their quest for salvation would lead them to reject the freedoms their shaggy-haired predecessors had embraced. It was the hippies, after all, who had questioned the dogmatic faith in progress and science that had undergirded the postwar liberal consensus that now lay in ruins. Behind the evangelical ferment of the mid-1970s lay a hunger for meaning in a society where many people didn't know what to believe anymore, and where the crisis of values prompted by the upheavals of the 1960s left many feeling understandably lost. If the number of people turning to God in response caught the media by surprise, it's perhaps because the media had forgotten how religious a country America had always been. As the historian Garry Wills pointed out in a 1978 essay, while academic scholars had theorized excitedly about the "death of God" in the late 1960s, 98 percent of Americans told pollsters they were believers. More than twice as many Americans as Europeans said religion was very important to them. "There can be no revival because there is nothing to revive," noted Wills. "For revivification, no less than for a murder trial, one needs a corpse. The evangelical 'corpse' has been alive and kicking all through our history."

AND, ALL OF a sudden in the late 1970s, it was visible on the political stage. "I would find it impossible to stop preaching the pure saving gospel of Jesus Christ, and begin to do anything else—including fighting Communism, or participating in civil-rights reforms," a fundamentalist preacher named Jerry Falwell declared in 1965. Fourteen years later, after meeting with a group of conservative strategists, the preacher from Lynchburg, Virginia, launched the Moral Majority. Based in Washington, its aim was to mobilize people of faith against an array of secular evils: divorce, homosexuality, pornography, abortion. That eight million evangelicals did not vote was "one of the major sins of the church today," Falwell declared, words that delighted leading conservative strategists like Richard Viguerie, a direct-mail specialist, and Paul Weyrich, the founder of the Heritage Foundation.

What these strategists understood is that, although not every born-again Christian was a fundamentalist, and not every fundamentalist was politically conservative, many evangelicals were looking for a political counterreformation to join. In the span of a generation, they had watched the Supreme Court ban officially sponsored school prayer and legalize abortion, the taboo disappear from practices like premarital sex, and the feminist and gay rights movements emerge, developments that left many feeling, not without reason, that their values were under assault as never before—and that they had no choice but to fight back. Ever since the 1925 Scopes trial, when the media had portrayed them as backward rubes in thrall to silly ideas like creationism, fundamentalists had largely withdrawn from politics. Scholars leaped to pronounce fundamentalism dead. Yet as the historian George M. Marsden notes, fundamentalists didn't go away but rather continued to do what they had always done best— "evangelize and build up local churches." Many also entertained "lingering aspirations to a wider social, spiritual, and moral influence," since the post-Scopes disengagement from politics was, after all, a relatively new thing. During the nineteenth century, evangelicals had stood at the forefront of an array of causes, from abolitionism to temperance.

Convinced that evangelicals could once again be mobilized, New Right strategists flooded the mail with literature designed to awaken them from their isolationist slumber. "Your tax dollars are being used to pay for grade school courses that teach our children that *cannibalism, wife swapping,* and the *murder* of infants and the elderly are acceptable," read one such missive from a group called the National Conservative Political Action Committee. Through such appeals, an alliance took hold that would profoundly reshape the nature of American politics: a marriage between evangelical Christians who believed their values were threatened, and conservative strategists aware that social issues like abortion and homosexuality could turn people who didn't necessarily care about lowering the capital gains tax (and might not even benefit from such a change) into their allies. The trick was to roll everything together under the rubric of saving the republic from an invasive liberal state. It was activist judges who prevented children from praying in school—and who were also responsible for nettlesome environmental and labor regulations. It was liberals in Washington who were pushing the ERA—along with quasi-socialist measures that hampered free enterprise. It was Medicaid that paid for abortion, one more reason Big Government had to be rolled back. As Weyrich put it, "We talk about issues that people care about, like gun control, abortion, taxes and crime. Yes, they're emotional issues, but that's better than talking about capital formation."

Some pro-life Catholics were less than thrilled by the new alliance, particularly those whose opposition to abortion was part of a broader agenda that included support for welfare rights, opposition to the death penalty, and other progressive goals. "Unfortunately, there are many in the prolife movement who do not share the bishops' broad application of the respect-life principle," warned George C. Higgins, a Catholic monsignor. "They apply the principle selectively—to the unborn child, but not to prisoners on death row, nor to the poverty-stricken family in the inner city. . . . I would hope that prolife Catholics seriously consider the possibility that in collaborating with the right wing on abortion they risk defeat of the overall social justice agenda."

In 1979, the same year Jerry Falwell launched the Moral Majority, an evangelical minister named Francis A. Schaeffer embarked on a twenty-city film and lecture tour with a born-again pediatric surgeon named C. Everett Koop. The tour's purpose was to promote a new book and film series, *Whatever Happened to the Human Race?*, that aimed to stir evangelical opposition to something few non-Catholics had vocally opposed: abortion. The vast majority of evangelicals had been silent about *Roe v. Wade*. Some had even voiced approval of the decision, which the magazine *Christian Century* hailed as "a beautifully accurate balancing of individual vs. social rights." Schaeffer was determined to change this, having come to view abortion as the product of a depraved humanistic value system that placed man rather than God at its center, and having grown convinced that evangelicals could return America to its rightful biblical roots by jettisoning their escapist theology.

The irony was rich, for Schaeffer himself had spent much of his life holed up at a secluded shelter in the Swiss Alps, L'Abri, where he wrote a series of books linking the decline of western civilization to the rise of secular humanism. Not the subtlest reading of history, his work nevertheless struck a chord, inspiring a small cottage industry of books assailing secular humanism that began appearing on the shelves of Christian bookstores. With his goatee, flowing hair, and bohemian attire, Schaeffer was a sort of Abbie Hoffman figure in reverse—the "Guru of Fundamentalism," as *Newsweek* described him. It was Schaeffer who helped convince Falwell to reach across denominational lines in the battle against secular humanism. ("Listen, God used pagans to do his work in the Old Testament, so why don't you use pagans to do your work now?" he counseled.) In his 1981 book, *A Christian Manifesto*, he also laid out a rationale for civil disobedience in the struggle against abortion. "*The bottom line* is that at a certain point there is not only the right, but the duty, to disobey the state," he wrote. The book sold 290,000 paperback copies. Its author would inspire thousands of future pro-life activists, among them Randall Terry, the founder of Operation Rescue, and a visitor to L'Abri named James Kopp.

PERCHED AS IT was on the U.S.-Canadian border, in one of the more heavily Catholic sections of the country, Buffalo could not have been confused with the Bible Belt. Yet the area surrounding the Queen City had witnessed its share of religious enthusiasms in the past—more than its share, in fact. "For a dissolute young man looking to be struck by evangelical lightning in the 1830s, western New York was the place to be," observes Louis Menand in *The Metaphysical Club*. During the nineteenth century, the canal towns stretching from Albany to Lake Erie came to be known as the Burned-Over District. It was in this area, also nicknamed the "psychic highway," that the preacher Charles Grandison Finney made a name for himself, barnstorming from town to town to save souls at frenzied, camp-style revival meetings. The same soil gave rise to the Millerites, whose leader, William Miller, predicted the imminent return of Christ in 1843 and whose disciple Ellen G. Harmon would go on to found the Seventh-Day Adventist Church. Nearby Palmyra is where Joseph Smith, Jr., author of a six-hundred-page book of biblical prose called the *Book of Mormon*, grew up.

Buffalo, alas, proved less hospitable to these forces than most neighboring towns. "You have no idea," Sylvester Eaton, a local Presbyterian minister, wrote to Finney in 1831, "of the awfully stultifying, hardening influence which prevails here." The city's residents were simply too busy making money to pay much attention to spiritual concerns, Eaton complained.

A century and a half later, nobody talked much about the Burned-Over District. Buffalo was known, if it was thought of in religious terms at all, as a city of immigrant Catholics who practiced their religion quietly and who had good reason to be wary of Bible-thumping evangelicals. Yet the wave of spirituality that washed over the country did not leave western New York unmarked. In 1987, the National Association of Evangelicals held its annual convention in Buffalo, claiming 50,000 local supporters. A year later, Billy Graham preached for several nights before a mass audience at Pilot Field, the city's newly built baseball stadium. By then, numerous large evangelical churches had formed in Buffalo and its surrounding suburbs, many with booming memberships. It is from these churches that many of the shock troops in the city's rapidly escalating abortion war would, in the decades to come, be drawn.

PART 2

———

The Believers

■

· 6 ·

Cars gathered in the windswept parking lot of St. John the Baptist Church around 6:30 P.M. They lined up in a motorcade and proceeded down Delaware Avenue, circling past Millard Fillmore and Children's Hospital—places in Buffalo where abortions were performed—before stopping at St. Michael's Church, a sprawling brick and sandstone structure downtown. Inside, a small crowd had assembled to pray to overturn *Roe v. Wade*. "Let's don't give up until we turn this bad law back," declared the Reverend Barney Lee before an audience of 150 sympathetic listeners, among them a few local assemblymen and Hizzoner, Mayor Jimmy Griffin.

It was January 22, 1981, the eighth anniversary of *Roe*, and although the "bad law" to which Lee referred was still on the books, the forces pressing to overturn it hardly appeared to be giving up. That same day in Washington, D.C., 50,000 pro-life demonstrators took part in the annual March for Life on Capitol Hill. "We want life, yes we do; we want life, how about you?" the protesters chanted on the steps of the Capitol. "We want Reagan! We want Reagan!" they shouted closer to the White House. Although America's newly inaugurated president did not address the marchers in person, several representatives of the march organizers met with him in the Oval Office afterward. They presented him with a bouquet of long-stemmed red roses to express their gratitude.

It was Ronald Reagan's first official meeting with a public organization of any kind, and a fitting conclusion to a campaign during which the Republican Party had dropped its long-standing support of the ERA and endorsed the idea of a constitutional amendment to ban abortion. The party that since the end of World War II had stood for two things—rigid anticommunism and limited government—had begun the transformation that eventually made it home not only to libertarians and supporters of big business but also to social conservatives and the Christian Right.

A new era was beginning, one in which the dispirited mood of the Carter years would give way to the buoyant optimism of Reaganism, which fused its message of renewal with a pointed critique of liberalism. "We're not, as some would have us believe, doomed to an inevitable decline," President Reagan declared in his 1981 inaugural address, in marked contrast to his predecessor, Jimmy Carter, who in his own inaugural four years earlier had urged Americans to recognize that "even our great Nation has its recognized limits." Limits? The only kind Reagan acknowledged in the years to come were those—burdensome taxation, a culture of dependency among the underclass—that could be blamed on the government. After a decade of bitter setbacks that had profoundly shaken public faith in Washington (Vietnam, Watergate, the Iranian hostage crisis), this proved to be a winning message, not least because the man disseminating it projected such sunny faith in the basic goodness of America. Faith, too, in the power of conservative solutions to seemingly insoluble problems. Stagflation: Reagan promised tax cuts that, through the magic of supply-side economics, would pay for themselves. The Cold War: a space-based missile defense shield would make the United States invulnerable again. It didn't matter that these ideas were based on (suspect) theories rather than facts. What mattered was that Reagan believed in them. When he promised to lead the United States into "an era of national renewal," nobody could doubt the sincerity of his words, which had a soothing effect on the nerves of his fellow Americans.

In Buffalo, the hunger for better times led to something different: not bold new policy initiatives plucked off the shelves of conservative think tanks but a public relations campaign, launched by a group of area businessmen, to refurbish the battered city's image. Its centerpiece was a jaunty music video that began airing on local TV stations in 1980:

> *Buffalo's got a spirit,*
> *Talking proud, talking proud,*
> *Listen up and you'll hear it,*
> *Talking proud, talking proud*

So sang a Buffalo-born actress, Terry Licata, alongside a chorus of foot-stomping residents. It sounded like the theme song for a sports team, and, as it happens, the campaign took on a life of its own on November 22, 1980, when the tune blared over the public address system at Rich Stadium after the Buffalo Bills defeated the reigning Super Bowl champion Pittsburgh Steelers, 28–13. "Talking Proud" T-shirts, pennants, and banners soon inundated local retail stores. The Buffalo Sabres etched a Talking Proud logo onto the ice at Memorial Auditorium. The Fillies—cheerleaders for the city's professional indoor soccer team, the Stallions—performed a specially choreographed Talking Proud routine. Andrew B. Craig, president of M&T Bank, called it "the most extensive and far-reaching effort in the history of Buffalo aimed at upgrading and improving the [city's] popular image."

Proud or not, Buffalo, like the rest of the country, was slipping back into recession; apparently, renewal would not come as easily or painlessly as Reagan's supply-siders hoped. Once again, jobs were leaving a city whose residents thought they had lived through the worst during the 1970s. A few days after Christmas, 1982, *The Buffalo News* reported that unemployment in the Buffalo area had climbed back up to 15.3 percent. That same year, Bethlehem Steel, which had once operated the nation's third largest steel plant, in nearby Lackawanna, announced that it was shutting down virtually all operations there. The facility, known simply as the Plant to locals, was being mothballed, its towering blast furnaces reduced to hulking ruins on account of cheaper foreign imports, the rising value of the dollar, and outdated technology. Politicians, including Mayor Griffin and U.S. senator Daniel Patrick Moynihan, expressed shock. In August 1983, a group of workers chose to express their anger

A sign outside a
restaurant in
Buffalo, 1982

another way: by raising an upside-down American flag 12 feet by 24 feet—the international distress signal—over a blast furnace in the middle of the night.

Reaganomics, for Buffalo at least, wasn't much help. By 1983, the share of funding to the city coming from the federal government had fallen from 30 percent to 13 percent; the cuts' impact would fall disproportionately on the poor.

THE VILLAGE OF Kenmore sits directly north of Buffalo, in the Town of Tonawanda. It is among the nation's oldest suburbs, the brainchild of Louis Phillip Adolph Eberhardt, a real estate agent with a handlebar mustache who, in 1888, began purchasing property in what was then a remote stretch of prairie dotted with farmhouses. Only a few years earlier, passenger service had begun on the Belt Line, the commuter railway that encircled Buffalo and would soon make it easier for locals to work in the city without living in it.

The first house Eberhardt built in Kenmore burned down shortly after he moved in; early residents struggled to find a supply of fresh water. But in 1894, what would become Kenmore's main street, Delaware Avenue, was paved with asphalt. A few years later, the first sidewalks were laid. By 1930, the village had blossomed into a prosperous middle-class community that was home to more than 16,000 inhabitants, its streets lined with elm trees, frame houses, and newly installed electric lights. Kenmore today has the more weathered look typical of many "inner" suburbs—the older houses could use sprucing up, and Dutch elm disease long ago wiped out the once splendid trees—but its worn appearance lends it a distinctiveness missing from some of the newer, more sterile subdivisions surrounding it.

On the corner of Kenmore Avenue and Colvin, at the line where Kenmore crossed into Buffalo, stood a two-story redbrick building that, in the mid-1980s, emerged as a flashpoint in western New York's abortion wars. The building bordered a parking lot with a Mobil gas station. It was subdivided into a number of units where several doctors rented office space. It is here that my father opened an office in the early 1980s, and here that pro-life demonstrators would soon begin massing to greet him at work.

Remove the protesters from the picture, and what you'd have is the story of an immigrant doctor fulfilling a fairly conventional, which is not to say unexciting, aspiration. To start up his own practice in America: in the bureaucratized world of Israeli medicine, no physician could dream of such a thing. In the United States, it was what every enterprising young doctor did, and my father, son of a socialist though he was, would prove no different, scratching the entrepreneurial itch that made medicine in America more personal—but also more of a business—than it is just about anywhere else. He liked the idea of seeing his own patients and being his own boss, factors that played a large role in impelling him to remain in America. He relished the challenge of finding out whether he could make it on his own, though he understood it might not be easy at first. He was, after all, still a newcomer in town, without the connections to draw an immediate group of patients, and, perhaps more crucially, without the outgoing personality that would have made bridging the cultural divide any easier. Linda Stadler, who was among my father's earliest coworkers, recalls trying with limited success to train him to remember to smile and say hello to patients. He was so shy and uncommunicative that she worried women would come for one appointment and never return. In truth, I'm not certain how his patients understood a word he said in those days, for his difficulty with English was a frequent conversation topic—and source of amusement—at home. "*Theeze* Dr. Press," he invariably answered the telephone at home, no matter how many times we instructed him to say "This *is* Dr. Press."

My father's linguistic deficiencies did not stop him from making a positive impression on at least some of his coworkers. Eileen Alt, a nurse who worked with him at the Erie Medical Center, confirmed that he wasn't the chattiest person in the office back then. "We used to ask your father a billion questions, but he was very, very quiet and difficult to understand," she recalled. "I always felt like I was translating for him." At one point, she told me, a rumor circulated that he carried an Uzi submachine gun in his briefcase (not true, though he did, and still does, own a handgun, and would on occasion practice his aim at the local firing range). "He was so serious, and of course we'd heard the story about him training Paul Newman during the filming of *Exodus*." But there were other times when he appeared more at ease. "Your father was very compassionate with patients," said Alt. "I remember he would put his hand on a patient's arm if something went wrong and tell them, 'It's okay, everything will be okay.' He was always going out of his way if someone was borderline or needed help."

Medicine was not a political calling to my father. But it was a barometer of virtue to him, a measure of the kind of person he could claim to be, which he viewed as a function not of whether he was pro-life or pro-choice but of how attentive he was to the people in his care, and how hard he worked. Some doctors placed limits on how many hours they spent at the hospital. Not my father. He sprang out of bed with a bounce in his step and never complained of being tired, even when he had to work straight through the night to do a delivery or, as was not uncommon, the entire weekend. Of course, between the demands of his patients and his puritanical work ethic—*Avodah ze chayenu*, "Work is our life," the saying in Israel went—something had to give, and often that something was time with us. On family vacations, he invariably left early. On weekends, he often worked both days. He was generally the last one home at night and the first one gone in the morning, which made me wish not infrequently that my father was a teacher, or a fireman, or a carpenter: anything but a physician "on call."

MY FATHER'S NEW office was a ten-minute car ride from Williamsburg Square. But by the time he started working there, we'd moved to the Village Green, a middle-class suburban enclave in Williamsville where the lawns were all neatly trimmed and the more lavish houses sported backyard swimming pools. Station wagons and minivans cluttered the driveways of the ranches and split-levels, whose carpeted interiors glowed with modern lighting and the aqua hue of television sets. Our own house on Exeter Road was a two-story yellow-brick affair. It had a wood-paneled living room, a brick fireplace, a spacious kitchen, and a winding staircase that led to four bedrooms upstairs, each of which would soon be furnished with beds and bookshelves purchased at one of the nearby shopping malls or department stores. Although there came a day when my sister and I viewed our new surroundings through a more jaded lens—oh, the boring, sterile suburbs—I don't recall feeling remotely cynical about them at the time. What we felt was lucky— as, having gone from Williamsburg Square to the cushy suburbs in less than a decade, we inarguably were. We no longer lived in the apartment of a family struggling to make ends meet but in the house of a physician whose practice would grow steadily in the years to come.

Few of my father's patients, particularly in the beginning, were calling his office about the procedure that would soon land his name in the headlines. Though it would be described as such many times in the years to come, my father's new office was not an abortion clinic. Women came there for regular gynecological checkups and care, with abortion only one of a range of medical services performed. Why so few obstetricians mimicked this arrangement (which would have obviated the need for specialized clinics) speaks to an uncomfortable fact that pro-choice activists rarely acknowledged and that my father somehow failed to grasp until it was too late. Despite all that had changed since the 1950s, including legalization, many physicians, even those who were firmly pro-choice, continued to fear the stigma associated with the term "abortionist." Its negative connotations had not gone away—despite *Roe*, despite feminism, despite polls indicating that a majority of Americans agreed abortion should be legal under at least some circumstances. For even people who felt this way rarely went around proclaiming abortion a *good* thing. Few doctors wanted to have anything to do with it, particularly in a predominantly Catholic city like Buffalo, and here was a second, related disincentive to arranging things the way my father did. In neighborhoods like South Buffalo, where Irish pubs and churches abounded, a doctor who did even a few abortions risked putting his or her entire practice in jeopardy. Risked, at minimum, losing patients who would be uncomfortable knowing abortions were performed in his office. Who in their right mind would want to deal with the icy stares from colleagues who disapproved? With the possibility that one's office would come to be viewed not as a medical facility that provided treatment to women but as a slaughterhouse where babies were killed?

My father was not unaware that some people in Buffalo felt this way about abortion. He'd even spotted a protester or two outside the doors of the Erie Medical Center on High Street. Yet he still had no idea how widespread the opposition to abortion was. He didn't think that performing abortions at his office would bring protesters to his door. The truth is, he didn't consider the political implications at all. He simply thought he was providing a medical service for which there was both a demand and a need.

It seems incomprehensibly naïve to me now: how could the same man who'd grown up obsessively tracking the news in Israel have been so clueless? In the early 1970s, okay, but by 1980? After Ronald Reagan's election? After the Moral Majority had formed? On the other hand, my father's detachment was of a piece with his lifestyle, which revolved around the traditional duties of supporting a family and advancing his career. As in so many immigrant households, the task of decoding the intricacies of American culture and politics would fall to the next generation—to my sister and me—although my parents didn't disregard politics altogether. In 1980, they became citizens, eligible to vote. It was an election year and so, on the first Tuesday in November, my father drove to a polling booth and cast his inaugural vote as an American. His choice was the first presidential candidate ever to receive an official endorsement from the National Right to Life Committee: Ronald Reagan.

The poor sap, you might think. Only, my father was not a liberal, at least by the standard American definition of the term. When it came to foreign policy he believed, like any good Israeli, in a strong national defense. When it came to domestic policy he believed in moderation. He was suspicious of ideological extremism, a sentiment that would deepen in the years to come, but Ronald Reagan did not seem like an extremist to him. He seemed like a politician who reflected my father's own optimism about America, a pleasant man who projected a folksy humility and told ordinary people that they had a right "to dream heroic dreams." Though this was the kind of phrase that made Reagan's liberal critics cringe, it had no such effect on my father, for what was he doing if not living out just such a dream?

By this point it was clear that my family was not going back to Israel, even if my parents avoided saying so directly. At home, English began replacing Hebrew in our conversations. More and more of our friends were non-Israelis. It was not long before my father was proudly calling me his "*American* boy." I played Little League for the Red Sox, wore sneakers, and collected playing cards. Soon I started teaching my father about a sport that would come to play a major role in our relationship: football. On Sundays in the fall, the game that had made O. J. Simpson and Jack Kemp into local heroes temporarily erased the class, race, and ethnic distinctions in Buffalo, turning everyone into a member of the same beleaguered tribe: Bills fans. One rainy August evening—I do not recall the year—my father put me in the passenger seat of his new car, a beige Monte Carlo, and drove to Rich Stadium, where the Bills were hosting a preseason game against the Denver Broncos. We sat beneath the upper-deck rafters, a strange farrago of odors—peanuts, beer, sweat, cigarettes—wafting over us. It poured nonstop and the Bills lost, but I could not have imagined a better time, not least because I had three hours of my father's undivided attention in an atmosphere where the sight of men hooting, hollering, and hugging one another was not only tolerated but expected. The Bills hadn't won a championship since

1966,* but this hardly mattered. To the contrary, as in Chicago and Boston, losing would only deepen the city's affection for its team. For my father and me, rooting for the Bills would become both a shared passion and a way to affirm that we belonged.

THE NEXT FEW years passed by uneventfully, or so it seemed. My father's practice continued to grow. His English (*slowly*) improved. My sister and I enrolled in elementary school, then at a private middle school in the city, still unaware that our father was doing anything that might be considered controversial.

Had we been living in Europe, this impression might never have changed. Even predominantly Catholic countries like Italy and France would somehow manage to legalize abortion without provoking significant unrest. "Outside the United States, serious opposition to abortion is rare," the conservative columnist Fred Barnes later observed. But America wasn't Europe. The culture wars were in full swing by this point and, with Reagan in the White House and evangelicals congratulating themselves on having played an important role in electing him, liberals were squarely on the defensive. The broad array of conservative single-issue groups that had emerged to fight disparate cultural battles during the 1970s—against abortion, against the ERA, against pornography, for school prayer—were now united under the banner of the New Right. As Frances Fitzgerald pointed out in a *New Yorker* profile of Jerry Falwell, the leadership of the Republican Party, once typified by the businessman on the golf links, looked increasingly "like William Jennings Bryan in a double knit and television makeup." Few Americans hadn't heard of Falwell by this point, just as few, regardless of political affiliation, were unaware that they were living through reverberations from the changes that the 1960s had wrought. In Buffalo, Jimmy Griffin had been reelected to a second term, and although Griffin was a Democrat (albeit one who in 1977 had run on the Conservative ticket), when it came to

---

*They *still* haven't.

social issues he might as well have been a newly minted Republican. On January 22, 1982, one year after Reagan had met with the organizers of the March for Life in Washington and nine years after *Roe v. Wade* became law, Griffin signed a proclamation officially declaring that date "Right-to-Life Day" in Buffalo. As he did so, fifty members of the Erie County Right-to-Life Committee marched around city hall singing "God Bless America." Another 200 local protesters traveled to Washington to take part in the March for Life.

Only the mood was not quite as buoyant as it had been a year earlier.

"MY FINEST HOUR," Jerry Falwell called the moment when he and the rest of America first learned that Ronald Reagan had trounced Jimmy Carter in the 1980 election, a feeling shared by many pro-life activists. Four years earlier, those activists had watched Congress pass the Hyde Amendment, legislation sponsored by Illinois representative Henry Hyde that barred federal Medicaid dollars from being used to pay for an abortion unless it was necessary to save the woman's life. Cora McRae, a pregnant Medicaid recipient, promptly challenged the amendment on the grounds that denying poor women what their wealthier counterparts took for granted was unconstitutional. On June 30, 1980, the Supreme Court issued a 5–4 decision against McRae, ruling that nothing in *Roe* assured a woman "a constitutional entitlement to the financial resources to avail herself of the full range of protected choices." In a stinging dissent, Justice William Brennan argued that Congress and the Court had "effectively removed . . . choice from the indigent woman's hands." The number of federally funded abortions indeed plummeted, from 350,000 per year to a mere 900 in the third quarter of 1978.

The Hyde Amendment was not the complete victory pro-lifers might have wanted, since states could still opt to continue funding abortion with their own Medicaid funds. New York was one of those states, though it did not maintain funding without resistance. In 1977, before a cheering gallery, the Niagara County Legislature voted 23–7 to defy Albany and bar any welfare funds from paying for abortions. The following year, a busload of activists from western New York traveled to the state capital to attend a rally in support of a bill prohibiting state Medicaid funds from underwriting the procedure. "It's murder, plain murder," Irene Sielski, a parishioner from Queen of Peace Church in Buffalo, told reporters on the sun-drenched lawn where the demonstration took place.

That Ronald Reagan should become the vehicle of hope for social conservatives of this sort was in some ways odd. The former California governor was a divorced Hollywood actor who did not attend church regularly and who, as governor, had supported the ERA, opposed legislation that would have barred homosexuals from teaching jobs, and signed a permissive abortion law that had led to more than a million legal abortions being performed in California.* His running mate in 1980, a Yale graduate and former CIA chief named George H. W. Bush, was known to be pro-choice.

Yet Reagan had said the right things during the campaign. "You can't endorse me, but I endorse you," he'd told an audience of evangelical leaders who had packed into Dallas's Reunion Arena a few months before the election. He held a press conference to complain that the Supreme Court had "expelled God from the classroom" and to urge that the biblical story of creation be taught as an alternative to the theory of evolution. Reagan understood the value of broadening the GOP's base—in a 1977 speech, he had wondered aloud whether it might be possible for a candidate "to present a program of action based on political principle that can attract those interested in the so-called 'social issues' and those interested in 'economic' issues." Almost as though he'd written the script to his own real-life movie, he then went out and did just that.

A mere six months into his first term, however, the man in whom millions of social conservatives had placed their trust gravely disappointed them. On July 7, 1981, President Reagan announced that he had

---

*Reagan would express regret for the decision, though, as his biographer Lou Cannon has shown, his claim that doctors had abused what he originally assumed would be a far more restrictive law is implausible. The bill's opponents had in fact warned him of its permissiveness beforehand.

selected a fifty-one-year-old judge on the Arizona Court of Appeals to replace retired Justice Potter Stewart on the Supreme Court. Her name was Sandra Day O'Connor. The first female nominee in history, O'Connor had well-established conservative credentials on most issues, but not the ones that mattered to the religious right, whose leaders drew immediate attention to her past support for the Equal Rights Amendment and cosponsorship of a bill in Arizona that had made family planning methods and information widely available. The religious right's misgivings were well founded, for in the years to come O'Connor cast a crucial swing vote in numerous cases affirming a woman's right to choose. The National Organization for Women praised O'Connor's nomination as a "victory for women's rights." Senator Ted Kennedy declared, "Every American can take pride in the President's commitment to select such a woman for this critical office." The National Right to Life Committee, the Moral Majority, and other social conservative groups were left to fume.

The news soon went from bad to worse for the religious right. In Congress, opponents of abortion simply didn't have the votes needed to pass a Human Life Amendment, which Helen Greene had described as her ultimate goal in an interview in *The Buffalo News* in 1976. That same year, Jimmy Griffin, then still a state senator, had sponsored a resolution also calling for a Human Life Amendment, which met with the same fate. In fact, five years later, a memorandum that circulated among pro-life leaders struck a decidedly pessimistic note about the prospects. "It is no secret that in spite of better than expected results in the 1980 elections, many of the most experienced right-to-life leaders are far less optimistic about the possibility of passing and ratifying an ideal amendment in the foreseeable future than they care to admit in public," the memo explained. "Some privately speak of 20 to 30 years being necessary to end abortion."

Part of the problem lay in the White House, which had done little to make good on its campaign pledge to support such an amendment. Reagan's administration hadn't even thrown much weight behind a more moderate measure, the Helms-Hyde Bill, cosponsored by Senator Jesse Helms of North Carolina and Congressman Hyde, that would have enabled states to ban abortion by declaring that human life begins at conception. Nor did Reagan endorse the Family Protection Act, an omnibus bill that included a bevy of measures (prohibiting abortion, restoring school prayer, barring federal funds from being used to promote homosexual or feminist values) championed by the New Right. Nobody believed such a bill could actually be enacted, but voicing support for it would have been symbolically significant. Instead, the administration told supporters it needed to focus on more pressing economic issues like tax cuts, an explanation that did little to comfort people like Paul Brown, executive director of the Life Amendment Political Action Committee.

"We are a movement in disarray," Brown told the press less than a year after Ronald Reagan had taken office. "Political reality has come home to the prolife movement, and it has been totally unpleasant."

At the core of the unpleasantness they were feeling was the fact that, a decade after *Roe v. Wade*, what had once seemed radical—legalizing abortion, at least under some circumstances—no longer did. Despite their superior organization and zeal, pro-lifers could not convince a majority of Americans that abortion should be uniformly banned. In January 1982, an AP-NBC News poll asked Americans, "Do you favor or oppose an amendment to the Constitution which would give Congress the authority to prohibit abortions?" Three fourths said they opposed such an idea and only 19 percent approved, poll numbers that undoubtedly influenced the White House's reluctance to invest political capital in the issue. In fact, the GOP had risked much in supporting an antiabortion amendment and opposing the ERA during the campaign, as a majority of Americans disagreed with both positions. The only reason Reagan hadn't been hurt by this political misstep is that many voters with more liberal views were willing to support him for other reasons. Now, it was becoming clear that while Republican leaders were happy enough to incorporate the foot soldiers of the religious right into their ranks, once in office they did not want to risk alienating middle-of-the-road voters by seeming too close to them. "What do you want to give them?" the Reagan biographer Lou Cannon asked a White House aide as leaders of the March for Life met with the president. "Symbolism," the aide answered, mentioning the Mafia member in *The Godfather* who lived by the motto "Hold your friends close, hold your enemies closer."

"We want to keep the Moral Majority types so close to us they can't move their arms," the aide explained.

Symbolism is what many social conservatives cynically came to expect from their supposed allies in Washington in the years to come; it was enough to appease activists on some issues. But what good was a symbol when the lives of unborn children were at stake? When more than a million legal abortions were being performed every year in a growing network of clinics? In Buffalo, on the same day Mayor Griffin announced that January 22 would become Right-to-Life Day, the Erie Medical Center held a ceremony celebrating its tenth year in existence. There were plenty of doctors in western New York (and throughout the country) who performed abortions by this point. While politicians like Reagan and Griffin paid lip service to banning abortions, the number of women seeking them wasn't declining.

Which is why some abortion opponents soon began advocating a more confrontational approach.

On a cool spring day in 1985, a tall man dressed in a three-piece suit dropped by my father's office.

"We're going to shut you down," he warned in a deep baritone voice. He handed a card to the receptionist and sauntered out the door.

The name on the card was Joseph Scheidler. When my father saw it, he shrugged and went on with his day: the name meant nothing to him.

The man in the three-piece suit would soon emerge as the leader of the radical wing of the pro-life movement, a wing he played a crucial role in helping to form. The founder of the Chicago-based Pro-Life Action Network (PLAN), Joseph Scheidler had come to Buffalo to promote his new book, *Closed: 99 Ways to Stop Abortion,* which, as the title suggests, was not written for people who equated being pro-life with sending politely worded letters to their senators. "Some of the work we must do now includes things some people don't think are nice," Scheidler told a small audience in the auditorium of St. Joseph Hospital in Cheektowaga, a heavily Catholic, heavily Polish suburb east of Buffalo, during his visit. "But remember, Jesus was not a 'nice' person. He was loving. He cared. But he was not 'nice.'"

If these sounded like fighting words, it's because the large, bearded man voicing them often seemed less like an advocate for a cause than a soldier in the trenches of a war—"the Green Beret of the pro-life movement," as Pat Buchanan admiringly described him. Scheidler had first made a name for himself in 1977, when he interrupted a commencement address that Senator Birch Bayh, an abortion-rights advocate, was delivering at St. Joseph's College, a Catholic school in nearby Rensselaer, Indiana. "Birch Bayh, the pro-abortion senator of Indiana, is bringing scandal to this college," bellowed Scheidler through a battery-powered megaphone as startled parents looked on.

Despite a reluctance to get arrested himself, Scheidler soon formed an organization, Friends for Life, that pioneered many of the tactics the more radical wing of the movement would adopt in the years to come. A devout Catholic who at one point had trained to become a Benedictine monk, Scheidler had never thought much about abortion before *Roe v. Wade*. But from the moment he learned of the decision, he became obsessed with the issue and soon set about channeling his prodigious energy into a more abrasive style of activism.* For years, pro-lifers had reacted defensively when accused of imposing their beliefs on others. Not Scheidler: "If we don't start imposing our morality, we are going to drown in their immorality." In place of the schoolmarmish housewife who handed out pamphlets at church on Sunday was Scheidler, an uncompromising firebrand who instructed his followers to spray-paint public placards with antiabortion graffiti. Once, Scheidler hired a private detective to track down the address of an eleven-year-old girl whose mother had scheduled an abortion for her. He then mounted a balcony to harangue the mother through a bullhorn before organizing a picket line in an attempt to block the mother and daughter from entering a public hospital. Scheidler flew around the country to meet with people who had carried out more extreme acts, such as bombing abortion clinics, which he pointedly refused to condemn—"I can't get too excited about some real estate damage."

Arguably the most important and influential of Scheidler's tactics was the so-called Chicago method of "sidewalk counseling," in which

---

*Scheidler had scarcely more tolerance for contraception, calling nonprocreative sex "disgusting—people using each other for pleasure."

demonstrators were instructed to confront women as they entered abortion clinics. "Counseling" might entail urging a patient to visit an alternative "women's center" where she would receive advice not to have an abortion. It could also mean screaming epithets at her. "Close your legs, whore," Scheidler once chanted through a bullhorn outside a clinic. If such language risked reinforcing the impression that opponents of abortion harbored contempt for women and for the very idea of female sexual pleasure and desire, it didn't seem to bother Scheidler, who understood that combative methods made for great street theater and thus increased the chances of generating press coverage, something he keenly appreciated. "Conflict is always newsworthy," he noted in *Closed*.

Thanks largely to Scheidler, by the mid-1980s the days when women could enter abortion clinics without brushing past protesters were over. The same went for doctors, whom Scheidler shrewdly identified as the "weak link" in the abortion "industry." Activists should do everything in their power to convince physicians to stop performing abortions, he argued, and, failing this, make their lives as uncomfortable as possible. "If you can't convert them, then get them to quit," Scheidler urged. "Call their wives . . . get their landlord to kick them out. . . . Leaflet the entire neighborhood."

In other words, make the battle *personal*, shaming everyone involved in the whole sordid business: patients, clinic escorts, above all the medical staff. "Know who your enemies are. Know who your abortionists are," thundered Scheidler before his audience in Cheektowaga. "Point these people out. Get them out of the business of killing."

ALTHOUGH MY FATHER didn't make much of Joseph Scheidler's visit to his office, he did notice that, shortly afterward, the size and intensity of the protests in Buffalo increased. Where formerly a few isolated demonstrators had shown up every now and then at 50 High Street, now several dozen started appearing a couple of times a week at clinics and doctors' offices throughout the city. Where formerly even the larger gatherings held each year on the anniversary of *Roe v. Wade* maintained a civil tone, now the atmosphere was shrill and combative. "*Murder!*

Abortion is MURDER!" blared the chant outside Buffalo GYN Womenservices, an abortion clinic that had recently opened on Elmwood Avenue. In 1985, a reporter from *The Buffalo News* dropped by on a sunny morning when the shopping plaza in which the clinic was located was full of both customers and protesters. Some carried signs emblazoned with photographs of blown-up fetuses, beneath which the words "Human Garbage" were scrawled. Others brought megaphones, through which appeals were voiced to the women inside.

"You up there," a demonstrator pleaded, "it's not too late to change your mind. Please come out of the clinic!"

The message for Marilynn Buckham, the clinic's director, was more pointed. Buckham's name blasted out from the megaphone. A man in sunglasses informed the *News* that, afterward, he planned to picket her home, where demonstrators had recently circulated a letter. "Dear Friends," it stated,

> One of your neighbors, Miss Marilynn Buckham . . . operates the Buffalo GYN "Womanservices." . . . This so-called clinic kills and mutilates preborn children every day. . . . Abortion, which is the murder of children, is one of the most evil, hideous sins against God that someone can commit.

Though he would soon enough be on the receiving end of similar messages, my father first witnessed this kind of scene not at his own office or in front of our home but in the parking lot at 50 High Street, where he occasionally worked. Since he parked his car in a different lot and entered the building through a door in back, the protesters didn't confront him at first. Indeed, they didn't seem to notice him, though he saw the signs, heard the chants, observed the size of the crowds and the increasingly combative atmosphere. His initial reaction was a typically subdued one: he passed by, took the elevator upstairs to the fifth floor, put on his scrubs, and went to work.

This was not just my father's reflexive Israeli stoicism kicking in. It was the response of a man who assumed that the demonstrations constituted a noisy but ultimately minor inconvenience, one he could not imagine serving as the prelude to a sustained campaign of civil disobedience. He hadn't been around during the civil rights movement. There had been no comparable phenomenon in Israel, where breaking the law to express political dissent was relatively rare. It was equally uncommon, or so it seemed to my father, in western New York. Although he had heard stories about young Americans burning their draft cards during the 1960s, the images he associated with those times were of students marching in places like Berkeley, California, not ordinary citizens taking to the streets of Buffalo.

In the past, at least, Buffalo had indeed been a law-and-order town. As the historian Mark Goldman has noted, while there had always been political agitators of one sort or another in the city, its residents, bound by neighborhood, church, and family, tended to be "suspicious and afraid of radicalism of any kind." Those who could trace their roots back a few generations had not forgotten that their beloved hometown owed its darkest hour to an assassination perpetrated by an anarchist. In subsequent decades, despite the presence of a large blue-collar workforce sympathetic to labor unions, Buffalo proved extremely inhospitable to radicals and Communists. In 1947, the city's Catholic leaders spearheaded anti-"Red" rallies in public parks throughout the city, a message greeted enthusiastically by the many working-class residents of Russian and East European extraction. Two decades later, few of the latter looked kindly on the demonstrations that erupted on the Main Street campus of the University of Buffalo, where, as throughout the country in the late 1960s, the student body grew radicalized. Spurred by the escalation of the Vietnam War, students at UB started organizing peace marches and demanding an end to all war-related research at the university. By decade's close, they were denouncing not just the Vietnam War but the whole capitalist system, not just Lyndon Johnson but the racism and inequality that pervaded every facet of American society—a message that played well on campus but not in Buffalo's working-class neighborhoods. When, in the spring of 1970, the turmoil at UB peaked—hundreds of riot-clad officers clashing with students after panicked administrators called in the police to occupy the campus—dozens of angry letters flooded *The Buffalo News*. The vast majority expressed outrage at the protesters, not the cops. "I very much resent the fact that our tax money is supporting these 'students,'" fumed one. "Close the college until all potheads are removed," demanded another. The 10,000-member Erie County Council on Veterans called on Governor Nelson Rockefeller to put an immediate stop to all "anti-American activities" at the university. What seemed to irritate the students' critics most was less what they were saying than the way they were saying it: The fact that they desecrated the flag and acted as though they were above the law. The fact that they were turning Buffalo's leading educational institution—a place many people could only dream of attending—into a circus. The fact that many hadn't worked a day in their lives yet were so sure what everyone else should think of America and its capitalist system.

THE DEMONSTRATORS WHO began turning up at 50 High Street in the mid-1980s were, of course, not out-of-town college students but locals. Instead of quoting Huey Newton and Che Guevara, they quoted Scripture. The principles the protesters were acting upon did not reflect the teachings of the New Left but those of the institution that in Buffalo commanded arguably more moral authority than any other: the Catholic church.

And yet, when demonstrators began turning up the volume outside doctors' offices and abortion clinics in Buffalo, it was not the Catholic church egging them on. At no point on his way past the protesters does my father recall seeing the face of Bishop Edward Head, the man who, in January of 1973, had come to western New York to head the Diocese of Buffalo, encompassing the city and eight surrounding counties: 1,200 priests, 2,870 nuns, nearly one million parishioners. By the time Bishop Head was installed, the days when Catholics in Buffalo were viewed as dangerous outsiders had long since passed. Figures like Cardinal Francis Joseph Spellman and John F. Kennedy had brought unprecedented stature to Catholics in America, whose flag-waving patriotism few questioned anymore. Fewer and fewer Catholics exhibited the "enclave mentality" that had once led Dorothy Day, the great cofounder of the Catholic Worker Movement, to describe members of her faith as "a nation apart, a people within a people." Many had left the old immigrant neighborhoods in cities like Chicago and Buffalo and moved to the suburbs, where new parishes were sprouting up everywhere.

The latter trend was, however, a mixed blessing: a sign, on the one hand, that Catholics were making it, but also of the vacuum that siphoned members out of dozens of older urban parishes. Churches, at the turn of the century, had been as ubiquitous in Buffalo as bars and factories: St. Stanislaus, a towering Polish cathedral on the East Side, in the heart of Polonia; St. Anthony of Padua, an Italian church on Court Street; Blessed Trinity, a Romanesque structure on Leroy Avenue. With their stained-glass windows and elaborate interiors, these churches spoke to the centrality of faith in the lives of Buffalo's immigrants. Yet by the mid-1970s, the combination of suburbanization, white flight, and economic decline had left many parishes struggling to survive. St. Nicholas, a church on Utica Street, in the city's Cold Spring District, watched its membership plummet from 3,000 in 1959 to 673 by the mid-1970s; St. Mary of Sorrows, on Genesee Street, went from 7,500 to 1,038; Sacred Heart, once serving 1,100 worshippers, closed. Between 1959 and 1974, parishes in the central city suffered a net loss of 34,584 members, one study found. As one might expect, the mood among ecclesiastical leaders was grim. "Neighborhood is going down," lamented Chester Meloch, the pastor of St. Stanislaus. "Much spiritual apathy is breeding," complained Father James Staebell, of St. Monica's. Lurking just beneath the surface, the pastors observed, were racial tensions. "They are mortally afraid of blacks," one pastor noted of the whites remaining in the neighborhood he served. "The black-white confrontation has polarized." In 1974, the Diocese of Buffalo organized a Peace and Justice Commission to assess the challenges facing the church in an era of wrenching social change. "Look at our city," the commission reported a year later:

> The exodus of business, disinvestment by private industry, investors, and the banks, the decline of housing stock, real estate speculation, unfair taxes, the refusal of the suburbs to engage in the process of social change, the destruction of once-flourishing neighborhoods by

programs of "urban renewal" have already adversely affected and alienated the people who remain in the city. They have had to bear the burden of all the social change in terms of their money, their security, their way of life. The city is decaying; the once-flourishing neighborhoods have withered. The human dimension is all but lost.

Bishop Head's appointment was officially announced on the morning of January 23, 1973, one day after the Supreme Court announced its decision in Roe v. Wade and a couple of weeks before my father arrived in Buffalo. At his first press conference, the bishop was asked about the ruling. "I feel it is tragic," he told reporters in the white-paneled Information Office of the Chancery on Madison Avenue, in New York City. "I do not believe that once life has begun that it should be terminated according to the whim of a woman who might find it inconvenient for that life to continue."

At no point in the years to come would the Catholic church in Buffalo waver from this view. In fact, the church had made its opposition to abortion known well before Bishop Head came to Buffalo. "We urge you most strongly to do all in your power to prevent direct attacks upon the lives of unborn children," a pastoral letter read from the pulpit of every Catholic church in Buffalo had declared nearly six years earlier, on the morning of February 12, 1967. Issued after a bill liberalizing access to abortion had been introduced in Albany, the letter bore the signature of James A. McNulty, Bishop Head's predecessor in Buffalo, and the bishops of the seven other dioceses in New York State. Never before had a joint appeal of its kind been issued.

"All in your power": this is what the Catholic church had directed the laity to do, a message that, prior to Roe, could be read as a simple call for civic engagement. Writing to your state senator or representative, signing a petition, venturing off to Albany to engage in a bit of lobbying: these were the activities that had characterized pro-life politics in the early days. But what did "all in your power" mean after Roe? Did it mean Catholics should run around chaining themselves to the doors of clinics so nobody could enter? Did it mean direct action of the kind Joseph Scheidler advocated? In 1975, the National Conference of Catholic Bishops appeared to lean in a more radical direction when it issued a

"Pastoral Plan for Pro-life Activities" calling for a nationwide grassroots mobilization against abortion. The plan envisioned the formation of "tightly-knit . . . pro-life units" at the parish level in every congressional district of the country in order to influence lawmakers and turn out protesters at demonstrations.

To liberals, feminists, and much of the mainstream press, the Pastoral Plan would be interpreted as a sign that the church would stop at nothing in order to overturn *Roe*. But the reality was rather different. As the reporters James Risen and Judy L. Thomas document in their book, *Wrath of Angels*, despite the NCCB's uncompromising rhetoric few bishops actually proved "willing to put their credibility on the line for an all-out social and political assault on *Roe*." Many feared that such a campaign would jeopardize the church's tax-exempt status. Others were resigned to the fact that the nation had moved toward a new consensus in favor of legalized abortion under at least some conditions. Others still believed the best way to spread the pro-life message was through dialogue, not confrontation. "We must be ready to reach out and share and educate," Bishop Head told an audience in 1980. Opponents of abortion should move ahead "quietly, calmly," he advised, in a spirit of "reconciliation."

Such language struck a balance between the church's fixed tenets and its reluctance to stir too much social unrest. It is a tension JoAnn Wypijewski, raised in a Polish-Catholic family in Buffalo, and as perceptive an observer of the city's social landscape as there is, views as a reflection of the church's conflicted identity. "The church is this great contradiction," she says. "It has always been the church of the people, the church of the poor, the working class, the immigrants, so it has this mass, populist base. But it is also very much the church of the state. Its institutions rarely sanction radicalism because it really does have the legacy of Rome, of Constantinople, of being the state religion. The idea of the hierarchy ruling is so profound that even though the church is more radical in its approach to the Gospel than many other faiths, its structure sort of disables the populace. It is a religion of 'don't rock the boat.'"

Many pro-life activists would come to feel that, indeed, caution guided the church when it came to abortion. "Prudence without fortitude" is how John O'Keefe characterized the hierarchy's approach. "Wimps for Life" is how Joseph Scheidler, and the protesters in Buffalo, started to describe those who believed abortion was wrong but failed to get out on the streets.

Behind such rhetoric lay a new reality. The pro-life movement was in the process of becoming two movements: "one mainstream and polite, focused on the corridors of Congress," as Risen and Thomas put it, "one radical and impolite, focused on the doorways of American abortion clinics." In Buffalo as elsewhere, there would be plenty of Catholics in the more militant camp. But there would also be plenty of born-again Protestants. The categories that had defined the abortion conflict during the 1970s—feminists on one side, Catholics on the other—were beginning to blur.

JUST HOW MUCH they blurred is evident in the family background of the woman who would become the first major target of the protesters' wrath in Buffalo. Before Barnett Slepian, before my father, before anyone else in the city started spotting demonstrators outside their offices or saw their name on flyers and picket signs, Marilynn Buckham found herself in the movement's crosshairs. The director of the abortion clinic on Elmwood Avenue, Buckham was a small, feisty woman with sparkling brown eyes. She had grown up part of a working-class family on the West Side, where, ever since Italian immigrants began living there, being Catholic was simply an assumed part of one's identity. As a young girl, she attended Mount St. Mary Academy. Like everyone else she knew, she went to church on Sunday and took Communion.

As was true for so many members of her generation, though, the Catholicism of Buckham's youth and upbringing was a looser-fitting faith than the one of her immigrant grandparents. Like many Italians and Poles in Buffalo during the postwar years, in the 1950s Buckham's parents had moved from the city to the suburbs—in their case, Tonawanda. By the time she enrolled at the University of Buffalo in the early 1960s, the winds of Vatican II had begun to blow. Catholics in

Buffalo started hearing the Mass read in English for the first time. More and more were, like Buckham, attending college, which meant exposure to ideas, and to people, outside the faith. After taking classes at UB, Buckham met a journalist, whom she started dating. In 1969, they decided to get married, even though she was Catholic and he was not. "We went to see the pastor at my church," she recalls. "He said unless Tom [her fiancé] signed a document stating that we were going to raise our children Catholic, they would not marry us. I thought it was ridiculous. So we went and got married in a Unitarian church instead."

A couple of years later, Buckham bumped into a woman at a cocktail party who told her that, now that the law in New York had changed, an abortion clinic would soon be opening in Buffalo. The woman asked whether Marilynn might be interested in working there.

Though she considered herself a freethinking person, Buckham admits the idea jarred her at first. To work at an abortion clinic? She thought about how the news would go over with various members of her family. "I was really taken aback [by the offer]," she says. "I wondered what my mom would think, what my family would think."

The more she thought about it, though, the more at ease with the idea, indeed even drawn to it, she was. Like many women in the late 1960s and early 1970s, Marilynn Buckham had come to develop strong views about the importance of reproductive freedom, views at odds with what she'd been taught in Catholic school. "Privately, I had long believed that women had been kept under the thumb because they were not free to make their own decisions about when to have children," she says. "I had never really acted on it, but I definitely felt I wasn't going to be forced into motherhood without it being *my* choice." Coupled with an emerging feminist consciousness was her sense that, when it came to the issue of birth control and family planning, the faith in which she had been reared was simply out of touch with reality. "All the Catholics I knew were practicing some form of birth control," Buckham says. "To say 'Every sperm is sacred,' the church's dogmatic opposition to all forms of family planning, it just seemed bizarre to me."

There were plenty of Catholics who would have considered such sentiments blasphemous. As polls conducted in the aftermath of *Roe* started to reveal, however, Marilynn Buckham was less of an anomaly among members of her faith than many people assumed. In 1978, a survey found that 44 percent of Catholics believed the church should "relax its standards forbidding all abortions under any circumstances." A year earlier, another survey had found that 45 percent agreed abortion should be permitted in the case of a woman who "cannot afford any more children." Catholics were even more out of touch with their ecclesiastical leaders on the matter of birth control, which the papal encyclical *Humanae Vitae* strictly forbade but which many had long been saying they practiced.*

In the years to come, studies confirmed that, contrary to popular perception, Catholics were no more unanimously opposed to abortion, either in their beliefs or in practice, than the rest of the population. In 1979, Barbara Howe published a study of the patients who showed up for abortions at 50 High Street, in Buffalo, during a three-month period in 1975. Of the 1,250 first-time patients, 52.9 percent were Catholic—slightly more than the percentage of Catholics in all of Erie County. Of those seeking a *repeat* abortion, 48 percent were Catholic. A few years later, in 1984, then–New York governor Mario Cuomo touched on the gap between doctrine and practice in a controversial speech, "Religious Belief and Public Morality: A Catholic Governor's Perspective," at Notre Dame University. In the speech, Cuomo explained that while he personally accepted the church's teachings on abortion, he felt compelled as a public servant *not* to impose this view on Americans who felt differently—atheists, Protestants, Jews, and some members of his own faith. "Despite the teaching in our homes and schools and pulpits, despite the sermons and pleadings and parents and priests and prelates, despite all the effort at defining our opposition to the sin of abortion," stated Cuomo, "we Catholics apparently believe—and perhaps act—little differently from those who don't share our commitment." New York Cardinal John O'Connor immediately denounced the speech.

---

*Issued by Pope Paul VI in 1968, *Humanae Vitae* provoked "more vocal and sustained [opposition] than . . . any other topic in the history of modern Catholicism," notes the historian John T. McGreevy.

Bishop Head told an audience in Buffalo that the church's position on abortion "cannot be altered or amended by anyone."

As a matter of what the Catholic hierarchy believed, this was inarguable. In terms of what a substantial number of Catholics practiced, however, Cuomo was right.

MARILYNN BUCKHAM TOOK the job at the clinic. Once she started working there, she saw a broad range of women—including Catholics— pass through its doors. She also deepened her commitment to choice, not least because of what she witnessed before *Roe v. Wade*. "Remember, I started in 1972," she explains, "and the phones back then just never stopped ringing. We were getting calls from Toronto, Montreal, Ohio, Pennsylvania, Michigan, Virginia. Women traveling long distances to get an abortion, sleeping in their cars because we didn't have enough time slots in the day to accommodate them. It was a flood, and I was just flabbergasted to see the need. I had always believed in a woman's right to choose, but I had never realized how desperate women were."

A decade later, by the 1980s, things had calmed down considerably. The deluge of out-of-state patients had diminished to a trickle. Buckham's friends and parents had long since accepted the decision she'd made. ("My mother was supportive," she says. "My father was quiet about it, but it was a quiet acceptance.") What headaches she experienced working at 50 High Street were mostly internal, logistical ones— in particular, run-ins with the out-of-town physicians who owned the facility and demanded it be run on what she felt was too tight a budget. "I was constantly being questioned on accounting, salaries, expenditures," she says. "It was awful. I did it because I loved what I did, but it was very, very difficult." In 1983, having worked her way up from answering the phones to serving as an administrator to, in effect, running the place, Buckham decided she'd had enough. She quit and, along with a couple of doctors and nurses she'd gotten to know, opened a clinic of her own at 260 Elmwood Avenue, on the second floor of a building in a shopping plaza, the ground floor of which was a Bells Supermarket. She had no trouble getting a lease; there were no indications that doing so would invite disturbances.

The clinic was called Buffalo GYN Womenservices. Buckham was the director, and she was proud of the place, which represented a marriage of her feminist principles and her business savvy.

Less than two years after the clinic opened, the protests began. First one, then another, then another still, eventually becoming loud, angry, in-your-face demonstrations, accusing Buckham of complicity in murder; of running not a health care facility serving the needs of women but a butchery—for profit.

As I would come to appreciate upon meeting her many years later, Marilynn Buckham was no pushover. She is a strong, self-possessed woman whose presence and voice fill a room. My father first met her in 1976, when he started working one afternoon a week at 50 High Street. Their relationship was a distant but respectful one. She struck him as a person who knew what she believed and did not hesitate to voice her opinions, a woman who did not suffer fools gladly or go through life afraid to do what she considered right.

Yet when the demonstrations began, Buckham was shaken. "I was freaked," she says. "I couldn't believe they could just print my name on a billboard with my phone number on it. It was on a huge sign on Elmwood, right outside the clinic, so people walking up and down the street couldn't miss it."

By the time *The Buffalo News* sent a reporter to visit the clinic on Elmwood in the fall of 1985, the situation was starting to seem like war. "We feel we're under siege," Buckham told the *News*. The feeling would not let up anytime soon.

· 8 ·

One afternoon, I traveled to Washington, D.C., to visit the headquarters of Faith and Action. Located in a sand-colored, three-
story brick town house across the street from the U.S. Supreme Court,
Faith and Action is an advocacy organization whose mission is "to reintroduce the Word of God into the public debate surrounding legislation and policy matters." It was cofounded in 1994 by a minister named
Rob Schenck, a self-proclaimed "missionary to Capitol Hill" who, before coming to Washington, had made a name for himself in another
city: Buffalo.

Dressed in a deep blue oxford shirt and dark slacks, Schenck greeted
me with a warm handshake and a welcoming smile. He apologized for
not remembering my name, which I had left with a receptionist a few
weeks earlier when I'd called to arrange the interview. An affable man of
medium height and a compact build, Schenck looked less like a minister than a Hill staffer, his sleeves rolled up, his dark hair cropped short,
his boyish face slightly suntanned. We sat in an elegant room on the second floor of the town house, sunlight streaming in through the windows,

beneath which a large yellow banner was hanging that I'd spotted on my way inside. On it appeared the four most contested—and, to Faith and Action, meaningful—words in the Pledge of Allegiance: ONE NATION, UNDER GOD.

An assistant brought me a glass of ice water as Schenck took a seat on the edge of the couch near the armchair where I sat. In this pleasant atmosphere, Schenck proved a gracious host, happily recounting the odyssey that led him to become a born-again Christian and, beginning in the late 1980s, a dedicated pro-life activist. His manner was open, and our conversation flowed easily, to the point that, several hours into the meeting, it seemed we were fast becoming friends. It was an admittedly odd feeling, for along with his twin brother, Paul, the man sitting next to me had led the pro-life movement in Buffalo during a period when the city's courtrooms regularly filled with protesters—and when going to work each morning became more and more of an adventure for my father.

"WE HAVE BEEN offended and defiled by this horrid act." So declared the Reverend Paul Schenck before roughly 200 protesters who had gathered to attend a mock funeral outside my father's office in Kenmore. The demonstrators filed past a series of open caskets containing the remains of four dead fetuses that a couple living nearby claimed to have found in a Dumpster. A spokeswoman from my father's office, interviewed in *The Buffalo News*, adamantly denied the story, noting that all such remains were forwarded to a pathologist as mandated under law at the time. A representative from the Erie County Health Department said he was not aware of any complaints about the improper disposal of fetal remains at the site. My father maintains that if anything was found in the Dumpster, it was black bags full of medical waste that could be legally disposed there. One of the fetuses displayed at the funeral was twenty-two weeks old; he didn't perform abortions at this stage.

Even so, the event made *The Buffalo News*: "200 Abortion Foes in Kenmore Protest 'Dumping' of 4 Fetuses," announced the headline.

The mock funeral at my father's office took place in September 1987.

Two months later, a group of pro-life activists from Buffalo boarded a bus to Philadelphia. A dozen or so others followed in a fifteen-seat van. They arrived in the evening, slept a few hours, and awoke to attend a rally in a parking lot. The activists, roughly 400 of them, formed a caravan and drove across the Delaware River to Cherry Hill, New Jersey, parking at a nearby Catholic church. From there, they tramped through the rainy predawn to the Cherry Hill Women's Center, an abortion clinic, where they sat down to blockade the doors. On a nearby wall a banner was draped: "Operation Rescue."

The sit-in that took place that morning marked the beginning of a grassroots campaign that, in Buffalo as elsewhere, would soon catapult abortion into the spotlight as never before. By the time the police cleared the entrance to the Cherry Hill Women's Center, 210 protesters had been arrested; 41 were from western New York. Drawing on a tactic that had been used sporadically in the past, the demonstrators blockaded the entrance to the facility so that women intending to end their pregnancies could not get in; thus were "rescued" the babies who would otherwise have been aborted that day. This strategy would soon spread to other cities and turn Operation Rescue, whose members carried out civil disobedience in the name of what they insisted was a higher law— God's—into one of the most powerful social movements in the country.

Nothing in his history or in what he had witnessed thus far in Buffalo prepared my father for such a thing, the irony being that the family background of Operation Rescue's leaders in western New York was not so different from his own. When it finally happened, my father's encounter with fundamentalism in America would come courtesy of twin brothers who grew up in a Jewish home in Grand Island, that sliver of land located between Buffalo and Canada that Mordechai Noah had once dreamed of turning into a Jewish state. The household in which Rob and Paul Schenck grew up was "a largely secular, fully assimilated Jewish home," Rob told me—and a liberal one. "Richard Nixon was *evil*—he was an evil man in our home," he said. "I don't even remember anyone talking about Republican candidates for office. It was as if they didn't exist." At age fourteen, Rob and Paul attended their first political demonstration, not to protest the legalization of abortion in New York but to demonstrate against the Vietnam War. A year earlier, they had helped form the Grand Island Association to Stop Pollution, a glass-recycling project.

These were the first signs of the compulsion they shared to shake up the world around them. For the most part, though, the Schenck brothers appear to have spent their youth doing what most teenagers with a rebellious streak did in the early 1970s. They dressed in ragged jeans and torn-up sneakers, Rob Schenck told me. They grew their hair long, smoked pot, and engaged in various "low crimes and misdemeanors," such as tossing firecrackers into the Niagara River. "My brother and I were very counterculture," Rob insisted, adding that he "had sex with whoever was willing to have sex with me." At one point, one of Rob's closest friends got his girlfriend pregnant. She ended up having an abortion, a decision Rob said he didn't think all that much about at the time. The only admonition he could remember receiving from his parents about sex was to make sure he used a condom.

I sat there trying to square the image forming in my head—a pair of nonconformist Jewish kids who would have fit right in among the stoners depicted in Richard Linklater's coming-of-age-in-the-seventies film, *Dazed and Confused*—with the reality of the clean-cut born-again Christian next to me. Then it occurred to me that being dazed and confused is perhaps what prompted the Schenck brothers to embark on the spiritual journey that would alter the course of their lives. While they were still in high school, Rob told me, Paul befriended the son of a Methodist minister. Rob initially thought of Charlie as a "Jesus freak" and worried his brother was getting drawn into a cult. One day, however, Charlie invited them both to a Friday night prayer service he attended. The Schencks agreed, slipping into the back row of a white clapboard church with a spire that sat in the middle of a Grand Island cornfield. They watched as members of the group sang and prayed—and felt instantly compelled to join. Once he got over his initial inhibitions, Rob told me, he found the people warm and welcoming. They seemed to know a different sort of God from the one he and his brother had grown up imagining: not the fearsome master of the universe evoked on their occasional visits to temple—"a great big angry ogre seated somewhere on a cloud," as Rob would later joke—but a personal, intimate God.

Several visits later, the Schenck brothers heard a minister from England preach about what it meant to know God through a personal encounter with Jesus Christ. Spellbound, they came forward that night and, at the minister's invitation, knelt down and prayed in repentance for their sins, an experience that would forever change their lives. They were born-again Christians now, a conversion that stunned their father, Henry, who "took it as a rejection of our family, our Jewish heritage," Rob told me. Yet the pull of their new faith proved stronger even than the fear of disappointing him. In the fall of 1974, Rob and Paul were baptized by a Salvation Army captain in the frigid waters of the Niagara River, which separates Grand Island from Buffalo. The river was so cold their lips turned blue, but this was partly the point. "It was sort of a test— you know, How serious are you about this?" Rob recalled with a chuckle.

Before long, the Schenck brothers could be spotted in the cafeteria at Grand Island High School and on street corners, delivering sermons, a turn that, on one level, marked a stark repudiation of everything they'd known and experienced until then. There would be no more drinking and partying with their friends in Grand Island. No more fooling around with girls. The lifestyle they'd formerly led, with its openness and experimentation, with its lack of clear boundaries about what was morally permissible, now seemed like a recipe for damnation to them.

And yet, viewed another way, the Schenck brothers' conversion to Christianity signified not the end of the rebellious phase of their youths but its culmination. The church they joined, Rob told me, was experimental and alternative. Many of its members were bohemian. "They were counterculture," he explained, "the last wave of what you would call hippie or flower children. You know . . . antiwar, pro–legalization of marijuana, free-love kind of lifestyle, but they were now Jesus people and were rapidly changing their personal morality and going to church." The Friday night prayer group the Schencks attended called itself Agape, the Greek word for spiritual love. Many of its members still wore jeans and grew their hair long. The prayer style was so intense, Rob recalled, that it unsettled the church's more traditional members, prompting the radicals to break off to form their own congregation.

What the Schenck brothers appear to have found in this world is what so many alienated young people had been searching for in the 1960s: a community bound together by an alternative set of values that encouraged expressions of fellowship and love, albeit on condition that one accepted the Bible as the true word of God.* After high school the Schencks started taking classes at the Elim Bible Institute, a small evangelical college located just outside Rochester, where they were exposed to the works of Francis Schaeffer and got to know another wayward youth turned born-again Christian, Randall Terry. As a teenager, Terry had dropped out of high school and drifted aimlessly from his hometown of Rochester to Galveston, Texas, where he slept on the beach and did drugs. He had seemed more interested in playing the guitar and becoming a rock star than in religion or politics. Like the Schencks, however, Terry would undergo a born-again experience that changed his life. A few years later, in 1986, under Schaeffer's spell, he would start organizing sit-ins at an abortion clinic in Binghamton, New York, from which he would spread the message (and the methods) of Operation Rescue.

It is to people like Terry and the Schenck brothers that leadership of the pro-life movement was passing—fiery young lay ministers who were, at heart, rebels, willing not only to raise their voices but also to break the law in order to purge America of the vices in which they themselves had once indulged.

A YEAR OR so after the mock funeral, my father arrived at his office one afternoon and found the entrance mobbed. A group of demonstrators had stormed the building and occupied the space in front of the

---

*Perhaps their trajectory was not so unusual. "What finally started attracting young people to Christianity was something the churches had absolutely nothing to do with: namely, the psychedelic or hippie movement," observed Tom Wolfe in his famous essay on the 1970s, "The Me Decade and the Third Great Awakening." "The hippies suddenly made religion look hip."

doors to prevent anyone from entering or leaving. A rescue was under way, one of dozens being carried out across the country by this point, one that left my father and his coworkers paralyzed.

"I walked up to the building, people were sitting on the floor, on the stairs, huge numbers," my father recalls. "I really couldn't go inside." Linda Stadler had gotten there earlier, before the protesters showed up. She remembers two men bursting through the doors and announcing, "There will be no murders here tonight!" She called the Kenmore police, which didn't do much good. "The protesters were trespassing, but nobody was pressing charges: we couldn't press charges, because we didn't own the building," Linda says. "The police really had never been confronted with a situation like that."

It took five hours for the police to clear the demonstrators away, too long for any patients to be seen that night, meaning the rescue was a success (though, as in Cherry Hill, New Jersey, the appointments were rescheduled). My father, Linda, and a few other workers ended up going out for chicken wings and burgers at Fitzgerald's, a local restaurant, where they tried to recover their equilibrium. "The workers were okay — they didn't like it, but they were not scared," my father says. And how was he? Also not scared, but frustrated, particularly because patients had had to be sent home, and, he admits, slightly disoriented.

"I must say it was . . . not a shock, but a surprise. What is this all of a sudden? Where did it come from?"

Where it literally came from was Binghamton, the home of Operation Rescue's founder, Randall Terry, and from a wave of fresh recruits who, in Buffalo as elsewhere, were transforming the pro-life movement from a Catholic phenomenon into a multidenominational one. Like Joseph Scheidler, Terry wanted the pro-life movement to be radical and abrasive, to shock people out of their complacency. Unlike Scheidler, he understood that the key to transforming the movement into a mass campaign lay in tapping into a new constituency: evangelicals. To convince his fellow born-again Christians to participate in the sit-ins he started carrying out in Binghamton, Terry framed his message in the explicitly biblical language earlier activists had avoided for fear of seeming preachy or sectarian. *"Our perspective is unashamedly Bible-based,"* he wrote in a 1987 recruiting manual, *To Rescue the Children*. "Why? First, the Bible is the absolute truth — the only absolute truth. Second, only the Word of God and a Christian world view give value to life." Terry drew on examples from Scripture to justify civil disobedience, calling on Christians to obey the "Higher Law" of the Bible. He also urged them to "re-educate" the "godless generation" of Americans who'd been brainwashed by the "liberal elite" and by popular culture ("the rock music gods have not only promoted sexual promiscuity, but drug abuse, rebellion against parents, violence, and Satan worship"). "The moral chaos America now lives in," he wrote, "with all the violent crime, killing of the pre-born, child molestation, and pornography, is the result of America abandoning God's law as the basis of right and wrong and replacing it with a humanist foundation of sand." The Word of God, Terry instructed his fellow ministers, "is a sword." This was Francis Schaeffer's language with an extra dose of militancy. It was also becoming the language of political conservatism in America, a form of right-wing cultural populism with a theocratic tinge.

You might think such a message would have limited appeal in a culture whose pop icons included Prince and Madonna. Yet such figures were precisely why many people felt attracted to the evangelical movement — and not only in the Bible Belt. "Evangelical Surge Stirring Ferment in Western New York Religious Life" rang the headline of a 1986 front-page story in *The Buffalo News*. As the author, David Briggs, reported, thousands of worshippers in the area were flocking to places like The Chapel, an evangelical church in Williamsville, and New Covenant Tabernacle, an Assemblies of God congregation. For people looking for clear answers about right and wrong, for a remedy to the "moral chaos" they feared was enveloping society — kids having sex earlier and earlier, young women bearing children out of wedlock, homosexuals infiltrating groups like the Boy Scouts — these churches offered a refuge. "Society, which is sick of sin and tired of the dead, social Gospel, is flocking to this evangelistic fire," one minister explained.

New Covenant Tabernacle, one of the churches featured in the article, was located in a former Jewish funeral home in Tonawanda. Its founder was Paul Schenck. New Covenant's membership had grown from a few dozen families to several thousand people in the span of a few years. The Schenck brothers' church provided the bus to transport activists from Buffalo to Philadelphia for Operation Rescue's first major blockade, in Cherry Hill, New Jersey, and would spearhead Project Rescue in Buffalo, the local branch of the movement launched by their friend Randall Terry.

A WEEK AFTER the first rescue at my father's office, the protesters showed up again. This time, armed with a signed complaint, the Kenmore police were ready to drag the demonstrators away in a van. Not long after they were arrested, the protesters returned yet again. It would go on like this for a while, a cycle of demonstrations and arrests that started to dominate the local news and turn the area outside my father's office, and several other places in Buffalo where abortions were performed, into battle zones replete with cameras, police paddy wagons, bewildered patients, and throngs of protesters jamming the entrances to save the unborn.

I was starting my senior year in high school at the time of the mock funeral at my father's office. I remember seeing the demonstrators clustered outside with their signs: the blown-up photographs of mangled fetuses; the placards emblazoned with his name. Though it was an eerie feeling, I don't recall thinking it was dangerous, perhaps because no major acts of violence had occurred in Buffalo. Nor did I harbor doubts about the kind of person my father was. My mother remembers that, on several occasions, she sat me down and asked whether I was troubled by the mounting turmoil and the demonstrators' allegations that my father was a baby-killer, a murderer. I told her no, that I was proud of my dad and thought what he was doing was right.

This was the truth, although it's also the case that, privately, a part of me felt uncomfortable, embarrassed, even somewhat ashamed. Why else did I manage never to talk with any of my friends about what was happening? Why else did I avoid bringing the subject up at school or mentioning it when people asked what my father did for a living? I did not believe what the protesters said about my father being morally depraved. How could I possibly believe such things about the person whose moral example I had grown up striving to emulate, who along with my grandfather Benjamin was the sort of man I hoped one day to become myself: the kind who did what he believed was right regardless of the cost? Even so, there was something I grasped intuitively about the protesters that made what they were saying difficult simply to ignore or dismiss: the undeniable passion of their convictions. Even from my guarded perspective, or maybe especially because of this, their fervor and their vehemence were hard to discount.

Sitting in Rob Schenck's office, I asked him what being at a rescue was like. "I found it to be one of the most spiritual exercises I had ever engaged in," he said, his eyes brimming with excitement, as though it had happened yesterday. He had just described a sit-in that had taken place in December 1988, outside the doors of a medical complex at 666 Colvin Avenue—666 being "the number of the anti-Christ in some interpretations of the Book of Revelation . . . so we laughed about that." I reached for the ice water and forced a smile; 666 Colvin was the address of my father's office. That morning, he had arrived at work to find a throng of protesters blockading the doors. As usual, they didn't move until the police carted them away, prompting other doctors working in the building to complain that the disruption forced them to delay procedures for their patients, including a blood test for a sick infant and treatment for a woman with suspected pneumonia. "This is just outrageous," Dr. Leonard Wohlin told *The Buffalo News* at the time. To Rob Schenck, it was exhilarating. "It was peaceful, it was prayerful, it was courageous," he told me.

If I place myself in Schenck's shoes, I can imagine his sense of exhilaration. At the time, I could not contemplate the idea that a noble impulse might be motivating the protestors—they were doing their best to make my father's life miserable, is what I understood. But if I step into the moral universe Schenck described to me—a world where every unborn child represents God's creation and life begins at conception, where this is not a matter of debate but of truth as handed down in Scripture—the ethical imperative is clear. I can see why it would have seemed entirely justified to clasp hands and blockade the entrances to a place like my father's office. I can also imagine how frustrating it must have been that, despite the life-and-death stakes, some people still refused to see the light: women who continued entering the clinics; doctors who went on working in them. If you believed that abortion was murder and that there was no other way to see it, it is easy to imagine why the preferred explanation for the behavior of those who sought and performed abortions was not that they held different views—and were moral agents in their own right—but that they refused to open up their hearts: women too ignorant or selfish to consider what they were doing; doctors who *profited* from it all.

This was the message my parents were repeatedly sent. One day my mother dropped by my father's office and parked her car. When she came back, a sign covered the windshield: PAID FOR WITH CHILDREN'S BLOOD. On another occasion, a woman screamed at my father on his way into work that he should go back to Israel and that his mother would be ashamed if she knew what he did for a living. There were messages left at his office warning him he was going to hell. There were threatening notes and letters. The locks to his office were mucked up with glue one day. Another day the parking lot and front door were splattered with red paint.

I suspect that, in the back of their minds, some of the activists knew that the women having abortions, and even physicians like my father, were not terrible people. Rob Schenck admitted as much to me. "I don't think that most abortion providers go into an abortion saying 'Let me just murder this pre-born human being,'" he conceded. "You probably have to believe in what you're doing." In the heat of the battle, however, there were few such acknowledgments: people like my father and Barnett Slepian were simply murderers, cold-blooded killers who were in it purely for the money, who deserved whatever abuse or discomfort they got, since, after all, what was a bit of invective aimed at an abortionist next to the lives of unborn children? Who could really feel sorry for such people, or their wives and children, or even their friends?

The slurs and accusations would have been difficult for any person to endure. Tough Israeli though he is, my father was not immune to their sting. He cared what people thought of him, cared especially that the people he knew viewed him as a morally upright person and a caring, dedicated physician. That was why he'd gone into medicine in the first place—to help people, the way the doctors trying to save the wounded soldier in his platoon back in Israel had. It was why he cherished every card and letter he got from a patient thanking him for delivering her baby. The pleasure of being an obstetrician rested, for him, in being able to share such moments with people who would otherwise have been strangers. He loved working in the one field of medicine where people associated late-night trips to the hospital not with illness or tragedy but with what often was one of the happiest moments of their lives.

For such a person, to suddenly be confronted by a movement that reduced one's entire life's work to an abominable sin was not pleasant. In his typically stoic manner, my father never complained, at least not in my presence. On the rare occasions when I asked about the protesters, he'd say they were extremists, that there was nothing much to worry about, and leave it at that. Beneath the tough veneer, however, the pressure was not always easy to shrug off. "It was hard on Dad, it was a lot of extra strain," my mother says. "Once I drove there with him and we saw all the people from far away with all the signs, an enormous throng. Dad sighed and said, 'Oh, what a circus.'"

"Psychologically, it hurt," my father admitted to me recently. "If somebody is calling you a killer, it hurts. Even if it's not the truth and you don't believe it, it hurts." The word—*hurt*—lingered in the air between us, a rare expression of vulnerability from a man who prided himself on concealing his emotions, who'd been raised to believe that merely to acknowledge feeling wounded was a sign of weakness.

"The work itself is hard, it's not easy," he went on. "You deal with patients under stress, so when they scream outside, it makes the patients more nervous, and it affects you somehow. I try to stay calm, but someplace it probably builds up and hurts.

"And it created tension," he added. "They started using the 'killing babies' slogan, and I was concerned that it's going to affect the practice."

• • •

BY THE TIME the sit-ins began, my father was dividing his time between the office on Colvin and a group practice he'd joined on Delaware
Avenue, near downtown Buffalo. As far as he knew, all the doctors in the
group were pro-choice. Some even performed abortions in the city's hospitals. But they didn't do them at the office on Delaware, in large part because they feared this might drive nervous patients away and damage the
business. My father harbored similar concerns. For a physician contemplating whether to incorporate it into his or her practice, abortion was actually a risky proposition. For who knew how much controversy it might
bring, how far the protesters might be willing to go to disrupt the practice,
how many patients they might succeed in scaring away. "Death threats,
obstruction and broken windows have taken their toll," *Time* magazine
reported in a 1992 article chronicling why, despite surveys showing that a
large majority of ob-gyns were pro-choice, fewer and fewer performed
abortions. There was another, more mundane reason, too, *Time* noted:
"Many doctors are inclined to see abortion as routine work that's poorly
paid by their standards." It was true that—as the protesters never tired of
pointing out—my father did not perform abortions for free. But it was also
true that, particularly as the pressure escalated, remaining a provider was
a risk, one he could easily have avoided if money and the stability of his
career had been his primary considerations.

I asked my father whether, given all this, it ever crossed his mind
to stop.

"No."

Why not?

"Because," he said, pausing to collect his thoughts, "I felt like what I
was doing was right."

My father had not suddenly become a feminist. But he didn't need
to be a member of NOW to understand that the protesters were challenging his authority as a physician—not to mention the moral agency
of his patients, who, like him, frequently had to run a gauntlet of protesters on their way to his door. To hear the cries of "Murder!" and
"Don't kill your baby!" ring out, and, on some days, to wait outside because the entrance to the building was blocked. The protesters had
every right to express such views, my father felt. But they had no right to

force their beliefs on other people who were making a decision that was already hard enough. "I respect people who are opposed to abortion," he said in an interview with Gene Warner, a reporter from *The Buffalo News*, in November 1988. "It's their view, their right. But it's unacceptable to me the way they're trying to impose it on other people."

Of course, the "other people" being imposed on included not only his patients but also himself. The point of Project Rescue was not to engage my father in dialogue. It was to force him to stop performing abortions—and, with enough pressure, to break his will. He reacted the way you would expect an Israeli in such a situation to respond: not by softening his stance but by hardening it. "It's probably made me more determined," he told *The Buffalo News*. "If I think I'm doing something right and somebody's harassing me for that, it will make me more determined. I wouldn't give up."

WORK WAS NOT the only place physicians like my father began encountering throngs of protesters. In 1988, the same year Project Rescue formed, a twenty-two-year-old Baptist minister named Daren Dryzmala launched Project House Call. Its aim was to bring the battle to the one place any person would assume they could let their guard down: home.

The truth is, Dryzmala wasn't the first person to do this. In fact, Joseph Scheidler's book, *Closed*, had recommended picketing doctors' houses. Years earlier, my mother recently told me, she and my father had come home one day to find a group of pro-life demonstrators on our sidewalk. My sister and I, both fairly young at the time, were home. My mother figured we'd probably been frightened. In fact, neither of us had noticed (I have no memory of the event, nor does my sister). A few years later, when I was shooting baskets after school one afternoon on our front driveway, I do remember seeing protesters on our sidewalk. They lit candles, sang, and prayed together as the late afternoon light grew dark. It felt creepy, even without anyone saying a word to me, but did not seem terribly threatening.

Project House Call was different. Its goal was to turn up the volume and frequency of such demonstrations. Dryzmala, a recent graduate of

Liberty University, Jerry Falwell's school in Lynchburg, Virginia, was an intimidating presence on the picket lines, whose loud voice could be heard blocks away and who had a flair for the provocative. One of the first Project House Call demonstrations took place on Yom Kippur, the holiest date on the Jewish calendar. Targeted that day was a slender, bearded obstetrician-gynecologist my father had met a few years earlier named Barnett Slepian, who was Jewish.

A few months later, on December 5, 1988, the protesters came around again—this time to two Jewish doctors' houses. It was Hanukkah. My mother was in the kitchen; my father wasn't home. Outside, the members of Project House Call sang Christmas carols and prayed. The group moved on to the Slepian residence, where Dr. Slepian was open-ing presents with his wife and children. STOP THE KILLING NOW, read one placard; SLEPIAN DOES ABORTIONS, declared another. Dr. Slepian's anger boiled over. Bolting out of the house with a baseball bat, he smashed the window of a van, and hit one of the protesters, Ronald Breymeier, bruising his hand.

I have thought about this incident often. It occurred ten years before Dr. Slepian would be murdered in his home. As far as I know, nothing links the two events. Yet I can't help but wonder whether what hap-pened on December 5, 1988, somehow played a role in the larger chain of events. Was this the episode that turned Dr. Slepian into Project Res-cue's leading target, the physician protesters seemed to revile most in the years to come and the one whose name one day lodged in the mind of his murderer?

I wonder, too, whether Dr. Slepian's reaction that evening contained a portent of its own. What he did was undeniably rash, but it was also something many people in his shoes might imagine doing, an effort to prevent the protesters from encroaching on "the one retreat to which men and women can repair to escape from the tribulations of their daily pursuits." The words are from a 1988 Supreme Court decision that up-held the constitutionality of a Wisconsin ordinance barring protesters from picketing in front of a person's home. While marching through a residential neighborhood was perfectly legal, the Court ruled, "there simply is no right to force speech into the home of an unwilling listener" by targeting an individual residence. "The home is different," ruled the Court in an opinion joined by its two most conservative members, William Rehnquist and Antonin Scalia, since the aim of picketing a house was not to educate the public about an issue but "to intrude upon the targeted resident . . . in an especially offensive way."

The target in that case was a physician who performed abortions.

If my father had been home that night, with us as we unwrapped Hanukkah presents, might he have stormed out of the house with a baseball bat? I am certain he would have been every bit as angry; and I know that he understood why Dr. Slepian responded the way he did. While it is hard not to wonder whether Dr. Slepian's reaction that night fueled the rage directed at him, who can say, in retrospect, that it was unjustified?

· 9 ·

One evening in the summer of 1987, a crowd gathered at the Mill-grove Bible Church in Alden, a small town thirty miles east of Buffalo, to attend a presentation on abortion. The church was located in a yellow brick building, down the road from an abandoned school and firehouse. It had roughly 200 members. Among them was a twenty-two-year-old woman named Karen Swallow Prior. Prior had blue eyes and sandy-blond hair that fell in curls around her shoulders. She had grown up on a farm in Maine, riding horses and dreaming of becoming a vet-erinarian, before her family moved to Buffalo. She sat in the back row of the church that night, unsure what she'd make of the presentation, since, although she was a devout Baptist, she'd never really thought much about abortion before. After a couple of speeches, the lights were dimmed and a video was shown. From where she sat, Prior could barely see the grainy black-and-white images flitting across the TV screen. But she had no trouble hearing, and what she heard moved her. "The child senses the most mortal danger imaginable," the narrator intoned. "The child is tugged back and forth . . . the body is now being systematically torn from the head. . . ."

Prior was watching *The Silent Scream*, a low-budget twenty-eight-minute documentary that had been making the rounds at meetings like this ever since its release in 1984. What it showed was an ultrasound videotape of an abortion, as narrated by Dr. Bernard Nathanson, a former abortion provider and reproductive rights advocate—he was one of the founders of NARAL—who'd had a change of heart and made a film to let the world know why. To its pro-choice critics, *The Silent Scream* was a crude piece of agitprop, in which Nathanson's subjective judgments—that the twelve-week-old fetus was a "child" whose pain and suffering could be seen on film—were presented as facts, while the voice of someone else, the pregnant woman whose womb was shown, was conspicuously absent.* But to people who were pro-life, *The Silent Scream* offered powerful confirmation of an incontrovertible fact: that what happened during an abortion was the violent dismemberment of a living soul, an innocent child crying out for help.

This was the conclusion Prior drew. She left the meeting that night certain that abortion was wrong, that women in crisis pregnancy situations needed help, and that as a Christian she was obligated to do something about it. A decade earlier, these feelings might have found expression in volunteer work at the Alden Pregnancy Information Center, the organization that had staged the presentation at her church that night and that counseled women in the area not to have abortions. Prior indeed began volunteering there. At the center, she soon heard about a new movement, Operation Rescue, sending people out to blockade clinics and doctor's offices. Prior had never engaged in civil disobedience before. When she broached the idea to her husband, Roy, he told her it was wrong: a Christian shouldn't go around breaking the law. She reluctantly deferred to him—it was a wife's duty to obey her husband, her faith taught—but she prayed he would come to realize that God wanted

---

*It is a legitimate complaint: in 2005, a study published in *The Journal of the American Medical Association*, based on a review of hundreds of scientific papers, concluded that it is unlikely that the nerve connections in the brain of a much older, twenty-nine-week fetus are sufficiently developed to feel pain. "From the available biological evidence, it seems very unlikely that a fetus experiences what we think of as pain before 29 weeks of gestation," said Dr. Mark A. Rosen, one of the authors of the report and the chief of obstetric anesthesia at the University of California, San Francisco.

her to do this because she was convinced what the protesters were doing was right. A short while later, David Anderson, the assistant pastor at the Priors' church, announced that he was going to New York City for a rescue. The weekend he left turned out to be a bone-chilling one. Roy Prior spent much of it thinking about his pastor standing outside in the frigid winter air. "I just keep thinking about Dave," he told his wife.

Karen's husband soon joined her at a rescue, their first. It took place in January 1989, at 50 High Street. The couple bundled up in many layers in anticipation of spending hours outside. Prior was nervous. She had never thought she would do such a thing. As she sat in the lobby singing and praying with the other protesters, her stomach churned. Then she heard a soothing voice from the opposite end of the room, a minister assuring the demonstrators to remain calm. It was Paul Schenck, who would soon become one of Karen's closest friends.

More than eighty people were arrested that day, among them Prior and her husband. She was soon arrested again, and again, and again. It was the start of a commitment that would culminate in Prior's serving as Project Rescue's spokeswoman in Buffalo, a role she admits was offered to her partly because she so effectively undercut stereotypes. In a movement perceived as male-dominated and *anti*-woman, Prior was an articulate female with career ambitions. She was not a minister but a doctoral candidate in English literature at the University of Buffalo. She dressed in jeans and T-shirts. She was self-possessed and levelheaded, fielding questions coolly and welcoming debate. When I first met her years later, she told me she would gladly become pro-choice if I could offer her a convincing enough argument (I failed). Prior had left Buffalo by this point, moving to Lynchburg to teach English at Liberty University. She opens each of her classes with a prayer, and, in our interviews, frequently grounded her arguments in passages from Scripture. But she also expressed admiration for writers not normally considered favorites in the Bible Belt: Jonathan Swift, Samuel Beckett, and Edward Albee. In one class, I watched Prior lecture critically about why evangelicals generally failed to understand the depth and brilliance of Flannery O'Connor, a Catholic writer she adores. Her poise and composure made her a natural as a teacher, just as I suspect they served her well as Project Rescue's point woman.

While serving in that capacity, Prior led a hectic life, hosting strategy sessions, speaking at high schools, conducting countless interviews. It was exhausting but exhilarating: the movement she had joined was saving lives, she was convinced, and also helping women. To Prior, there was no contradiction between being pro-life and being pro-woman: she simply couldn't imagine anyone going through what she'd witnessed in *The Silent Scream* and feeling empowered afterward. These were not views that proved popular among her academic peers. As her public profile grew, Prior felt a distinct chill from her colleagues at UB: icy glares in the hallways, nasty notes in her mailbox. One day, a coat hanger was placed on her car. Prior felt ostracized. She felt that people who claimed to be open-minded preferred to dismiss her as a reactionary zealot rather than engage her in dialogue. "They would ignore me or avert their eyes," she said. "It was very hard."

Listening to Karen, there was a part of me that didn't want to believe this, that preferred to think the intolerance in the abortion conflict existed solely on one side. We were sitting in her office at Liberty University. In the background classical music was playing. Bookshelves lined with literature anthologies covered one wall. Prior sat a few feet from me, speaking calmly but forcefully, sipping on occasion from a cup of coffee. She exuded an air of confidence that made it hard for me to picture her getting too upset about icy glares from anyone. Yet the longer we spoke, the more her experience sounded plausible to me, in part because I realized that I had come to our meeting holding some of the same assumptions about her myself.

IF ONE OF the goals of the movement Prior joined was to make life more difficult for people like my father, it was working. Throughout 1989, my father continued to arrive at work each morning uncertain whether the building might be blockaded. There were other worries as well. On several occasions, patients of his complained of receiving calls at home from protesters castigating them for having abortions. Another time, a woman who hadn't shown up yet for an appointment said she had received just such a call, prompting my father to worry whether someone in the office might be leaking people's names.

Meanwhile, the lease on his office on Colvin was about to expire. The owner of the building, a former internist, had been supportive throughout the protests. But my father heard that he was planning to sell the building, and feared he would have trouble renewing the lease with a new owner. After scoping out the possibilities, he decided to relocate to a shopping plaza under construction near Maple and Sweethome Roads, a busy location not far from our house. My father signed an agreement to purchase a 1,600-square-foot space. Shortly thereafter, he received a call from the owner, who told him that a woman had phoned him to warn that if Dr. Press moved into the plaza, massive blockades would follow. How she had learned of my father's plans is a mystery— most likely, by trailing his car after work one day. Whatever the case, the owner of the plaza told my father he could not sell him the unit, since doing so would scare off other clients.

My father was furious. Though not litigious by nature, he contacted a lawyer, who told him he had a solid case but also warned that the matter could take years to resolve. Linda Stadler urged my father to sue. He was tempted, but another part of him dreaded the idea of a drawn-out confrontation. For all his single-mindedness, he hated personal entanglements of this sort. Eventually, he decided to work out a deal in which the owner agreed to build him an office at another location at a discounted rate in exchange for the dropping of legal claims. Even so, the experience left him weary. "It was very frustrating," he said.

Marilynn Buckham's frustrations were greater. At least in Kenmore, the suburb where my father worked, the police did their best to minimize the disruptions. The situation was more nebulous in Buffalo, where the police took their cue from Mayor Griffin. In October 1988, 200 protesters blockaded the entrance to Buckham's clinic on Elmwood Avenue. The police appeared on the scene, but by day's end had made only two arrests. The next day, 400 demonstrators turned out. Eighty-one demonstrators were arrested, but the officers on the scene took their time, waiting several hours before removing a single one. The Buffalo police commissioner, Ralph Degenhart, claimed the problem was again the absence of a formal written complaint from the clinic. Buckham called this "baloney," saying she had notified the police the previous day that she was ready to sign complaints. Mayor Griffin, for his part, hinted that the delay was intentional. "We're not going to be having a stranglehold on people," he announced. Griffin had visited the protest site and come away impressed with the demonstrators' civility: "I thought the pro-life people behaved themselves very well." Gerry Matuszewski, the owner of Angelina's, a luncheonette located nearby, had a different view. "It was, if I can use the word, asinine," he told *The Buffalo News*. "My breakfast business was devastated. Lunch was terrible. They intimidated my customers."

Adding to Buckham's frustration was the fact that, when arrests did occur, the charge was trespassing, a minor violation that carried no significant fine or jail term. Predictably, the protesters would soon reappear. Cases that made it to court kept getting strung up on technicalities. City Judge Joseph D. Figliola dismissed trespassing charges against 125 demonstrators because the police failed to describe the specific acts of misconduct perpetrated. Another judge dismissed charges because prosecutors forgot to include the date of the alleged offense in a deposition.

THE VEHICLE THROUGH which Marilynn Buckham and her allies chose to fight back was the Pro-Choice Network of western New York. The organization formed in the fall of 1988, shortly after several hundred people attended a pro-choice meeting at a Unitarian Universalist church in Buffalo and decided to form an organization. Afterward, a small group of women began to meet regularly, women whose commitment to reproductive freedom didn't necessarily grow out of their feminist upbringings. Helen Dalley, one of the Pro-Choice Network's most committed members, was the daughter of a Pentecostal minister. She had grown up in a strict fundamentalist household, where, as Dalley told me when we met not long ago in her modest two-story house in

Tonawanda, "everything was decided by the Bible. If you were a woman you couldn't cut your hair short, you couldn't wear makeup, you couldn't dance or wear jewelry." Dalley's belief that women were smart and capable enough to run their own lives took shape against this backdrop, and is part of what inspired her to begin serving as a clinic escort. It infuriated her to see women hectored in the streets by people who were certain they knew what was best for them. She soon found herself helping to coordinate events like the speakout organized by the Pro-Choice Network in March 1989, where women gathered to describe their personal experiences with abortion. One participant recalled getting pregnant at age sixteen in the era before *Roe*, at which point her family and boyfriend abandoned her. She was sent to a home for troubled girls, where she was raped and force-fed Valium and other medications. She eventually had the child, who suffered from birth defects and was put up for adoption. "Safe, legal abortion was not an option for me," the woman told the audience. "I for one will not let what happened to me happen to my children or grandchildren."

My father did not attend events like this. He was too busy working, he says, and anyway continued to view himself the way he always had: as a physician carrying out his professional responsibilities, not an advocate for a cause. But he didn't fail to notice that there were people around who cared deeply about the issue. I know, too, that his views were slowly altering within the crucible of events. The phrase "The personal is political" might still have sounded foreign to him, but he had a sense now of what it meant. He understood, too, that the party occupying the White House could influence more than just the state of the economy and the balance of power in the Middle East. The days when he would cast a vote for a Republican—at least one who was opposed to a woman's choice—were over.

The emergence of the Pro-Choice Network made people like my father feel less isolated, even though the group failed to muster the passion and energy Project Rescue did. Part of the problem lay in the complacency that *Roe* had bred: while the decision lit a fire under a new generation of pro-life activists, it had the opposite effect on a younger generation of women, many of whom had no memory of the days when abortion was a crime. Two decades earlier, feminists had been the ones organizing demonstrations and demanding change. Now, the insurgents challenging the status quo were people like Karen Swallow Prior and the Schenck brothers. The sense of urgency, like the momentum in the conflict, had switched sides.

ANOTHER PROBLEM WAS demographic. The makeup of the PCN was, as one of its members admitted, "95 percent middle-class and 95 percent white." The problem has dogged modern feminism since the publication of Betty Friedan's *The Feminine Mystique*, which had chronicled the discontent of middle-class housewives trapped in the claustrophobic suburbs while ignoring, some critics would later complain, the experiences of less privileged women struggling against racism and poverty.

Two decades later, instead of offering an expansive vision that linked reproductive freedom to fair wages, educational opportunity, and racial equality, many women's groups had boiled the struggle down to a single goal: preserving choice. NARAL framed it as a question: *"Who decides—you or them?,"* "you" being the pregnant woman in consultation with her loved ones, "them" being meddlesome politicians trying to poke their noses into the personal realm. Behind this shift lay a sober realization that, with the political climate shifting to the right in the mid-1980s, liberals needed a message that would resonate with as many voters as possible. The solution put forward at the time was to present abortion in libertarian rather than feminist terms, as a matter of freedom from government interference. As the journalist William Saletan has shown, in states like Alabama only 42 percent of voters endorsed a woman's *right* to an abortion. But 71 percent agreed that the decision was "best left up to a woman and her doctor without government interference." The only problem was that, soon enough, conservatives would use identical arguments—that the government should stay out of it; that the decision should be left to families—to advocate all kinds of restrictions on abortion (bans on public funding; parental consent laws) that proved popular.

Which, in turn, served to reinforce the impression that, when it came to less fortunate women, groups like NARAL couldn't be bothered. What good was choice, after all, to the millions of poor women who could not afford to *pay* for an abortion? What—in the absence of prenatal care, child care, access to affordable contraception, better education, and decently paid jobs—did it do to alter the life prospects of women growing up in places like East Buffalo?

NOT LONG AGO I paid a visit to Arthur Eve, the African-American assemblyman from Buffalo who lost the mayoral election to Jimmy Griffin in 1977. We met on a warm mid-summer day. Eve was dressed in shorts and a pink-and-white-striped tennis shirt. He sat in a black leather chair behind an oak desk. A broad-shouldered man with a distinguished bearing, he was, by the time we met, on the brink of retirement after nearly four decades in the New York State Assembly. He'd witnessed a lot through the years, including demographic trends that had left him understandably dispirited about the state of life in the community he represented. When Eve first arrived in Buffalo in the 1950s, he told me, it had been a magnet for blacks fleeing the South. He himself came to the city after attending West Virginia State College, and immediately landed a unionized job at a Chevy plant. Two generations later, such jobs had become increasingly scarce, and the pattern was reversing itself. "We lose a lot of people who are leaving this community for the South because it now offers greater opportunity for blacks than the Northeast," said Eve, shaking his head in disgust. "We are going *backwards*."

I had come to see Eve to ask him about what turned out to be the single most agonizing decision of his career: the vote he cast on the 1970 bill proposing to legalize abortion in New York. A deeply religious man who'd been raised Episcopalian, Eve was personally opposed to abortion. But he was also aware that a disproportionate number of the victims of illegal abortion were black. In the run-up to the vote, Eve received a coat hanger in the mail from local members of the NAACP, a reminder that black women were far more likely to be injured or hospitalized from illegal abortions. He also received a call from his mother, who had worked for years as a cashier at a black movie theater in Miami. She told him that young women routinely showed up to have their pregnancies terminated on the theater's balcony and often wound up in hospital emergency rooms. Eve's mother had had to call the ambulance herself on occasion. "It was the only time my mother ever called me about a vote," Eve told me. After hearing her out, Eve threw his support behind the bill, which proved pivotal: the legislation ended up passing by a single vote.

Two decades later, black women in Buffalo did not have to visit places like that movie theater to get an abortion. Even the poorest among them could get a safe, legal abortion, since Medicaid in New York, unlike in so many other states, covered the procedure. Yet one could hardly blame Arthur Eve for wondering how much progress had been made. In 1986, a study found that Buffalo had the highest rate of teenage abortion in New York. It also had the third-highest rate of out-of-wedlock teen pregnancies. To Eve, neither trend suggested that young women in Buffalo were making informed, empowering decisions about their reproductive lives. As he watched more and more black teenagers become mothers during the eighties, Eve started pulling them in off the streets to find out where they had learned about sex. From TV; from magazines; from friends, they told him. One said her boyfriend had assured her that if she held her breath while they had intercourse everything would be fine.

Not a single girl told Eve she had learned about the subject in school, which is what The Buffalo News also found when it surveyed adolescents on the topic in the early 1990s. By this point, Buffalo's teen pregnancy rate had climbed even higher: the city ranked first in New York State. (In 1989, in spite of all the shouting outside places like my father's office, the number of women in Buffalo under age twenty who had abortions was second highest in the state, after only New York City.) Yet, as the News reported, "contraceptive counseling and sex education have been limited or non-existent" in the public schools. "Those statistics [on teen pregnancy and abortion] are mind-boggling," complained Elaine Blyden, an African-American woman who cochaired a committee appointed by the Buffalo board of education to review the health education program. As Blyden told me in an interview, the school system in Buffalo did teach abstinence, but not how to obtain and use contraception.

The schools were not the sole source of the problem. Many young girls getting pregnant, *The Buffalo News* reported in its survey, came from abusive homes. Many evidently lacked access to adequate prenatal care. By 1991, Buffalo's infant mortality rate had risen to an alarming 15.5 per 1,000 live births, which was not only the highest rate in New York but also eclipsed the rate of Bulgaria and Costa Rica.

Focused as it was on countering Project Rescue, the Pro-Choice Network in Buffalo had little time to consider the range of what it was *not* addressing. It didn't have the resources to campaign for universal prenatal care or public investment in the inner-city neighborhoods where many young women having abortions lived. Of course, had it tried, there's no guarantee the effort would have succeeded. In the late 1970s, a group of feminists in Buffalo actually did launch a reproductive rights organization that attempted to bridge the city's race and class divides. It was called the Committee for Abortion Rights and Against Sterilization Abuse (CARASA). Its founders were veterans of the antiwar, civil rights, and women's movements, feminists aware that, all too often in the past, family planning programs targeting minorities had been designed not to empower women but to limit population growth. In the 1920s, some eugenicists had embraced the birth control movement in order to prevent those whom they viewed as lesser breeds from reproducing, and, although her own motivation was to empower women of all social backgrounds, Margaret Sanger at times tailored her message to their ears, at one point bemoaning the burden of the "unfit" in a speech. Six decades later, few people spoke this way, but concerns about the "unfit" spawning too many children had hardly gone away. The 1980s were, after all, the years when "welfare mothers" from the inner city were being demonized for having too many kids. In the black community, abortion and family planning were still often viewed with suspicion for this reason.

CARASA tried to calm such suspicions by acknowledging that, for many women, the choice *to raise a child* was often the one that seemed most out of reach. "In addition to abortion," the group's mission statement proclaimed, "CARASA is committed to the elimination of forced sterilizations of poor and disabled women, access to effective contraception, sex education, social conditions supportive of those who choose to become parents. . . . In our view, reproductive freedom, including abortion, is a precondition for sexual, racial and economic equality." This was the sort of language groups like NARAL had abandoned by the mid-eighties. CARASA's success in reaching a more diverse audience, however, was limited. "Our hearts were in the right place and we really did care about the issues as they affected everyone, but it's hard to just show up in a community and say, 'You know, you really should care about these issues' without being *of* that community," Laura Grube, one of CARASA's founders, told me. Like the members of the Pro-Choice Network, most of CARASA's members were middle-class and white. Few had to struggle with the difficulties confronting residents of the city's poorer, predominantly black neighborhoods. "It seemed at the time and probably still is the case that feminism was just not the most important thing in the black community here," Grube said. "The issues of race and poverty were just so central."

Of course, feminists weren't the only ones who failed to calibrate how race and class might shape how their message was received. The pro-life demonstrators I recall seeing in front of my father's office were also overwhelmingly white. None of their posters drew attention to the social conditions that might have led a woman from one of Buffalo's more impoverished neighborhoods to think twice about raising a child—or, for that matter, to wind up pregnant in the first place. Comprehensive sex education? This is what people like James W. Comerford, a member of the Buffalo board of education and a staunch foe of abortion, vigorously fought *against*. In 1990, Comerford campaigned to have books on teen pregnancy removed from public school libraries. Why? Because the books mentioned organizations like Planned Parenthood, which Comerford likened to "a Nazi death camp" at a rally. ("How they murdered the Jews was more humane than how they murder babies," Comerford declared, a comment he later insisted was not meant to minimize the Holocaust.) In a manner my father found incomprehensible, many pro-life leaders denounced birth control and sex education in the same breath as abortion. On the day he signed a proclamation declaring October 1990 Respect for Life Month, Mayor Jimmy Griffin was asked whether he thought more sex education might be needed in Buffalo's public schools to address the escalating teen pregnancy rate. "No I don't," Griffin replied. "I believe sex education should begin at the home and the church, and we should get back to the basics at school of reading, writing and arithmetic."

BACK ON THE streets, Project Rescue's tactics appeared to be growing bolder. On February 17, 1989, a group of demonstrators arrived at my father's office around 11:00 A.M. Several of them entered the building and fastened themselves together with sophisticated horseshoe bicycle locks. The locks proved impervious to a drill, forcing the police to negotiate with the protesters' attorney to get them to leave. A few months later, more than fifty protesters barged through the doors of my father's office and occupied it. Once again, several chained themselves together with bicycle locks. As it happens, my mother had come to the office that morning to help out with some paperwork. When the protesters arrived, she tried to shut the door to keep them out, but was pinned back against a wall; she ended up with a deep bruise on her forearm.

A video of this scene in my father's office, recorded on a handheld camera he owned, captures the atmosphere. In it, the protesters are splayed out on the beige carpet of a waiting room. They are dressed casually, in jeans, T-shirts, and sweaters that look as if they came from JC Penney or Sears. Many are shielding their faces with a yellow pamphlet on which the words "Project Rescue" are printed. When the camera passes by, one older woman points to a miniature plastic fetus. The room is roughly evenly divided between men and women, most of whom are middle-aged; they seem like the kind of people who can afford to spend a weekday occupying a building rather than going to work but who also weren't born with silver spoons in their mouths. They look like residents neither of the inner city nor of the affluent subdivisions in

Amherst and Williamsville but of the more modest, inner-ring suburbs like Kenmore (where my father's office was located) and Tonawanda (home of the Schencks' church).

At first glance, the class identity of these people might have seemed murky: were they down-on-their-luck factory workers or pampered suburbanites? Viewed through the prism of the nation's culture wars, however, their status is clear. "The clinics are run for profit—we're a nickel-and-dime organization," a spokeswoman for the protesters had told *The Buffalo News* in 1985. This was the new language of populism in America, pitting ordinary, churchgoing Americans against a corrupt secular elite. By the time the video at my father's office was shot, class in America no longer existed in popular consciousness as a signifier of how much money people made. Instead, it had been redefined as a function of education and cultural background. If you believed that the Bible was the word of God and that traditional values were under assault, you belonged among the subjugated masses. If you believed in evolution and read *The New York Times* regularly, you were privileged. If you attended church on Sunday and were convinced that the people running Hollywood, the courts, and the media were bringing America to ruin, you were marginalized. If you thought there were bigger problems out there than homosexuality and abortion, you were a snooty elite. In blue-collar Buffalo, a place where factory workers once attended night classes on the class struggle—but where, as elsewhere, churches increasingly played the role unions once had—this was how the social pyramid was increasingly imagined and seen.

IN THE VIDEO of my father's office, none of the protesters are talking. But the room is hardly silent. Throughout the sit-in, hymns and protest songs ring out. The most persistent refrain is a pro-life twist on the old civil rights–era spiritual:

> Be a hero, save a whale,
> Save a baby, go to jail,
> Keep your eyes on the prize,
> Hold on . . .

Face-to-face with a movement that claimed a direct line of descent from the struggle for black equality, my father could not help but feel befuddled. As far as he knew, the goal of the civil rights movement had been to expand the rights of a minority group. Operation Rescue's goal, as far as he could tell, was the opposite of this—to *limit* the rights of women. In the video of the protest at his office, an exchange can be overheard between my father, a nurse, and a distraught patient who has just made her way past the protesters. "You okay?" the nurse asks. "No!" the patient exclaims. "Outside, they were screaming at me!" "Oh, don't worry about that," my father says, trying to calm her. "Don't they realize we have a choice?" she says, unappeased. "I'm just as mad as you are," he tells her—and he was. Nothing upset him more than to see patients arrive in such a state. Nothing did more to deepen his resolve.

To Karen Swallow Prior, the appropriateness of the analogy with the civil rights movement was clear. "Abortion is a civil rights issue to me," she told me. The rights in question, she explained, belonged to unborn babies, whose lives surely took precedence over the feelings of women like the one my father counseled that day, women who—Karen felt— would come to regret the decisions they'd made. She had met would-be mothers who, years later, expressed grief and pain about the abortions they'd had; the goal of the movement was to spare them this fate. Its chief tactic, civil disobedience, came straight from Martin Luther King, Jr.

Between the civil rights movement and Operation Rescue there was indeed one undeniable connection: both movements were strongly animated by faith. In his book *A Stone of Hope*, the historian David L. Chappell convincingly likens the civil rights movement to a religious revival, showing how black Southerners inspired by the prophetic tradition of the Old Testament spearheaded the drive to abolish "the sin of segregation." "It is hard to imagine masses of people lining up for years of excruciating risk against southern sheriffs, fire hoses, and attack dogs without some transcendent or millennial faith to sustain them," notes Chappell. "It is impossible to ignore how often the participants carried their movement out in prophetic, ecstatic biblical tones." Although the risks were considerably less grave for Operation Rescue activists in the late 1980s, much the same can be said of their inner experience. No other issue in Buffalo stirred such passion and dedication. No other local group inspired as many people to take to the streets.

If a spiritual thread connects the civil rights movement and Operation Rescue, however, this does not mean they were cut from the same cloth. However tempted he may have been, Dr. King did not castigate segregationists as devils or sinners. In the spirit of Jesus' injunction to "love thy enemy," King preached an ethic of love, calling on civil rights activists to recognize the humanity of even their most rabid opponents, and thus to rise above the cycle of hate into which movements for social change can often descend.

Operation Rescue labeled its opponents a different way—"pro-aborts," "murderers," "baby-killers." When a group of ministers in Buffalo sympathetic to abortion rights held a meeting, a protester assailed them as "ministers of Satan." When the police moved too quickly to clear demonstrators from the entrance to one clinic, Paulette Likoudis, who preceded Karen Swallow Prior as Project Rescue's spokeswoman, likened them to Nazi storm troopers.

The effect of such language was to dehumanize anyone who did not subscribe to the movement's views, and to make Project Rescue come across as strident and shrill even to people who were of mixed mind about the issue at hand. The success of the civil rights movement resided, in the end, not in its spiritual roots but in the fact that the more familiar Americans grew with it, the more just its actions seemed. In Buffalo, the daily confrontations with women, the yelling and screaming and the mounting arrests, left a different impression. "It is becoming quite a burden and all the men are physically exhausted," Police Commissioner Degenhart complained after blockades forced him to assign thirty-five cops to handle the disturbances at clinics. As their patience wore thin, police and local judges started levying stiffer fines and penalties, a step that outraged members of Project Rescue but almost no one else. In 1989, in conjunction with a one-hour TV special, *The Abortion Battleground*, the local affiliate of CBS News conducted a poll about the protests. They asked the people of Buffalo what they made of the rescue movement: 67 percent of those surveyed said they believed the demonstrators had "gone too far."

MY FATHER WAS not interviewed for that special, which does not surprise me. Although reporters had begun showing up regularly to cover the sit-ins at his office, he rarely talked to them. In the news clips I collected from this period, his name appeared frequently enough. But lengthy quotes did not.

This was partly a reflection of personality: my father was shy, something his still-rudimentary command of English exacerbated. To this day, when we argue about politics and he has something important to say, he says it in Hebrew. It was a reflection, as well, of the cynicism he'd developed for the profession I would join. When my father read stories in which he was quoted, he often couldn't recognize the words. Reporters don't actually write what you tell them, he would later tell me (a problem I assured him was not characteristic of my work). He had a good rapport with one reporter at *The Buffalo News*, Gene Warner, but when other journalists called, he generally preferred not to comment. In the local papers and on TV, the person from his office quoted most frequently was not my father but Linda Stadler.

There was a third reason for this: my father was reluctant to draw attention to something that was already generating far more publicity than he would have liked. Some people thrive on being the focus of controversy, on finding themselves thrust into the public eye. My father was not one of them. He liked to go about his business quietly, to blend into the crowd and leave the headlines to someone else.

By this point, thanks to choices he'd made whose consequences he hadn't foreseen at the time, blending into the crowd was no longer an option.

· 10 ·

In the spring of 1991, my father moved into a new office, a one-story red-brick facility built by the strip-mall owner he'd nearly sued. It stood alone, on a lot where there had been a house, so that no other businesses could possibly be affected by whatever might occur. The location was not what my father had originally imagined, but it was a nice enough office just the same, with a laboratory, a series of examining rooms, a spacious reception area, a kitchen for staff, and a waiting room stocked with the usual assortment of medical office magazines. My father had involved himself in planning virtually every detail of the place, from the color of the carpeting to the wallpaper, a level of fastidiousness that tested the patience of his coworkers ("Oh my God, what it takes for that man to make a decision," Linda Stadler joked with me) but that at least left him satisfied in the end. More than satisfied, he was proud, and understandably so, having gone from medical resident to established ob-gyn in eighteen years.

It did not take long for the protesters to learn of my father's new location and begin gathering out front, waving their placards as cars turned in to the parking lot and patients approached the door. It was not the message he would have hoped to convey to his new neighbors. Yet for the remainder of that year, although the demonstrators continued turning out, no blockades or sit-ins took place. This was not because Project Rescue had decided my father could use a break. The previous fall, a federal judge had issued a restraining order calling on its members to stop blockading the entrances to abortion clinics and doctors' offices or face a $10,000 fine. The injunction came after Buffalo GYN Womenservices, the clinic Marilynn Buckham ran, and several local physicians, including my father, filed a complaint alleging that the penalties meted out to protesters were doing little to deter them. It was by no means clear that the judge hearing the case, Richard J. Arcara, a lifelong Catholic and Republican, a former altar boy appointed to the bench by Ronald Reagan, was sympathetic to abortion rights. ("Arcara is a Catholic. You can't win this thing," a pro-life attorney snapped at his pro-choice counterpart before one hearing.) But Arcara believed in the rule of law. By the time his restraining order went out, courts in numerous other cities had issued similar rulings, and the fines against Operation Rescue had begun to pile up.

When I came home in August to visit my parents before going back to college, at Brown University, I thought perhaps the pressure on my father had eased for good. We talked less about abortion than about the prospect of the Bills reaching a second consecutive Super Bowl—the year before, they'd made it to the big game, which I had watched in a hotel room with my best friend from Buffalo and his brother, imagining the celebratory phone call I'd be making to my father when the final seconds ticked down. Instead, my friends and I sat in stunned silence as a last-second field-goal attempt by Bills kicker Scott Norwood, which would have won the game, sailed *wide right*, a phrase that would soon enter the lexicon of sports fans everywhere as a synonym for heartbreak. Now, a year later, our hopes were pinned on the upcoming season. We didn't talk much about politics during my visit, or about what had happened just a few weeks earlier, in Wichita, Kansas.

Wichita is where the Summer of Mercy took place, a campaign of sit-ins orchestrated by Operation Rescue that law enforcement officials had expected to last a week but that instead continued unabated for forty-six days. Ignoring the threats of fines and jail terms, protesters from around the country participated in a series of protests that once again thrust Operation Rescue into the national headlines. The images from the trenches—demonstrators lying down in front of cars and jostling with federal marshals—were searing. The Summer of Mercy culminated with a rally of 25,000 people at Wichita State University's football stadium, where Pat Robertson, who had recently launched the Christian Coalition, exhorted the crowd to return America to its biblical roots. "Ladies and gentlemen, we will not rest until this land we love so much is truly, once again, one nation under God," Robertson declared.

I went back to college a week or so after the Summer of Mercy had drawn to a close. A month later, in early October, Randall Terry paid a visit to Buffalo—a "fact-finding" mission to scope out the city as a possible target for a similar campaign. "Do you plan on turning Buffalo into another Wichita?" Terry was asked in a phone interview on a local radio station.

"No," he answered. "And do you want to know why? Because it will be bigger than Wichita."

A few months later, Terry sent out a letter to his fellow activists. "Greetings in the name of Jesus!" it began.

> I just arrived back from Buffalo, New York. What a weekend! The Buffalo rescue movement has announced a major spring offensive they are calling "The Spring of Life."
> The event will take place between April 20th and May 16th. Their stated goal to the press, the city, the church—the nation—is to rid Buffalo of two of its child-killers. I am so excited, I can not tell you. . . . Please pray for a great move of God in Buffalo.

When Judge Arcara issued another federal injunction warning demonstrators they would be fined $10,000 for blockading clinics, Terry dismissed it, saying, "Get ready, pro-aborts. The best is yet to come."

THIS PROSPECT BROUGHT a smile to the face of at least one local politician. When word first circulated that Randall Terry was coming to Buffalo to assess its virtues as a site for a Wichita-style campaign, Mayor Jimmy Griffin announced he would "welcome him with open arms."

What of the fact that Terry's followers would likely be breaking the law? "I want to see [Operation Rescue] in this city," Griffin told the press. "If they can close down one abortion mill, they've done their job."

Others felt differently. On January 7, 1992, the Buffalo Common Council voted 11–1 to adopt a statement telling Operation Rescue it was not welcome. "I don't want Buffalo police officers taken off the East Side or anywhere else to be standing guard over lawbreakers," said Fillmore council member David A. Franczyk, the resolution's author. The Erie County executive, Dennis Gorski, weighed in with a similar view. "During these tough times, when taxpayers are pushed to the limit, the last thing we need is someone coming to our community to intentionally break the law and waste taxpayers' hard-earned money," said Gorski, noting that the Summer of Mercy had cost Wichita more than $100,000 in law enforcement expenses.

As opening day of the Spring of Life approached, a couple of officers from the Amherst police department dropped by my father's office, suggesting that it might be a good time to take a vacation. My father appreciated their perspective. "They said there will be confrontation and it will require a whole lot of manpower from them," he recalls. Other abortion providers in the area, including Barnett Slepian, with whom my father was in regular contact by this point, had agreed to keep their offices closed for at least a couple of days. My father arranged to have a special fence put up around his office, and placed an extra lock on the doors. He refused, however, to take up the Police Department's suggestion. "I told them that I would like to continue my work, that I don't think these people have the right to stop me," he says. "I was not looking for confrontation, but I felt it would be wrong to close the office."

It was a typical reaction from him: to stand firm in the face of pressure, just as he'd been taught throughout his life. I can't imagine it is what the Amherst police wanted to hear. Yet, as vexing as my father's determination might have been, in retrospect it may have proven strategically wise. In Wichita, the police had persuaded local abortion clinics to shut down for a week—the length of time they expected the demonstrations to last—only to see the move backfire. Instead of reducing friction on the streets, the decision emboldened pro-life activists, who at boisterous rallies celebrated the fact that their presence was turning Wichita into an abortion-free city and decided that they should carry on. The clinic shutdown was not the only decision that played into Operation Rescue's hands. By the time the Summer of Mercy took place, thousands of feminists around the country had participated in workshops on clinic defense, learning to lock arms around facilities in order to prevent pro-life activists from blockading the doors. The Feminist Majority Foundation and other national groups volunteered to send clinic defense teams to Wichita. But the local ProChoice Action League refused the offer on the grounds that the presence of counterdemonstrators would increase the risk of tensions spiraling out of control. It was an understandable position, but it meant that Wichita was left with few people to challenge Operation Rescue's presence on the streets.

In Buffalo, the leaders of the Pro-Choice Network of Western New York leaned toward a similar strategy. Engaging in clinic defense might cause "confusion for the patient," the group wrote in its newsletter, *Speak Out!* In February 1992, the PCN board voted not to take part in clinic defense and instead to let the police do the job. It was a naïvely optimistic (and classically liberal) approach, one with which my father agreed. He, too, feared things could get ugly if both sides braced for a fight.

There were other people in Buffalo who held a different view: who believed the best way to counter Operation Rescue was to go toe-to-toe with it. "We were determined that Buffalo was not going to be another Wichita," says Kathy McGuire, who had grown increasingly frustrated by what she perceived as the passivity of the Pro-Choice Network, which in her mind was too reluctant to engage in the sort of direct action Operation Rescue undertook. "I had been on the board [of the PCN] since 1989," she says. "I went to meeting after meeting . . . and it seemed to me the PCN was all about doing nothing, letting the powers that be take care of everything." The best way to defend women's rights, she felt, was to train massive numbers of activists to surround the clinics during the Spring of Life.

McGuire wasn't sure how the idea would go over in Buffalo. Nonetheless, she soon began hosting meetings at Buffalo State College, in the women's center at Bacon Hall. Much to her surprise, hundreds of volunteers showed up.

• • •

THERE WOULD BE volunteers from outside the city as well. Earlier that same spring, I received a call from a classmate of mine at Brown who had heard about my father from a mutual friend. She asked if I might be willing to come talk to a group of pro-choice students who were planning to take buses to Buffalo during the Spring of Life.

I had never spoken publicly about my father before; the idea made me nervous. But, perhaps because I knew the audience would be a sympathetic one, or at least I thought it would, I agreed. A few days later, I made my way to a room on campus where I'd been told the meeting would take place. Inside, roughly eighty students had gathered. The vast majority were women. Many wore their hair cropped short; others sported nose-rings. Finally, I thought, a room full of activists who viewed my father not as a greedy villain but as an embattled hero, although the scene would likely have been no less bizarre to him than seeing his name on the protesters' signs. My father had never claimed to be either a hero or a villain. Had he been there with me that night, I'm fairly certain he would have appreciated how many people had turned out. But I also suspect he would have felt completely out of place.

For me, however, speaking to my classmates brought home something I suppose I'd always known but never quite understood: just as there were many people who wanted my father to stop providing abortions, so there were many others who wanted him to go on. Granted, the students in the room were not your typical cross-section of America: many were feminists at a university where being conservative was enough to qualify you as a freak, where members of the religious right were easily outnumbered by members of the sectarian left. At the meeting, I told those planning to engage in clinic defense that, according to my father, the police, at least in Amherst, had no love for Operation Rescue, and indeed seemed sympathetic to the physicians being targeted. This didn't sit well with one member of the audience, an older man I recognized as a member of the International Socialist Organization. Activists shouldn't necessarily trust what doctors said, he warned, since after all they were elites interested in preserving the status quo.

Great, I thought, wait till my father meets this guy. Most of the students in the room, however, were there because they feared that a fundamental right that mattered to them was under threat, and they were hardly the only ones who felt this way. A few days earlier, in Washington, D.C., half a million people had flooded the Mall to attend the largest abortion-rights demonstration ever. Hovering over the event was the fact that, before the end of the 1992 term, the Supreme Court was to hand down a decision in *Planned Parenthood of Southeastern Pennsylvania v. Casey*, in which the constitutionality of abortion would again come under review.

It was by no means clear that *Roe v. Wade* would survive. Since 1973, Republican presidents had appointed six new justices to the Court. In 1989, in the case of *Webster v. Reproductive Health Services*, the Court had upheld an array of restrictions on abortion in Missouri. While the decision did not undo *Roe*, Chief Justice William H. Rehnquist gave every indication that that might happen soon, declaring "constitutional law in this area a virtual Procrustean bed." Inside the courtroom, Justice Blackmun announced in a dissent that *Roe* had been preserved "for today, at least." But, he added, "the signs are evident and very ominous, and a chill wind blows."

Were Blackmun's fears borne out, I realized standing in the room that night, a massive backlash of a different kind would likely follow. I hadn't thought about this much while growing up in Buffalo, perhaps because all the anger I'd witnessed seemed to come from one side, or perhaps because I'd never had to consider how an unplanned pregnancy might upend *my* life. Plenty of political causes at Brown required little sacrifice on the part of students and seemed to have a distant, abstract relationship to our lives. In this case, the link was direct and personal; a roomful of my classmates cared enough to travel to Buffalo for this reason. Walking out onto the main green afterward, I thought about this and about my father, who maintained that his actions weren't political, yet whose dedication and commitment mattered greatly to far more people than he likely realized, and I felt a powerful surge of pride.

· · ·

WHEN THE SPRING of Life began on April 20—two weeks after the abortion-rights rally in Washington and just as the Supreme Court began to hear oral arguments in *Casey*—Buffalo and the rest of the country were ready. That evening, the Spring was the lead story on all three national evening newscasts. Not since the Blizzard of '77 had the spotlight shone so directly on western New York.

The networks were anticipating a repeat of Wichita, which was not, initially at least, what they got. Instead of more than 1,000 out-of-town protesters swarming into Buffalo, as had been speculated days earlier, only 300 had shown up by the first day. The police were managing to keep things relatively calm, with pro-life demonstrators on one side of the barricades, their pro-choice counterparts on the other. For the next forty-eight hours, reporters and photographers from across the country—everyone from CNN to *Life* had a correspondent in town—tromped around town in search of colorful copy. The most headline-grabbing anecdote revolved around Baby Tia, a dead fetus that Rob and Paul Schenck brandished on the picket lines, saying she had been aborted after twenty-five weeks. The Erie County medical examiner's office disagreed, stating that Baby Tia was slightly more than nineteen weeks into gestation and that it could not confirm whether she had been aborted. Operation Rescue's leaders insisted otherwise. "Is this real? Is this real?" pleaded Rob Schenck when a police officer questioned Baby Tia's authenticity. "It's the most beautiful aborted baby I've ever seen."

On April 22, day three of the Spring of Life, the tempo of the protests picked up, especially at my father's office. Early that morning, my father went to Children's Hospital to see some patients, then headed for his office. On the way he came upon a set of barricades: the police had cordoned off the road. After he showed his ID, the officers directed him onto an alternative route that enabled him to reach his office from the opposite direction. As he approached, he says, a group of demonstrators spotted him and swarmed around his car. One man leaped onto the hood. Others stood in front, obstructing his path. My father pulled his Explorer to a stop while the police began arresting demonstrators (by day's end, they would book roughly 200 at his office alone). When the space around his vehicle had been cleared, the police motioned for my father to open the door. He got out, and half a dozen officers armed with billy clubs formed a human barricade around him, then escorted him through the parking lot to the door of his office.

Footage of the demonstration, recorded by my parents from a local TV news report aired that night, depicts the surreal scene. It shows my father in a gray sport coat, walking calmly in the middle of a circle of cops. He looks small among them, his head a foot or so below theirs. He is holding a beige leather briefcase in his hand. His back is turned toward the camera, so that the expression on his face can't quite be seen. But the way he is carrying himself—head tilted slightly down, arms at his side, gait even but deliberate—speaks both to the tension of the moment and to his fierce determination not to appear rattled. This was his office, he had patients to attend to, he wasn't doing anything wrong: thoughts like these would have prevented him from even considering, say, attempting to sneak into the building undetected, or scurrying by with a coat over his head to shield his identity, as a frightened patient of his featured in the same news clip does. In the news segment that aired, the only comment from my father's office comes (as usual) from Linda Stadler, a terse statement of fact: that the office remained open, that patients were being treated. As on other occasions, my father strained to avoid engaging the protesters in any way.

In this he differed from Barnett Slepian, who, against the advice of Marilynn Buckham and surely many others, had taken to rolling down the window of his car on occasion to chat with the demonstrators. On one occasion, a few years after the explosive confrontation outside his house during Hanukkah in 1988, Dr. Slepian went out to breakfast with a couple of them. His aim, I imagine, was to defuse some of the rancor and bitterness. I can't help but wonder whether, instead, the tactic ended up having the opposite effect, making his critics only more determined to change *his* mind—and, when he didn't change, turning him into more of a target.

Then again, there was no way to avoid becoming a target during the Spring of Life, as Operation Rescue ratcheted up its focus on the so-called weak links of the abortion industry: individual doctors. The pattern had begun in Wichita, which had been selected in part because it was the hometown of Dr. George Tiller, a physician who performed late-term abortions and whom the protesters called Tiller the Killer.

A scene from the Spring of Life

The accusations were no less pointed, and personal, in Buffalo, where, soon after the Spring of Life began, radio ads singling out my father, Barnett Slepian, and a handful of other physicians were aired. "Some doctors deliver babies. Some doctors kill babies!" blared the ads. On the corner of Maple and Exeter Roads, a quarter mile or so from my parents' house, a six-foot red banner reading PRESS KILLS CHILDREN was unfurled. Leaflets conveying the same message were distributed to my parents' neighbors. "Our intention in this neighborhood is to expose Shalom Press and his brutal exploitation of women," Rob Schenck explained of this aspect of the Spring of Life, which was dubbed Operation John the Baptist. "We are appealing to the neighbors to please encourage your neighbor to end his profiteering at the expense of unborn children."

As it turns out, at least within our neighborhood, Operation John the Baptist had the opposite effect. Several neighbors, appalled by the invasion of my parents' privacy, called to express their support. My parents, for their part, did their best to tune the message out. They found it more challenging to ignore the message of the vigil held outside my father's office on the eleventh day of the Spring of Life. It took place on Yom Hashoah, a national holiday in Israel commemorating the victims of the Holocaust. "This place is where the Holocaust continues to happen," Keith Tucci, Randall Terry's successor as head of Operation Rescue, told a crowd of 1,500 gathered for the vigil. Two doctors were mentioned by name: my father and Dr. Slepian, both Jewish, both guilty of continuing "a horror that brought so much suffering to their own families," in the words of Rob Schenck.

I learned only years later that my father drove by the vigil without getting out and saying anything. It wasn't the first time he had heard his ethnicity addressed by the protesters. "You are a Jew with a circumcised heart!" a demonstrator once told him. On another occasion, the Schenck brothers showed up at his office in *tallitot,* prayer shawls, and insisted he was ignorant of the teachings of his faith. There were the protests that had taken place on Jewish holidays in front of his house and Dr. Slepian's. "It was part of the battle, part of the intimidation," my father told me, the words of a man who, despite being raised in a secular household, took enormous pride in his Jewish identity.

My mother was in the car with my father on the night of the vigil. I can picture her glaring through the window on the passenger side, silently taking in the scene in which abortion was equated with the genocide that had cost her sister's life, and very nearly her own and her parents'. Recently, I asked her what she had made of it. She fell silent, then offered a single word: "Disgusting."

RANDALL TERRY TOLD the media that Buffalo had been selected for the Spring of Life because it was a "very strong pro-life city." About Mayor Griffin, who donned a "Pray for the Spring of Life" button during the tumult, there can be no doubt he was right. But the city as a whole was another matter. On the eve of the demonstrations, a poll commissioned by *The Buffalo News* found that just 6.8 percent of local residents unconditionally welcomed Operation Rescue to town. An additional 50 percent welcomed the protesters "providing they obey the law," while 43.2 percent didn't welcome them at all.

The same survey found that, despite all the protests in recent years and the area's heavily Catholic makeup, 64.4 percent of local residents described themselves as pro-choice, just 35.6 percent as pro-life. Does this mean the attitude toward abortion in western New York was no different than that at, say, Brown University? Not exactly. In 1989, a survey by a local polling firm found that only 22 percent of western New Yorkers believed abortion should be permitted under "all circumstances." But an even smaller number, 16 percent, said it should be allowed under "no circumstances." The majority, 57 percent, favored permitting abortion under "some circumstances," a position in line with that of most Americans, whose attitudes were often more nuanced than conventional labels (pro-life, pro-choice) allowed. The same poll found that only 11 percent of Buffalonians felt that abortion should be permitted at any point during pregnancy, but 68 percent believed it should be permitted during the first trimester (when roughly 9 in 10 abortions in Erie County were performed). To most people in Buffalo—as, for that matter, America—the question "Are you for or against abortion?" prompted the response "It depends": on circumstance, on timing and, one presumes, on a variety of other factors.

Perhaps this is why, when the Spring of Life finally happened, the vast majority of people in Buffalo did their best to ignore the hype. As during the 1960s, others expressed resentment at the mayhem that was unfolding. "I thought I was in Beirut," one woman who lived near a clinic complained to *The Buffalo News*. "I've had no sleep in five days," grumbled another. "What worries me is that when they gather, you don't know when they will begin to act crazy," said a third.

Even some people with potentially sympathetic views seemed to keep their distance. In retrospect, the most important constituency Operation Rescue failed to win over consisted of people like Michael Sutter, whom I met years later through a mutual acquaintance. Sutter lives in Grand Island, where the Schenck brothers grew up. He was raised Catholic but, in 1977, having lived a fairly rebellious lifestyle after college, became a born-again Christian. (His conversion came shortly after his father died.) A passionate outdoorsman, he runs a successful wildlife control business out of his home. He is also pro-life, telling me it upset him deeply to see people using abortion as a casual form of contraception. We met in his kitchen on a pleasant spring day, a decade or so after the Spring of Life. I wondered whether it had occurred to him to join the protests back then. He told me he had indeed driven past the demonstrations out of curiosity. He believed that many of the protesters who came to the city were "sincere." But he did not like all the noise and shouting; nor did he endorse the idea of blockading buildings, not least because, as a hunter and staunch advocate of the Second Amendment, he'd heard some members of the animal-rights movement promote similar methods. "What I didn't like was some of the tactics they used," he said.

In her journal entries from the time, Karen Swallow Prior recorded different reactions: from couples who saw what was happening and contacted Operation Rescue to ask whether they could help; individuals who decided to become pro-life activists for the first time. "Every week new people come out," Prior wrote excitedly. "It's weird—wild." The goal of Operation Rescue was never to win a popularity contest, she told me. It was to stop abortion and to raise consciousness. As she watched the protests in Buffalo unfold, Prior believed the Spring of Life was succeeding, even if, privately, she also harbored reservations about how certain matters were handled. There was, for example, a subtle tension between her and some of the national leaders, a tension whose gender dynamics did not escape her. "All the national leaders are men," Prior noted in her journal. "They seem not to oppose the leadership of women in theory, but have more difficulty applying it in practice." David Montgomery, a reporter for *The Buffalo News*, published an article headlined "The Rescue Honchos: Boys Will Be Boys," that mockingly depicted the Spring of Life's predominantly male leadership as a bunch of guys on a testosterone kick. At the time, Prior considered the piece a cheap shot. "I was *so* mad," she told me. But, she said, "the more I thought about it, the more I realized it was partly true."

Prior also couldn't understand why people like Randall Terry invariably mentioned homosexuality ("the vulgar Sodomite lifestyle," as he would later put it when running for Congress in 1998) at rescues. What exactly did this have to do with saving babies? Terry, she says, pointed out that a disproportionate number of the protesters on the opposing side were homosexual, which was true: the gay and lesbian community in Buffalo played an active role in organizing clinic defense teams. Terry's rhetoric, however, did little to mitigate the impression that the movement's ultimate goal was to create a theocracy that would police people's personal lives.

When the dust had settled and the Spring of Life was over, some 600 people had been arrested. According to Operation Rescue, a dozen women planning to have abortions were persuaded to change their minds (their identities were not revealed, making the claim difficult to verify). But there was little question as to who had won the war of images and, to a large extent, the confrontation on the streets. As *The Buffalo News* observed:

> No clinics were closed, even for a minute. No doctors were driven out of the abortion business. Mainstream Buffalo turned its back on Operation Rescue, even as a nation watched.

"Operation Fizzle," *Time* magazine called it. The event's "big winners," wrote *The Buffalo News*, were "the pro-choice loyalists who locked arms in front of clinic doors before dawn each day to keep the doctors' offices open." Indeed, for the first time in Buffalo, pro-life activists were met on the streets by equal numbers of pro-choicers, a rainbow coalition of artists, students, gays, lesbians, mothers, and kids. When it was all over, people like Kathy McGuire could not help but feel elated. "There was victory party upon victory party," she says.

MY PARENTS WERE not among those celebrating, but they certainly shared the city's general sense of relief. At long last, the protesters and camera crews were leaving.

First, though, something unusual happened: a profile of my father appeared in *The New York Times*. The date was April 29, 1992, the piece a one-page story accompanied by a photograph. In the photo he is wearing a light jacket over a sweater and white-collared shirt. His head is turned slightly to the side, as though he's staring at something in the near distance—a mêlée involving some protesters, perhaps. At fifty-two, he looks fairly young for his age, but the two decades that have passed since his passport photograph was taken are apparent. His once dark hair is now fringed with gray, and is thinner, especially around the temples. The black-rimmed glasses he wore in his early thirties have been replaced with wire-framed ones. The skin beneath his chin has slackened a bit. It is the photograph of a man who is closer to retirement than to youth, who has lived to watch his children grow up, who has been through a tumultuous couple of years and should (but won't) start to think about slowing down.

But there is another aspect to the picture that is timeless: the fixed expression on my father's face, the slightly narrowed eyes and closed, serious mouth. It is the same expression that appears in some of the photos of him back when he was a raw-boned kid in the Israeli army: focused, calm, a look of steely determination in his gaze. Maybe time would have softened this quality a bit had things been different. But, if this picture is any indication, the events of the past few years had only made it more pronounced.

I asked my father why he sat down for the profile, given his general habit of avoiding the press. In part, he told me, it was because *The New York Times* is the most celebrated newspaper in America. But the bigger motivation was the opportunity to have his side of the story told, to let people know that, however hard the demonstrators pushed, there were doctors in Buffalo who weren't going to back down. "I think the services are essential and necessary and they should be done legally and professionally," he told the paper. "And they should be provided by physicians trained to do them." He also took an uncharacteristic jab at the protesters. "If they put all this effort into birth control and education, we can reduce the number of abortions that way," he said. "But these people oppose that, too."

After the story appeared, my parents received dozens of supportive calls from people across the country. Cards and letters also poured in from friends and patients in Buffalo. Had no one acknowledged the piece, my father probably would have said nothing. But he saved every one of those letters, and he still remembers those calls.

· · ·

TWO MONTHS AFTER the profile ran, spectators gathered in the Supreme Court's great hall to hear its much-anticipated ruling in *Casey*. The fate of *Roe v. Wade* was hanging in the balance and, with five seemingly firm opponents of abortion now on the Court (Rehnquist, Scalia, Byron R. White, Anthony Kennedy, and Clarence Thomas), speculation swirled that a reversal was in the offing.

"We conclude the central holding of *Roe* should be affirmed," announced Sandra Day O'Connor, who, along with David Souter and Anthony Kennedy, coauthored the majority opinion in *Casey*. Restrictions on abortion that did not impose an "undue burden" on women were permissible, the ruling held, a standard that effectively replaced the trimester formula enshrined in *Roe*. But the core of Harry Blackmun's ruling was retained, on the grounds of personal liberty ("The destiny of the woman must be shaped to a large extent on her own conception of her spiritual imperatives and her place in society," wrote Kennedy in one section) and stare decisis, the principle that courts, lest they be seen as succumbing to political pressure, should adhere to precedent even in cases that have stirred immense controversy. "Only the most convincing justification under accepted standards of precedent could suffice to demonstrate that a later decision overruling the first was anything but a surrender to political pressure," wrote Justice Souter.

The ruling prompted a withering dissent from Justice Scalia. "By foreclosing all democratic outlet for the deep passions this issue arouses, by banishing the issue from the political forum that gives all participants, even the losers, the satisfaction of a fair hearing and an honest fight . . . the Court merely prolongs and intensifies the anguish," he wrote. "We should get out of this area, where we have no right to be, and where we do neither ourselves nor the country any good by remaining."

A few months later, Bill Clinton was elected president of the United States, thanks to the votes of 44.9 million Americans. Two of those votes belonged to my parents. They liked Clinton's intelligence, his articulateness, and his vow to do what he could to advance the cause of peace in the Middle East. They were also aware that he was committed to protecting a woman's right to choose.

When Clinton was inaugurated on the steps of the Capitol a few months later, you could hardly blame people like Marilynn Buckham, and my father, for breathing a sigh of relief and assuming the worst was over. This is certainly what I recall thinking at the time.

It is an assumption that could not have been more wrong.

PART 3

A Soldier of God

■

D on't stop thinking about tomorrow!" The Fleetwood Mac song blared through the loudspeakers in Ellicott Square as supporters pressed toward the stage and balloons filled the air. It was November 2, 1993. The victory anthem that a year earlier had played for Bill Clinton was now playing for Democrat Anthony Masiello, a former New York State senator who had just been elected mayor of Buffalo, ending the sixteen-year reign of Jimmy Griffin, who after four consecutive terms had decided not to run. A six-foot four-inch former basketball star at Canisius College, where he was nicknamed "Big Red," the tall, red-haired Masiello was, like Griffin, the product of a working-class Catholic up-bringing. He'd grown up on West Street, on a mostly Italian block lined with modest two-family houses. Unlike Griffin, Masiello was a baby boomer who campaigned on a theme — "the politics of inclusion" — that would have made his politically incorrect predecessor sneer. During the campaign, Masiello reached out to members of Buffalo's gay and les-bian community (Griffin had referred to homosexuals as "fruits and queers"). He had a good reputation among the city's African-American leaders, and had promised that all of the city's ethnic and racial groups would be represented in his administration. The message went over well, which did not mean that running Buffalo would be as easy for Big Red as sinking a jump shot had once been. "Savor the glow," a columnist for *The Buffalo News* advised the incoming mayor, noting he was about to take over a city "where nearly one in five households depends on welfare, where barely 10 percent of families have incomes exceeding $50,000."

Actually, in some respects the Queen City was in far better shape than it had been when the Griffin era began, a fact owed at least partly to Griffin himself, who during his tenure had pushed a series of creative downtown revitalization projects, including the construction of Pilot Field, a baseball stadium, and done his best to persuade business leaders that Buffalo was not, in fact, on the decline. The unemployment rate that had ballooned so alarmingly during the 1970s had dropped back into single-digit range. Buffalo's economy had made a slow, painful recovery, its laid-off steelworkers and machinists gradually finding other jobs, albeit in occupations that were far less likely to be unionized, to offer health benefits, or to pay a living wage than in the past. In 1991, an article in the *Buffalo Law Review* noted that the new "high growth" sectors in Erie County offered mostly the kinds of jobs—in retail, as stock clerks, as restaurant workers, typists, receptionists, cleaners, maids—where the average wage was $5.60 per hour. There was still some heavy industry in Buffalo—a Ford plant here, a Fisher Price factory there—and still plenty of union members around, but the old blue-collar economy had given way to a low-skill "pink-collar" one. In many of western New York's fastest-growing sectors, female employees now outnumbered men, by one measure a sign of progress, but not if living standards were taken into account. In the year Anthony Masiello was elected, one in four Buffalonians was living in poverty. The number of western New Yorkers in higher income brackets (more than $60,000 per year) had increased during the 1980s, but the number of poor people had grown even more. Buried in these statistics lay a fact of no small relevance to the nation's culture wars: by the early 1990s, it simply wasn't possible for most families to survive without two, three, sometimes four jobs. It was easy to blame feminism for steering too many women away from their traditional roles as mothers and housewives, but the reality was that being a stay-at-home mom was a luxury fewer and fewer women in Buffalo (or, for that matter, the rest of the country) could afford.

The mayor-elect nevertheless struck an optimistic note. "We want to make Buffalo the best possible place to live, work and raise a family," Masiello announced to his supporters on election night. A few months later, he moved into the wood-paneled office that Jimmy Griffin had occupied for nearly two decades. Reporters would have trouble recognizing it at first. Gone were the photograph of Harry Truman and the map of Limerick, Ireland, that had adorned the walls. Gone was the clock on which the letters of Griffin's first and last name had stood in place of numbers. Gone, too, was the familiar blue-and-white "Abortion Kills Children" sign that had greeted visitors in Griffin's day; although he was Catholic, Anthony Masiello was pro-choice.

It was yet another reason for the reproductive rights community in Buffalo to breathe a sigh of relief: the new mayor would not be rolling out the welcome mat for Randall Terry if he should come again.

And yet relief is not what anyone closely following the abortion conflict was feeling by this time.

"I'VE NEVER BEEN this afraid," Marilynn Buckham told *The Buffalo News*. It was March 20, 1993. Ten days earlier, a thirty-one-year-old man dressed in a suit and tie had lingered in the parking lot of Women's Medical Services in Pensacola, Florida, his right hand buried in his pocket, while a protest was taking place. He waited for David Gunn, the clinic's sole physician, to open the door of his car, then pumped into the doctor's back three bullets from the .38 caliber Smith & Wesson revolver he was holding. "I've just shot Dr. Gunn; he's dying," he told a police officer moments afterward.

It was the first killing of an abortion provider—the first pro-life murder—in the United States. The man who carried it out, Michael Griffin, was a chemical plant worker and former Navy submariner who, a few months earlier, had been shown a couple of graphic anti-abortion videos, including one that depicted a woman preparing her fetus for a funeral. Griffin had attended a number of fundamentalist churches in the Pensacola area. He had a reputation as a quiet, hardworking father and husband, though also, according to court papers filed two years earlier by his wife, for succumbing to "great fits of violence." He had fallen under the influence of John Burt, a militant abortion foe (and former Ku Klux Klan member) who appeared at some rallies with a five-foot effigy of David Gunn with a noose around his neck and blood on his hands. On it a verse from Genesis was inscribed: "Whosoever sheds man's blood, by man his blood shall be shed."

This would soon become the rallying cry of the pro-life movement's radical wing.

At the time of the shooting, I was living in the Boston area, which is where, nearly two years later, a mentally imbalanced loner named John C. Salvi—claiming to have been inspired partly by Michael Griffin—would walk into two abortion clinics and open fire, leaving two people dead and five wounded. A week or so after learning of Gunn's murder, I remember, I came across a newspaper article about a boot camp in Florida where Operation Rescue activists were being trained. Among the tactics described were tracing doctors' license plates, videotaping them at home, and learning the ins and outs of electronic surveillance. It sounded creepy to me, as did the debate that unfolded among those in attendance about what had just happened in Pensacola. The majority, the article reported, felt what Michael Griffin had done was wrong, but a few were less certain.

The article was not exactly reassuring, yet I do not recall thinking at the time that the pattern might spread, let alone that someone might soon repeat the act in Buffalo. Neither does my father. In the *Buffalo News* article quoting a frightened Marilynn Buckham, his reaction was recorded as well: "I believe that abortion should be available as part of the service obstetrician-gynecologists provide. I didn't give in to pressure before, and I'm not going to in the future." Terse and defiant, as usual, yet the truth is he still didn't believe someone in Buffalo might resort to violence. Like most physicians who performed abortions, he had received his share of death threats through the years. At the advice of the police, he'd purchased a bulletproof vest, and on occasion he wore it. Even so, he assumed the shooting in Pensacola was an isolated act, something that not incidentally had happened in the South, which not only had its own peculiar history of vigilante justice, but also was the location of the Bible Belt.

My father was not alone in his opinion. He remembers discussing the incident with his coworkers: they, too, thought it was terrible but, like him, did not seem worried. The Spring of Life was over, after all. The crowds of protesters on the streets of Buffalo had thinned. In Washington, a new administration favored abortion rights. Soon, with David Gunn's children on hand, President Clinton would sign the Freedom of Access to Clinic Entrances (FACE) Act, legislation passed by Congress that made it a federal crime to impede access to abortion clinics. Enacted in the aftermath of Dr. Gunn's murder, the FACE law would effectively bring the rescue movement to an end.

It did not occur to anyone to think that, having one door shut in their face, some pro-life activists would seek other, possibly more violent means. In fact, plenty of them had already embraced violence by this point, albeit in less lethal forms. In 1993, the same year David Gunn was shot, Dallas A. Blanchard, a sociologist from Pensacola, and Terry J. Prewitt, an anthropologist at the University of West Florida, published a study entitled *Religious Violence and Abortion: The Gideon Project*. The book took its title from an incident that had occurred nine years earlier, also in Pensacola, when, in the early morning hours of Christmas Day, two men dressed in black SWAT pants and dark green ski masks set off timers and blew up three abortion clinics simultaneously. The perpetrators, James Simmons and Matthew John Goldsby, were devout Christians who believed that God had instructed them to stop abortion. They drew their inspiration from the passage in the Book of Judges in which Gideon set out to destroy the altars of Baal, the false god to whom firstborn children were sacrificed. They described their act as "a birthday gift for Jesus."

In 1984, thirty abortion clinics in America were bombed or torched. There were twenty-three such incidents in 1985 and 1986. To understand more about those who did this, Blanchard and Prewitt visited prisons; they tracked other perpetrators down by phone. The portrait they drew made for a striking contrast with the mostly Catholic women Kristin Luker had interviewed a decade earlier. Blanchard and Prewitt's subjects were mostly men, nearly all under forty. They came from lower-middle-class, often blue-collar, backgrounds. Many lived on the fringes of cities or in small towns. Some were loners; others belonged to small, cultlike churches and interacted solely with like-minded people who shared their "solitary worldview." Their religious affiliations varied— they were Lutheran, Baptist, Mormon, Catholic—but one element united them: all were "religiously ardent," Blanchard and Prewitt reported, and all were "dualists" who viewed the world "in clear-cut black and white" terms.

IT IS AMONG such hardcore activists that the Army of God Manual, a blueprint for violence and sabotage, began making the rounds in the early 1990s. "This is a manual for those who have come to understand that the battle against abortion is a battle not against flesh and blood, but against the devil," its opening sentence declared. What followed was a brief excursion through a surreal world where making bombs, blowing up clinics, and plotting chemical attacks were depicted as the righteous duties of God-loving Christians. One section detailed the contents of pyridine, a flammable liquid derived from coal, and proclaimed: "So there it is, brothers and sisters. Just waiting to be spread all over this land!" Another laid out a nine-step process for making a highly dangerous chemical compound called C-4. Interspersed with this were quotations from Scripture, denunciations of "the God-hating, mother-molesting, baby-killing Amerikan system," and a smattering of lifestyle tips— "Celibacy: The Final Solution (for Life)," for example. Early versions of the manual stopped short of endorsing murder. The revised edition, completed after FACE was enacted, declared, "All of the options have expired. Our Most Dread Sovereign Lord God requires that whosoever sheds man's blood, by man shall his blood be shed."

In its rage and its righteousness, as well as in its pitch-black vision of an America on the brink of apocalyptic doom, the Army of God Manual accurately reflected the mood of bitterness and desperation among many hardcore activists in the aftermath of Operation Rescue's collapse. How disorienting that collapse must have been occurred to me while I was talking to Rob Schenck. One minute the Schencks were on the

cover of *Life* magazine as leaders of the most successful political and social movement in their hometown. The next minute, Rob Schenck was
at an ATM, unable to withdraw money because his assets had been
frozen—the result of one of the many judgments levied against him in
court. By 1994, both Rob and Paul owed tens of thousands of dollars in
fines for defying Judge Richard Arcara's court order. Paul Schenck had
also been sentenced to a month in federal prison for false representation
under oath (he'd denied exchanging glasses and neckties with his
brother at a protest, a claim that videotapes of the event belied). Like so
many other members of the movement, the Schencks had believed the
power of their convictions would awaken a nation's conscience and alter
the course of history. Instead, they found themselves defeated in court,
drowning in debt, and facing the grim reality that *Roe v. Wade* was not
about to go away anytime soon.

The Schenck brothers would eventually land on their feet, albeit not
in Buffalo. Paul Schenck soon moved to Virginia Beach to join the
American Center for Law and Justice, a Christian legal group founded by
Pat Robertson, while Rob Schenck made his way to Washington, where
by the mid-1990s he was spending his days handing out marble tablets of
the Ten Commandments on Capitol Hill and conducting prayer sessions
for congressional staffers. Thanks to a deftly timed change of scenery, the
rebellious twins from Grand Island found a place for themselves in the
growing network of evangelical Christians in Washington.

But not all of their comrades were content to travel this route, particularly not those who had come to believe that more radical measures were
required. In the Army of God Manual, a "Special Thanks" section identified various individuals in this camp. Among them was "sweet-Shaggy
West," whose real name was Rachelle Ranae (Shelly) Shannon. In August
1993, Shannon, a housewife from Grants Pass, Oregon, made her way to
Wichita, Kansas, a .25-caliber pistol in hand, and shot George Tiller, the
physician who had been targeted two years earlier during the Summer of
Mercy (Tiller survived the attack). Also thanked was "Atomic Dog," the
nom de guerre of a man authorities would later identify as James Kopp.

After Shelly Shannon came Paul Hill, a tall man with blond hair and
a fixed smile who, on July 29, 1994, cocked his rifle and unleashed a

barrage of bullets that killed Dr. John Britton, the abortion provider in Pensacola who had replaced David Gunn, and his volunteer escort, James Barrett. Barrett's wife, June, was injured.

This turn to violence provoked some notably equivocal responses from pro-life leaders. "While we grieve for [Gunn] and for his widow and for his children, we must also grieve for the thousands of children that he has murdered," said Randall Terry after the first attack. Meanwhile, more than two dozen pro-life activists signed a statement soon to be posted on the Internet defending the murder of abortion providers as "justifiable homicide."

AS THE SHOOTINGS began to sink into public consciousness, stories appeared about doctors inserting bulletproof glass in their offices and about younger gynecologists at medical schools who, thinking about their families and what kind of lifestyle they wanted to lead, were deciding not to provide abortions even though they were pro-choice. Around this time, my father remembers, he spoke with Barnett Slepian about the mounting sense of danger. Dr. Slepian had begun his medical residency a couple of years after my father and, the community of ob-gyns in Buffalo being fairly small, they'd gotten to know each other through the years. Recently, they'd started covering for each other on weekends, not performing abortions but doing the part of the job that gave both of them the most satisfaction, delivering babies. They had another bond as well, having been among the handful of physicians targeted by Operation Rescue.

Save for the Salvi shootings, the attacks up to now had happened in distant places. But Dr. Slepian had evidently given serious thought to a possibility my father had not—namely, that the same thing could easily happen in Buffalo. He told my father that he now avoided sitting by the windows in restaurants. Maybe the fact that his children were younger made him more conscious of such risks. Or maybe he just lacked the denial mechanism that made my father incapable of acknowledging even the slightest measure of concern about his own safety. Many times in the years to come I would ask my father whether the protests ever caused him to lose sleep or to worry. Each time, in the same calm voice, he would say no, with a firmness that leads me to believe this was not meant merely to reassure me but simply reflected the truth.

In August 1994, two weeks after Paul Hill shot John Britton, a letter about the violence appeared in *The Buffalo News*. It was written by Dr. Slepian. "The members of the local non-violent, pro-life community may continue to picket my home," he wrote.

> They may continue to scream that I am a murderer and a killer when I enter the clinics at which they "peacefully" exercise their First Amendment Right of freedom of speech.
>
> They may do all of the above to me and other abortion providers of this community. But please don't feign surprise, dismay and certainly not innocence when a more volatile and less restrained member of the group decides to react to their inflammatory rhetoric by shooting an abortion provider.

Reading the letter—which suggests that Dr. Slepian saw exactly what was coming, yet refused to be deterred from doing what he felt was right—gives me chills.

My father, for his part, was more shaken by the news of another murder that took place in the mid-1990s, one fueled by a volatile conflict that generated its share of headlines and that was carried out by a man who believed he was acting on orders from God. Only that killing didn't take place in America.

ON NOVEMBER 4, 1995, after seeing some patients at Children's Hospital, my father called home.

"Have you heard the news?" my mother asked him, in a tone that suggested something serious had happened.

"No," he said.

At a peace rally in Tel Aviv that night, my mother informed him, Yitzhak Rabin, the prime minister of Israel, had been shot.

"My God, I knew it!" my father exclaimed. "I knew he didn't have enough security."

He assumed, as most Israelis who first heard the news would, as I myself did, that the person who shot Rabin must have been a member of Hamas, the Islamic fundamentalist group that, one year earlier, had begun carrying out suicide bombings in Israel in order to disrupt the peace process. It turns out that Rabin and his wife, Leah, had discussed this very possibility on their way to the peace rally that night.

"No," my mother replied, "Rabin was not shot by an Arab. He was shot by a Jew"—a twenty-five-year-old religious student named Yigal Amir.

More than the spate of shootings of abortion providers, more than any event since the outbreak of the 1973 Yom Kippur War, the murder of Yitzhak Rabin left my father grief-stricken and stunned. His shock was partly rooted in the fact that an Israeli leader he greatly admired, the man who had served as the Israeli's army's chief of staff during the 1967 Six Day War, had been brutally slain. Yet its deeper source lay in the jarring realization that the nation where he'd grown up—where, as a child, he'd marched through the streets on Independence Day proudly waving the blue-and-white Israeli flag; where citizens were bound together like members of an extended family, he'd always thought—had produced bloodshed of this sort. That an Israeli citizen would assassinate a prime minister on the basis of some ideological precept was inconceivable to my father. It upended everything he thought he knew about his country. That evening, my parents went over to the house of some Israeli friends to grieve. The mood was somber. "It was a very shocking experience, I was very shaken emotionally," my mother says. "And Dad was—maybe his pain was deeper."

My father drew comfort only from the fact that at least he didn't have to share the news with his own father. Six months earlier, my grandfather Benjamin, who I'd grown up thinking would live forever, passed away, at eighty-nine, from prostate cancer. The last time I saw him was roughly a year before his death, on a visit to Israel during Passover. His mind and memory were as sharp as ever, but I remember how gaunt his face looked. I remember, too, his expression when we said good-bye, a wistful smile that suggested he sensed there might not be a next time. We spoke on the phone in the spring of 1995, a brief conversation during which I promised I'd come to visit him soon. A few weeks passed and, before I'd even begun looking into buying a plane ticket, he was gone.

My father flew to Israel hoping to see him one last time. By the time his plane landed, it was too late. "It wasn't easy," he would tell me later of the night he spent alone in his parents' apartment. The rocking chair where my grandfather used to sit each evening to watch the news was empty now. The kitchen counter where he used to slice watermelon for us on summer evenings was bare. Soon the letters and photographs chronicling the various stages of his life would be boxed up, including the correspondence between my grandparents when my father was a little boy and his father was away fighting in World War II. (He wrote a letter to my grandmother every single day, and she saved every one of them.) At least, though, my father was spared the burden of having to inform *his* terminally ill father that Yitzhak Rabin, whom he'd known personally and with whom he'd worked in the Labor Department, had been assassinated at a peace rally in a public square in Tel Aviv by an Israeli citizen convinced he was performing a mitzvah. It would have broken my grandfather's heart to hear this, my father told me, just as I know that it broke his.

AT THE TIME, my father did not link the murder of Rabin to the shootings of John Britton and David Gunn. Neither did I. The bullets fired by Yigal Amir, Michael Griffin, and Paul Hill struck different targets, in different countries, for reasons that seemed to have nothing to do with one another. Yet, in retrospect, there is a connective thread: extreme fundamentalism, the virulent strain of militant faith that, in the mid-1990s, began to lead individuals from seemingly disparate movements to carry out violence in the name of their spiritual beliefs. Speaking to interrogators after he was arrested, Yigal Amir said he had no regrets about what he'd done: it was consistent with his understanding of Judaism. "According to Jewish law, the minute a Jew gives over his people and his land to the enemy, he must be killed," Amir explained. "My whole life has been [spent] studying the Talmud and I have all the data."

He sounded not unlike Paul Hill, who, after murdering John Britton and his escort in Pensacola, likewise insisted his actions had fulfilled the tenets of his faith, telling a reporter he was a "minister of the Gospel" who had answered his calling.

To the vast majority of people of faith, these are the words of fanatics. But Yigal Amir and Paul Hill were not isolated crackpots; they were products of the militant strains of piety that took root within their respective subcultures. In these radical pockets of pure belief, the logic of violence flowed from a set of absolutes, a Manichean view of reality in which doubt was eliminated and militant action urged. The Jewish underground Amir inhabited consisted of messianic Zionists who believed with unwavering certainty that the West Bank—land Israel had occupied in 1967—was sacred Jewish property that could not be relinquished without endangering the lives of other Jews. In the mid-1980s, members of this underground carried out bombings that crippled two Palestinian mayors. They also plotted to blow up the Dome of the Rock, the Muslim shrine located above the ruins of the Second Temple; the Dome's destruction, they believed, would hasten the Messiah's return and the redemption of the Jewish people. In the company of my father and grandfather, I had walked by the Dome of the Rock countless times. It was ten minutes from my grandparents' apartment on Balfour Street, its glistening gold dome and beautiful mosaics part of what made Jerusalem special to me. We never talked about what might have happened had the zealots who set out to destroy it succeeded, perhaps because it hadn't sunk in that, for those who believed every inch of the West Bank belonged to Jews, compromise was unthinkable—whether it be with Palestinians or moderate Israelis.

To bring that home took the murder of a prime minister, a murder that did not arise out of a vacuum. In the period prior to the assassination, protesters had gathered on the streets of Jerusalem to denounce Rabin as a traitor and murderer. A month before his death, a group of Jewish mystics stood outside his home and recited a cabbalistic curse: "I deliver to you, the angels of wrath and ire, Yitzhak, the son of Rosa Rabin, that you may smother him and the specter of him. . . . Put to death the cursed Yitzhak."

The militant members of the pro-life movement likewise viewed politics through a prism of absolutism that left little room for compromise. While Randall Terry told America that the spirit of the pro-life movement was nonviolent, reality was always more complex. For if abortion was murder, as all of the movement's leaders insisted, and if breaking the law was acceptable—"The difference is between right and wrong, not legal and illegal," Paul Schenck once explained—where should the line be drawn? If it was okay to block women from entering clinics, what about damaging the equipment inside? If the equipment was fair game, what about the facilities themselves? What about threatening the people who worked in them?

In her book, *Articles of Faith*, Cynthia Gorney describes the intense tactical debates that took place among right-to-life activists through the years. Some watched the conflict escalate and concluded that confrontation was dangerous, even counterproductive; the only way to prevent women from having abortions was, ultimately, to win their hearts. Others likened themselves to abolitionists who had to take extreme measures against an institution as evil as slavery. Nobody Gorney met endorsed shooting doctors. But her narrative stopped in the early 1990s, which is precisely when a small circle of frustrated militants began to cross the line. As is often the case in social movements, what pushed them over the edge was not the prospect of victory but the sense of impending defeat. "Religious terrorism arises from pain and loss and from impatience with a God who is slow to respond to our plight," writes the Harvard scholar Jessica Stern in her book, *Terror in the Name of God*. To shed light on what can lead devout people to conclude that God is instructing them to kill, Stern spoke with militants from three major faiths: Islam, Judaism, and Christianity. Although their beliefs could not have differed more, their motivations—a deep sense of humiliation, a hunger for purity, a spiritual high rooted in the knowledge that they were making the ultimate sacrifice for God—were strikingly similar.

ONE MORNING I drove to Grand Island, where the Schenck brothers grew up, to interview a woman named Mickey van de Ven. We met at St. Stephen's Church, a sprawling brick edifice on Baseline Road, where Van de Ven works part-time and attends mass every Sunday. The late April sky had turned a shade of gray that made one wonder if the weather gods had decided to deprive Buffalo of spring yet again. The day before, it had snowed briefly. By the time I turned into the driveway at St. Stephen's, the snow had melted, and the sky was brightening a bit.

Van de Ven was waiting for me by the entrance to the church. She is a shy, soft-spoken woman with brown hair, round glasses, hazel eyes, and a warm, matronly manner. She directed me into a small white-walled room where we sat on a pair of light-blue armchairs. Between us lay a tray of cookies and a thermos full of coffee, which she politely offered me.

I had come to see Van de Ven to learn more about sidewalk counseling, something she had begun doing in the 1990s, at the same time that members of the movement's more militant wing started to insist that violence was the only effective method to rescue the unborn. Van de Ven is a devout Catholic who, before this, had served as a "prayer warrior," meaning she stood outside abortion clinics and prayed the rosary. She didn't participate in rescues; blocking doorways and getting arrested was not for her. When she started sidewalk counseling, she knew it would be challenging since, as she told me, "I'm not very forward." Yet she felt God was calling her, and, gradually, she fashioned a method tailored to her personality. Van de Ven didn't scream "Don't kill your baby!" at the women entering the clinic. She preferred asking, "Can I offer you some information?" If the women nodded, she would hand them literature like the pamphlet she gave me, depicting the various stages of fetal development. ("I'm here!" the pamphlet began. "At the moment the nuclei of the father's sperm and mother's egg unite a new and unrepeatable human being comes into the world.")

I asked Van de Ven whether the method was effective. She pulled out a blue spiral notebook, and, smiling, showed me photographs of various "saves"—women who'd stopped to talk to her and decided to go through with their pregnancies. There was a pretty brown-haired woman holding a blond-haired girl in pigtails. There was a light-skinned African-American infant. Van de Ven stared at the photographs as though the children were her own. She admitted there was more frustration than success. Sometimes, weeks passed without a single positive encounter. Sidewalk counseling was hard work, and, even in her church, not everyone appreciated it. She had seen the dismissive expressions when she tried to pass out pro-life literature after services sometimes. ("Just because you're Catholic doesn't mean you haven't had an abortion," Van de Ven wryly confided to me.) Yet she continued serving as a sidewalk counselor twice a week because, as she put it, "I felt it was God's calling."

Afterward, we drove out to Marilynn Buckham's clinic on Main Street, a brick building equipped with twenty-four-hour surveillance cameras and armed guards. Van de Ven showed me the line behind which she and other demonstrators had to stand because of the protective zones imposed over the years by courts. In 1997, the Supreme Court had upheld the constitutionality of a fifteen-foot buffer zone protecting clinic entrances, on the grounds that, as Chief Justice William Rehnquist wrote, "We have before us a record that shows physically abusive conduct, harassment of the police that hampered law enforcement and the tendency of even peaceful conversations to devolve into aggressive and sometimes violent conduct." The case, *Schenck v. Pro-Choice Network of Western New York*, grew out of the protests in Buffalo. In the same ruling, the Court struck down the "floating buffer zones" that Judge Arcara had imposed to prevent protesters from coming within fifteen feet of people entering clinics.

Van de Ven directed me to an area near a gas station where she normally stood, a good distance from the clinic. I could see why some protesters might view the buffer zone as a restriction on free speech, though it also occurred to me that, if every sidewalk counselor had conducted him- or herself the way Van de Ven did, the Supreme Court might have seen the matter differently.

I asked her whether her routine changed at all during the winter, when it was cold and blustery and people in Buffalo did their best to avoid spending prolonged amounts of time outside. She shook her head. I asked her whether it ever occurred to her to quit. She shook her head again, repeating that this is what God calls her to do.

IN HER QUIET, understated way, Mickey van de Ven was living proof of something that was easy to forget as the headlines filled with news about violence in the 1990s: it was still possible, even after the FACE law, even after Operation Rescue's collapse, to channel one's opposition to abortion into peaceful forms of activism.

On the other hand, Van de Ven was also a reminder of how much patience and perseverance this required, qualities not everybody had. I met Van de Ven in the spring of 2005. Twelve years earlier, in November 1993, a protest took place outside the clinic where Dr. Slepian worked, the same facility where Van de Ven did her sidewalk counseling. It was organized by the Lambs of Christ, a group whose founder, a Catholic priest named Norman Weslin, trained his followers to act as "victim-souls for Jesus Christ." The protest was held on a windy, overcast day. In the background a trumpeter played the "Battle Hymn of the Republic" while demonstrators sang and prayed. One voice rose above the din— that of a slender, dark-haired man delivering a furious jeremiad. "It's like AIDS was a warning to homosexuals," he howled. "He loves them, but he is trying to warn them to repent. Eternity in hell or eternity in heaven.

"You cannot escape death," the man intoned. "We are all sinners. We all will die. . . . God's wrath is getting ready to pour out."

Five years later, a video of this protest would be turned over to the FBI on suspicion that the man delivering the apocalyptic sermon was the person known within the Army of God as Atomic Dog—James Kopp. Investigators would eventually determine that he was not the speaker that day. But when I watched the tape not long ago, it nevertheless unnerved me, perhaps because the sermon proved prophetic all the same. One year later, in the fall of 1994, Garson Romalis, an abortion provider in Vancouver, was shot in his house while preparing breakfast. The next year, Dr. Hugh Short, an abortion provider in Hamilton, Ontario, was shot in the second-floor study of his house. Both physicians were injured but not killed. Two years after this, a bullet sailed past the head of an abortion provider in a suburb of Rochester, missing him by inches. A few weeks later, another doctor was shot and wounded in Winnipeg. In all of the attacks, the victims were struck in their houses by bullets from a high-powered rifle fired by someone who clearly had trained for the task.

The Winnipeg shooting took place in the fall of 1997. A year later, after another long winter and summer had passed and the leaves had turned, the violence would visit western New York.

· 12 ·

The Town of Amherst is perhaps the last place in America one would expect a headline-making murder to occur. In 1996, Amherst topped the list of *Money* magazine's "Safest Cities," even though, technically speaking, it was not a city but a town, and for that matter not a town so much as a collection of leafy subdivisions crisscrossed by commercial strips (Main, Sheridan, Niagara Falls Boulevard) that together formed Buffalo's premier suburb. Amherst often seemed like the city's lucky, spoiled twin, with everything a model suburb was supposed to have: tennis courts, ice rinks, country clubs, shopping malls, office complexes, good schools, lush green lawns, well-stocked supermarkets, and backyards where kids raced around playing touch football and freeze tag.

Amherst even had a university campus, whose location in the suburbs had come, alas, at Buffalo's expense. Back in the 1960s, the board of trustees of the State University of New York selected a plot of land in the middle of a floodplain in Amherst as the site for a sprawling new campus for the University of Buffalo. They did so even though Whitney M. Young, Jr., the executive director of the National Urban League, then-mayor Frank Sedita, and a coalition of local community groups, the

Committee for an Urban Campus, all advocated building the new campus in the city, where they argued it could help revive downtown Buffalo and decrease the isolation of the urban poor. A majority of the UB faculty, the alumni, and a number of local civic leaders, however, favored the suburban site, and, unfortunately, their arguments prevailed. Three decades later, Amherst had its campus—a chain of ugly buildings on a windswept plain surrounded by a grid of parking lots—while the Buffalo waterfront had none of the shops and cafés that might have proliferated in the presence of a thriving university. Downtown Buffalo did have a theater district, as well as a handful of restaurants and bars, but the people who frequented them were more likely to be suburbanites dropping in for the night than students or professors living in the neighborhood, which after midnight turned into a ghost town. You could chalk this up to faulty planning. You could chalk it up, as well, to three decades of inexorable sprawl. Between 1960 and 1990, the amount of developed land in western New York increased by 76 percent, even as the region's overall population declined by 9 percent. As in so many parts of the country, the area's geographical boundaries kept creeping outward, while the city shrank.

The fact that Amherst was the seat of privilege in western New York did not make it a bad place. All in all, it was a good place, with neighborhoods where children set up lemonade stands in the summertime, with couples raising families in what, for many, were their dream houses. In 1992, having put their kids through college, my parents began to consider building such a house themselves. Why not buy one of the beautiful old houses in the city? I suggested. There were parts of Buffalo—the North Park district, home to a cluster of houses designed by Frank Lloyd Wright—where the architecture was as elegant and as pleasing to the eye as anywhere I'd seen. My mother had other ideas. She and my father scoped out a plot in the suburb of Clarence, a lakefront property in a wooded area where a bunch of luxury houses were going up. In the end, my father decided the location was too far from the various hospitals where he worked. They eventually settled on a lot in Williamsville. It did not occur to them at the time that the other decision might have been a fateful one—that building a house on a lake by the woods might have proven not just inconvenient but dangerous.

. . .

ON OCTOBER 14, 1998, a college professor named Joan Dorn set out on her usual morning jog. Dorn lived in Amherst, a quarter mile or so from Roxbury Park, the L-shaped street where Dr. Barnett Slepian lived with his wife, Lynne, and their four children. On her way, Dorn spotted a car she'd never seen before. She also saw a man dressed in dark warm-up clothing trotting slowly. He seemed overdressed for the weather, and the car seemed a bit run-down for the neighborhood. Dorn jotted down the license plate of the vehicle, a black 1987 Chevrolet Cavalier with Vermont plates, in her runner's journal, joking with her husband that if anything happened to her he would know whom to suspect.

"Wacky car," she wrote.

Ten days later, after having breakfast with an old friend from college, I was standing in an office on Ninth Street in Brooklyn, where my friend was meeting someone, happily contemplating what to do with the rest of my day—it was Saturday, a week before Halloween, and the weather was beautiful—when I overheard a snippet of conversation that made my stomach drop.

"Yeah, do you believe it?" a woman at the opposite end of the room said. "Someone shot an abortion provider up in Buffalo—Slepian, Barnett Slepian."

It took a second for my mind to process the words and then for the physical reaction—much like the feeling you have on a roller coaster when everything suddenly dips but your body is still suspended in midair—to kick in. I ran down to the street, made a beeline to the nearest pay phone, and called my mother. She answered on the first ring; she'd been trying to reach me all morning. "We found out last night," she said, sounding as if she didn't quite believe what she was telling me, as I myself did not. Her voice was quiet and subdued. She said she'd spoken to Dr. Slepian the previous evening. A few hours later, he was shot in the back by a sniper hiding in the wooded area behind his house. My mother told me the police had come by within an hour to tell her and my father what happened—and to make sure the blinds throughout their house were shut. They then drove to Millard Fillmore Suburban

Hospital to see how Dr. Slepian was doing. As she relayed the details, I could feel my heart thumping. By the time they got there, shortly before midnight, Dr. Slepian had already been pronounced dead. My mother ended the conversation by saying, "I could be a widow right now."

The next forty-eight hours exist in my memory as a blur. I remember talking to my sister about how surreally close we had just come to losing a parent. I remember speaking with a friend who'd first heard the news on the radio—"abortion provider in Buffalo shot . . ."—and had assumed the victim was my father. I remember wishing it were all a bad dream and that I would soon wake up, an idea that did not seem so far-fetched in light of how ill-prepared for this moment I'd been. It had been six years since the Spring of Life, six comparatively quiet years. Randall Terry had long ago disappeared from the headlines. The FACE Act had all but ended the rescue movement. True, there had been a series of shootings of abortion providers in Canada and the United States—one each year, at roughly the same time, since 1994. But while Dr. Slepian had apparently received a fax that morning from the National Abortion Federation warning him to be extra vigilant for this reason, my father had not. At no point in recent years had we even discussed the pattern of attacks, or whether FACE and the demise of Operation Rescue might have had something to do with the sharp *increase* in violence since the mid-1990s: shootings like the ones in Pensacola, Boston, Kansas; bombings like the one that occurred on January 29, 1998, at the New Woman All Women clinic in Birmingham, Alabama, which killed an off-duty police officer named Robert Sanderson and maimed a nurse. (In 2005, Eric Rudolph would plead guilty to the attack, as well as to the 1996 Centennial Olympic bombing in Atlanta and an attack on a gay nightclub, saying "abortion, gay rights and the federal government" motivated him.) The attack in Alabama was one of more than fifty arsons or detonations that struck abortion clinics throughout the country between 1994 and 1998.

On the Monday following the murder, I called my mother and told her I was coming home, partly to offer support, partly because the thought of being there somehow made me feel safer. She told me there was no need: everything was fine and patrol cars were passing by the house constantly.

I told her I was coming anyway.

· · ·

I ARRIVED IN Buffalo on October 27, four days after Dr. Slepian was murdered, two days after Joan Dorn told the Amherst police about the wacky car she'd spotted on her morning jog earlier in the month. Before this, one person involved in the investigation would later inform me, "nobody had a *clue* who did it, and nobody had any idea whether the person responsible might strike again." A check of Vermont's motor vehicle records would reveal that the car in question was registered to a man named James C. Kopp of St. Albans, a sleepy town not far from the U.S. border with Canada. Its owner had been arrested dozens of times at protests outside abortion clinics through the years, authorities learned. In 1988, he had traveled down to Atlanta with Randall Terry to participate in a series of rescues that coincided with the Democratic National Convention. He was among the activists who prayed together in a wing of Atlanta's Key Road Detention Facility, an experience that lasted for weeks and that deepened the dedication of many of those on hand. Among the activists who spent time in that jail were Shelley Shannon, the housewife from Oregon who would later shoot George Tiller, and Norman Weslin, founder of the Lambs of Christ, the group that had organized the protest outside the clinic where Dr. Slepian worked in 1993. James Kopp was linked to the Lambs. At some point, Kopp acquired the nickname "Atomic Dog," which appeared in the acknowledgments section of the Army of God Manual. He was known in the movement for his skill in designing impenetrable locks that protesters could use to chain themselves to cars and furniture.

The black Chevrolet Joan Dorn had seen was eventually found in the parking lot of Newark International Airport, by which time its Vermont license plates had been replaced with New Jersey ones. The vehicle had been dropped off on November 4 and its driver had vanished, but on the floor by the passenger seat a Tasco binocular case was found. A pair of Tasco binoculars had already been discovered inside a black garbage bag buried in the woods behind the Slepian family's house. In the same bag, investigators found a wristwatch, a flashlight, a protective gun muffler, earplugs, a baseball cap, and an emptied box of cartridges whose caliber matched that of the bullet that struck Dr. Slepian.

None of this was known yet when I arrived at the Buffalo airport. My mother met me outside the baggage claim, exactly where she'd picked me up on a visit for Rosh Hashanah a few weeks earlier; that now seemed like eons ago. On the phone, she'd sounded numb, as though the reality of what had happened still hadn't sunk in. When I got in the car, she burst into tears. A friend of hers had just called to tell her she should present my father with an ultimatum: either stop serving as an abortion provider or risk losing her. Throughout all the years of harassment, she had never once leaned on him this way, even though there had been times when she wanted to pack up their bags and leave Buffalo because the pressure was so intense—not only for the man she loved but for herself. Strangers would walk up to her and say, "Your husband's a murderer!" Once, she recalls, a protester trailed her to my father's office, then glowered at her as she walked through the parking lot. "He was trying to intimidate me," she says. It never worked— for all her propensity to worry, she was ultimately no less tough or resilient than my father. But I can't imagine she didn't wish my father would come home one day and say, "Okay, I've had enough." Not because she didn't support what he was doing—like him, she believed the decision about abortion should be left to a woman and her doctor, though she felt abortions should be limited to the first trimester of pregnancy—but because her philosophy of life was to keep risks and hassles to a minimum. My father never did quit, yet, typically, my mother never complained. She gave him the unwavering support of a wife who, having seen her own parents survive far worse ordeals by sticking together, having always believed one's first loyalty was to one's family, would not have considered offering her husband anything less.

With the assailant's whereabouts unknown and calls pouring in from friends and relatives concerned about my father's safety, my mother's sense of loyalty came crashing up against the weight of her own history and the fear she felt. Upstairs in my parents' bedroom, she pleaded with me to talk to my father about no longer putting himself in danger. In her hand she held a letter that had just arrived from George Schillinger, an old friend of theirs. George, like my father, was a physician; like my mother, he was a Holocaust survivor. "Listen," my mother said as she began reading from it:

> Dear Shalom,
>   Undoubtedly, I'm not the only one who calls you or writes to you expressing concern about your safety. But I am one who survived Bergen Belsen, Russian jail etc. and therefore have the right to say that survival is the utmost duty, one that supersedes every idea, principle, even pride.
>   Please, save your family from the potential horror that visited the Slepians!

My mother turned to me at this point, her expression taut. In that letter was distilled the worldview that had colored the experiences of her parents, for whom abstract principles like justice and equality were all well and good, but not at the price of endangering one's life. It was a view common among survivors, a form of risk-averse realism that, given the circumstances of my mother's birth and upbringing, as well as the forces that had shattered her parents' once serene lives, she understandably shared. It's no wonder that at that moment, as terrible as she felt for the Slepian family, as much as she wanted to support her husband, what mattered most to her was that he be safe.

MY FATHER'S SAFETY was what mattered most to me, as well, although the thought of urging him to stop doing something he believed was right made me feel queasy. To do so would violate the ethical code I knew lay at the core of his identity, a code that had shaped me as well. To back down in the face of a threat or otherwise alter one's conduct in the face of danger: it is what every Israeli was taught *never* to do.

I had not grown up in Israel. I didn't react to the news of a bombing the way my father did. A part of me had come to view the stubborn defiance Israelis invariably displayed when their mettle was being tested as a sort of national pathology: a destructive impulse that too often closed the door to alternatives and compromise. Even so, I was my father's son, and the lessons he'd absorbed growing up were ones to which I'd been exposed as well. When I was a child, my parents took me to a screening of *Operation Thunderbolt,* a film that re-created the dramatic 1976 raid at the Entebbe airport in which Israeli commandos rescued one hundred hostages. I choked back tears as the film ended and we learned that the operation's hero, Jonathan Netanyahu, had died (he was one of three Israelis to die in the mission). As was undoubtedly the filmmakers' intention, the movie made me want to grow up to be just like Netanyahu, a person willing to risk his life for a larger cause—the kind of person I knew my grandfather and father to be. Two decades later, I'd become a journalist in part so that I could tell the stories of people who went to similar lengths—human rights activists who braved death threats in dictatorships; whistle-blowers who risked their careers to expose wrongdoing. These were the people most worthy of admiration in my eyes, so, in theory, I should have flown home determined to support my father in whatever he chose to do; I should even have gently prodded him not to give up. Instead, after speaking to my mother, I felt as she did: that he should stop.

When my father came home later that night, I gave him a hug at the door. He put his briefcase down and shook his head. He looked pale, tired, somber. It occurred to me then how integral to his personality a certain cheerful, boyish optimism was—and how much I missed seeing it just then. We sat down for dinner, during which he poked at his food distractedly. No tears filled his eyes but I could tell from his reticence and lack of appetite that he was no less shaken than my mother was. (By week's end he had lost five pounds.) While concern for his safety was the primary emotion my mother and I felt, grief and incredulity—at the sudden loss of a colleague, at the thought of what Dr. Slepian's wife and children were experiencing—were what appeared to most consume him. On the Sunday following the murder, he told me, he'd gone to visit Lynne Slepian, who was staying in a house off Maple Road with her parents and children. As he pulled up, he saw her standing outside by the front door. He expressed his condolences, offering to do anything he could to help out. I asked him whether she said anything in response. He looked up at my mother and me. "She said, 'You shouldn't be out—you should hide.'"

After dinner, we continued talking. I did not want to admit that I'd been thinking similar thoughts—not that he should hide, but that the murder made it untenable to go on as though everything were fine. "Dad, you're not a young man anymore," I said. He nodded. "You're nearing retirement, you've been through a lot"—I paused, trying to think of a subtle way to put it—"maybe it's time to leave this part of your practice to some younger doctors." There was silence; then he cupped his chin in his hand and sighed. We were sitting on the edge of the same beige carpet where my mother and I had been a few hours earlier. With his legs crossed and his shoes off, he looked small and isolated, a solitary figure backed into a corner—first by so many others and, now, by me. He looked over in my direction with weariness in his eyes, but no hint of fear or acquiescence. He started telling me about his upbringing, how he used to play with the shells of bombs as a child, how he grew accustomed to living in the midst of danger. At this point, my mother walked in.

"It's wrong, Carla, wrong," he said to her suddenly.

"What's wrong?"

"To give in to fanatics, to terrorists. So what if they'll kill me—then they'll kill me. Giving up is wrong."

In my bloodlines two strands of history had merged, one winding back to the khaki-clad pioneers of the Zionist movement, the other to the camps enclosed by barbed wire in Transnistria; one symbolized by the defiant soldier in battle fatigues storming a hillside, the other by my mother's family who'd left Yampol simply thankful to be alive. Now, judging by the tension in the room, and the warring voices inside my own head, the two strands seemed in danger of unraveling. Wasn't my father right that giving in would send whoever had shot Dr. Slepian the message that violence worked? But wasn't my mother also right to demand that, for her sake as well as for his own—and for my sake, and the sake of everyone else who cared about him—he consider his safety for once? The murder of Dr. Slepian touched on a division within my family about where to draw the line between high-minded principles and the bare necessity of surviving in the world. I had grown up thinking that I knew the answer: where my grandfather would draw that line; where my father would. But what I knew was an abstraction. Now that the abstract had turned personal, and the protagonist in the story was not a human rights activist in some remote country but my own father, what I wanted was for him to relax his standards—even as I knew that he would not. And even as knowing this filled me with respect and admiration for him, though also with a desire to see him change his mind.

The next morning, around 10:00 A.M., as I was talking to my mother, the phone rang. She picked it up. I watched the color drain from her face and saw her drop to her knees. She handed me the receiver. It was the Amherst police, calling to inform us that *The Hamilton Spectator*, a newspaper in Ontario, had just received a death threat against my father. There had been death threats before, but this one was different, coming as it did several days after a murder and, apparently, from someone with possible links to the crime. As I mentioned earlier, Dr. Slepian's murder was the fifth in a series of shootings, each of which took place around Canada's Remembrance Day; three of the other attacks had taken place on Canadian soil. *The Hamilton Spectator* had received a series of packages filled with antiabortion literature over the past year, including a recent one containing a photograph of Dr. Slepian with an "X" drawn through his face. As if this weren't enough, a few days before Dr. Slepian was murdered, Linda Stadler had spotted a white car with Ontario license plates in the parking lot of my father's office.

As I held the phone, I could feel the sweat beading down my neck and back. I could also feel my shoulders and arms shaking, not with fear but with anger. This was a rage as pure and palpable as anything I'd ever felt—fury at whoever was toying with my family this way, someone who remained hidden while we were exposed. A coward. I went to the bathroom after hanging up, toweled off, and thought of how much I would love to let whoever it was have it. I could have punched a hole through a wall. Then I realized my anger was directed not just at whoever had issued the anonymous threat but at all the protesters who'd stood through the years with their signs—Murderer. Baby-killer. At my father's office. At our home. At Barnett Slepian's.

The phone rang again. It was my father, calling from Sisters of Charity Hospital. "Dad, come home," I said, "right away." "Okay," he said, sensing my unease, "don't be nervous." An hour later, we were all sitting in the living room with an officer from the Amherst police. In the meantime, my mother had been pacing the house. Her face did nothing to conceal her worry. I had knots in my stomach. The only remotely relaxed member of our family was my father. Standing in the eye of the storm, he looked calm. It was a place that was familiar to him.

"Okay, Doctor," said the officer, a thick-set man with thinning brown hair and a heavy Buffalo accent, "here's what happened. We just learned that a paper in Hamilton received a threat saying, 'Shalom Press is next. Our American cousins have their list. We have our list.'" He asked my father what level of protection he thought the threat warranted.

"Well," he replied, glancing across at my mother, "the maximum, I think."

Two days later, during which the Amherst police stationed a patrol car outside our home virtually around the clock, a team of U.S. marshals arrived. They mounted surveillance cameras on every corner. They scoped the surrounding area, chopping down clumps of weeds where an intruder might hide, making sure all the windows were covered. I didn't know it at the time, but their presence was owed not to the threat *The Hamilton Spectator* had received but to a direct order from Attorney General Janet Reno. A few days earlier, Reno had attended a meeting in Washington to discuss how the federal government should respond to the latest murder of an abortion provider. Among those on hand were Vicki Saporta, the president of the National Abortion Federation, and Marilynn Buckham. Reno listened as Buckham described how, in her view, the authorities in Buffalo had too often minimized or condoned the intimidation directed at her clinic in the past. Now a doctor who worked there had been murdered in order to prevent women from exercising a constitutionally protected right. If the federal government was serious about defending that right, Buckham said, it would deploy federal marshals to protect the remaining abortion providers in the Buffalo area and would create a special task force to combat terrorism against reproductive health workers.

BOTH DEMANDS WERE soon met, a minor victory in an otherwise nightmarish week for Buckham. "I have never cried that much in my entire life," she later told me of the days following Dr. Slepian's murder. "And"—a sentiment I recognized—"I was as angry as I have ever been. My anger was so overwhelming." She wondered at first whether she had the wherewithal to keep Buffalo GYN Womenservices open. What got her through was the thought of all the women in Buffalo who would have nowhere else to go, as well as the support of other members of her staff, in particular Melinda DuBois, a strong-willed woman who in recent years had assumed growing responsibility for day-to-day management of the facility, and who did not waver for a second after the attack.

One other factor drove her not to quit: the thought of Dr. Slepian and his family. It was his nature, she told me, "not to be cowed" by pressure. On the morning after the murder, Lynne Slepian reinforced the message to her. "She said, 'I hear you're thinking of closing,'" Buckham recalled. "She said, 'You can't close—they will have won then, and that's the last thing Bart would have wanted.'" Buckham resolved to do everything in her power to keep the clinic open, even if it required flying physicians in from other cities to work there. It did: nobody in Buffalo wanted to fill Barnett Slepian's shoes just then. In the aftermath of the murder, while federal marshals escorted doctors back and forth from the airport to Buckham's clinic, only one abortion provider from the greater Buffalo area remained: my father.

IT WAS ONLY after the marshals appeared that I began to think seriously about what Lynne Slepian and her children were going through. On the night of the killing, having returned home from temple with her husband, Lynne was standing in the kitchen. She watched Bart put a bowl of split-pea soup in the microwave. Then she heard a loud pop and saw his glasses fly off. "Lynne, I think they've shot me," Bart said to her. He collapsed in a pool of blood on the kitchen floor. All four of the couple's sons, Michael, Philip, Brian, and Andrew, were home. One of them ran to get towels to stanch the bleeding while Lynne screamed for the children to take cover. She dialed 911. By the time the police arrived, the assailant had vanished.

I wrote Lynne Slepian a card telling her how sorry I was. As I dropped it in the mail, I thought of how futile expressions of sympathy can seem at such times, how little they do to alter the cold facts facing people whose lives have been engulfed by tragedy. The tragedy, in this case, could as easily have been mine. Thinking of that made me ashamed that I had urged my father to stop performing abortions in the aftermath of his colleague's murder. And it made me proud that he had resisted my advice.

As if witnessing the death of their father were not enough, the shooting that ripped a hole in the lives of Dr. Slepian's children soon provoked the predictable reaction: sympathy from some; thinly veiled satisfaction from others. Outside Dr. Slepian's medical office on Maple Road, several hundred people gathered for a vigil the night after the murder. They brought flowers, candles, and signs affirming their support for reproductive rights; one person pinned to the door a photograph of Dr. Slepian with a baby he'd recently delivered. Bishop Henry J. Mansell of the Buffalo Diocese condemned the shooting as a "cowardly, disastrous . . . vicious, heinous act." President Clinton, who later paid a personal visit to Lynne Slepian, said, "No matter where we stand on the issue of abortion, all Americans must stand together in condemning this tragic and brutal act."

But, as with prior shootings, not everybody did. A slash went through Dr. Slepian's name on a web site called the Nuremberg Files, where the names and addresses of abortion providers and clinic workers throughout the country were posted. Its creator, Neal Horsley, denied any prior knowledge of the murder but expressed no remorse about it. "I have no doubt that, just as John Brown's actions against slavery were morally justifiable, it is possible to morally justify the slaughter of Americans that murder God's children," Horsley told *The Buffalo News*.

Meanwhile, eight days after the shooting and outside Dr. Slepian's former medical office, the Reverend Robert Behn, who had assumed leadership of the pro-life movement in Buffalo, announced that the following April the city would play host to a reunion of the Spring of Life. "I think God has chosen Buffalo as a battleground where He's going to fight abortion with great strength," Behn announced. Also on hand was Rob Schenck. Before a phalanx of TV cameras, Schenck led a prayer service for the slain physician whom he and his brother had spent years vilifying, and dropped off seven roses for the Slepian family—one for each of his sons, one for Mrs. Slepian, one for Dr. Slepian, and one for hope.

Lynne Slepian bundled up the roses and sent them back, with a note:

> My message to you, Mr. Schenck, is to look within yourself for forgiveness. You certainly won't receive it from me or my family. It's your "passive" following that incited the violence that killed Bart and took away both my and my children's future.
>
> Keep your damned roses and look elsewhere for media attention!!!

A few months later, Schenck returned to Buffalo and announced that he regretted the whole incident, explaining that it was not the right time for the Spring of Life reunion, and that he would not be participating in it.

At least one local columnist suggested that the event's organizers spare the city as well. "It'd be nice if Buffalo were known for something other than the Bills and blizzards," wrote Donn Esmonde of *The Buffalo News.* "But fashioning a reputation as the prime battleground in the abortion war isn't what we had in mind." Although organizers claimed the idea had been in the works for a while, Esmonde noted that it was difficult to avoid the impression that the Spring of Life reunion was "piggybacking on the killing of Barnett Slepian, capitalizing on a tragedy that again put this area on the abortion map." The whole region of western New York could have used a break from being associated with tragedy, given two signature incidents of violence in the mid-1990s: Buffalo was where superstar turned murder suspect O. J. Simpson had earned his reputation as one of the icons of the 1970s; nearby Lockport was where Gulf War veteran turned government-hating terrorist Timothy McVeigh was born. Now there was a third headline-making crime, even though, like Leon Czolgosz, the Cleveland native who'd come to the city in 1901 to assassinate William McKinley, the man who pulled the trigger was from out of town.

Timothy McVeigh blew up the Alfred P. Murrah Federal Building in Oklahoma City on April 19, 1995, the anniversary of the attack on the Branch Davidian compound in Waco, Texas. April 19 was the date on which the Spring of Life reunion was slated to begin.

· 13 ·

Though he would maintain his innocence for a good while longer as articles began appearing on pro-life web sites suggesting he was being framed, nobody in the law enforcement community heard from James Kopp after the FBI issued a material-witness warrant in November 1998, seeking to question him about the shooting at 187 Roxbury Park in Amherst, New York. Nobody heard from Kopp except the small network of activists and supporters with whom he remained in touch. One of these people was Jennifer Rock, an IBM employee and right-to-life activist from Vermont who, a week or so after the shooting, received a phone call from Kopp. He asked her to withdraw $7,000 she'd once deposited for him in a bank account and to meet him at a mall in White Plains, New York. Rock complied. From White Plains she drove Kopp to the Nuevo Laredo airport in Mexico, a two-thousand-mile trip completed at breakneck speed. "I know you're innocent," she told him along the way, at which he apparently nodded. During the trip, Kopp bleached his hair blond to match a false West Virginia driver's license. He was a fugitive now.

While Kopp disappeared from sight, investigators slowly pieced together details about his background. In the news clips and magazine stories I would soon begin gathering about the man suspected of murdering Barnett Slepian, a portrait emerged that did not conform to easy liberal stereotypes. James Kopp did not grow up in the Bible Belt, reading about the evils of abortion, nor was he home-schooled by strict fundamentalist parents. He was born in 1954, the son of a corporate lawyer and a nurse who raised three daughters and two sons in the laid-back atmosphere of Marin County, California, north of San Francisco. A photograph of the Kopp family in 1960 shows young James and his twin brother, Walt, dressed in bow ties, sitting between their parents on a sunlit porch. Their father, Charles, is wearing a pair of neatly pressed dark slacks and a tie. Their mother, Nancy, sports a matronly dress. Kopp's three sisters are standing in back, their heads poking up above a ledge; a dog is sitting between James and his mom. It is as wholesomely American an image as one could imagine dreaming up. The toddler in the bow tie sitting closer to his mother later became an Eagle Scout who played the trumpet in his high school band. James Kopp was a quiet, bookish teenager who liked to ride his bike around the county, avoiding getting in trouble with the law or falling in with the wrong crowd. After high school he enrolled at the University of California at Santa Cruz, where he graduated with honors. In 1982, he earned a master's degree in biology from Cal State University at Fullerton.

Shy, soft-spoken, gentle: this is the way Kopp's classmates would remember him, just as those in the pro-life movement did. Unlike some of his fellow travelers, he didn't talk about blowing up abortion clinics, didn't sign his name to statements calling for physicians to be shot, didn't routinely stand on street corners blaring through a megaphone about the corrupted values of the broken secular world. And yet there are reasons to believe that, in the eyes of Barnett Slepian's assassin, the world was a profoundly broken place where it was dangerous to invest one's trust in people, where the line separating the sacred and the profane was clear, and where a single-minded devotion to stopping the evil of abortion served as the sole steadying force in a life buffeted by disappointment, loss, and pain.

• • •

THIS, AT LEAST, is the way James Kopp seemed to one member of his extended family. Lynn Kopp lives in a one-story brick house with blue shutters on a quiet suburban street in Irving, Texas. When I first contacted her, she seemed reluctant to talk. But as we chatted on the phone, she warmed up, and eventually agreed to meet in person. On the day I visited several weeks later, her white poodle, Peppy, greeted me at the door with a series of barks. Lynn Kopp emerged moments later, smiling and offering me a seat on one of the white wicker chairs on her front porch. She was wearing light-blue cotton pants and a matching blouse embroidered with a floral pattern. Her reddish-brown hair was cut short. She moved about gingerly, the result of a recent knee operation. She looked to be in her mid-sixties, about the age a younger aunt of James Kopp's might be.

But Lynn Kopp was no aunt, and, if it had been up to James Kopp, might never have been a member of his family at all. One evening back in 1981, Charles Kopp, his father, attended a dinner party in Dallas where he was working on a trial. Among the other guests was an attractive, recently divorced secretary named Lynn Hightower. They struck up a conversation, and instantly hit it off. At no point during the many dinners, phone calls, and romantic evenings that followed did the tall, charming, hard-drinking lawyer from California intimate to Lynn that he might be married, though he did mention his kids on occasion, leading her to assume he was divorced. They saw each other and corresponded regularly. Then, on July 4, 1984, as she was getting ready to go out to dinner with her parents at a country club, the phone rang at Lynn Hightower's home. "I understand you're a friend of my father's, Charles Kopp," the young man on the line said. "Oh, yes," she replied, not recognizing the voice. The caller informed her that his mother had seen some of the letters she'd been sending to his father, and did not appreciate them. "Well, I don't know why she should be bothered by it," she said. "Well, she's been married to him for almost forty years," he replied.

The son who had tracked down Lynn Hightower was James Kopp. Unbeknownst to her, the man she'd been seeing for three years had been leading a double life. As she struggled to think of what to say, James Kopp turned the conversation in a curious direction: he asked her to pray. Although she was a Baptist who regularly attended church, she found it odd that he would trot out his religion in this way, as though he were expecting her to repent over the phone. Yet, understanding how upset he must have been, she went along, and promised that, so long as his father was married, she would consider their relationship over.

Less than a year later, Nancy and Charles Kopp were divorced. Soon after that, their children received a wedding announcement in the mail: their father had married Lynn Hightower, who changed her name to Lynn Kopp.

If the disintegration of his parents' marriage came as a shock and disappointment to James Kopp, it was by no means his first encounter with deep and potentially wrenching loss. His younger sister, Mary, a schizophrenic, died of leukemia at the age of twenty-one. His one significant romantic relationship was with a college girlfriend named Jennifer, for whom he moved down to Texas after graduation. She ended the relationship in a manner that by all accounts left him heartbroken. "This was going to be my commitment for my life," he would later tell Doris Grady, a friend of his in the pro-life movement. Lynn Kopp heard this story from her husband—who provided an additional detail. Before the breakup, Chuck Kopp told her, Jennifer had gotten pregnant. She ended up aborting what Jim came to view as "his baby." "That's what his father told me," Lynn Kopp said. "That's what his father believed."

Whether the story is true or not—James Kopp later denied it, saying his girlfriend had thought she was pregnant but turned out not to be— one need not strain to imagine why this chain of events (death, betrayal, divorce) might have led a shy, sensitive young man to be extra wary of people, or why the promise of salvation through God, along with the notion that morality was something fixed and absolute, might have proven attractive to him. Kopp's quest for salvation would later take him to L'Abri, the retreat in the Swiss Alps founded by Francis Schaeffer; there he converted to Presbyterianism and gave himself over to Jesus Christ. Lynn Kopp first met him after he'd returned from South America in 1986, where he'd worked as a missionary. He showed up with a bouquet of flowers at the hospital where his father was recuperating from a stroke, a thin, wiry man in dark slacks, a colored T-shirt, and thick glasses. He and Lynn went down to the cafeteria together. As they spoke, he alternately chewed on his fist or his glasses.

Only later, when she began to receive collect calls from jail from a person identifying himself as Mad Dog, did Lynn Kopp realize the extent to which abortion had come to define her stepson's life. He would call asking for legal advice from his father, she explained. After these conversations, Charles Kopp would emerge from his study shaking his head. "Chuck would grit his teeth and do this"—she clenched her fists into two tight balls—"he couldn't understand why Jimmy would do this." Once, at dinner with several members of the family, Walter Kopp mentioned that he'd seen his twin brother on TV the night before, at a demonstration outside a Planned Parenthood office. "Damn fool," Lynn Kopp recalled her husband murmuring. The irony, as she saw it, was that the son whose behavior so confounded his father was clearly trying to impress him with his willingness to go to battle for a higher cause. During one visit, she remembers Jim mentioning passing through Quantico, Virginia, where his father, an ex-Marine, had completed his officer training. "In Jim's mind, he was being a soldier in the way his dad was a soldier," Lynn Kopp said. "He was a soldier for the abortion issue."

AS HARD AS he found it to connect with people, James Kopp evidently found it easy to identify with the victims of an act that symbolized everything wrong with a world in which God's laws were being mocked. To his supporters and fellow activists, the reason for this was simple: he was a devout and gentle person who felt with special acuteness the agony of the most helpless and innocent among us. That Kopp internalized the anguish he imagined being experienced in America's "abortion mills" was thoroughly reflected in his nomadic existence, which took him from demonstration to demonstration and led him to abjure ordinary comforts. He wore ill-fitting clothing that he washed in a bucket by hand. He worked menial jobs and had few material possessions. The regimen of self-abnegation to which he was drawn might have worn on someone with a family to support or career ambitions to pursue. But James Kopp had none of these things. The belief that abortion was murder drew him into a Spartan existence that revolved around one all-consuming objective: to save the lives of unborn babies trapped inside the wombs of women seeking to terminate their pregnancies.

This commitment started, Kopp would later insist, not with his girlfriend's decision to abort his child but at Stanford Hospital, in 1980, when a physician showed him the victim of a late-term abortion. Kopp was completing his master's degree in biology at the time. According to Kopp, the doctor flipped the baby back and forth "like a rag doll," remarking on its imperfectly developed genitalia and six fingers. "When you see stuff like this, you really start to believe in abortion," the doctor told him, pointing out the birth defects.

Kopp was horrified, and would soon channel the sympathy he felt for the unborn child into a range of activities whose evolution mirrored that of the pro-life movement itself: from the establishment of a crisis pregnancy center in San Francisco to participation in Operation Rescue's blockades to designing the unbreakable locks that would earn him the nickname Atomic Dog. What looked to others like a descent into extremism was, from Kopp's perspective, a logical progression, pursued out of frustration that, however hard he and others tried to shut down America's death camps, they kept operating. Counseling pregnant women not to kill their babies? Kopp had tried that. Civil disobedience? He tried that, too, joining Operation Rescue, for which he was rewarded with fines and prison sentences. The arrests that Lynn Kopp viewed as a sign of a young man's life veering off course were, in his eyes, a reflection of how a godless culture treated those trying to prevent mass murder. At one point Kopp expressed his feelings in an affidavit to a judge: "My jury and/or judge must hear, to rule fairly, my evidence about FORCED ABORTIONS being performed in the mill. I refuse to be stifled when talking about Jesus, His babies and the justification defense."

This was 1990. Two years later, by which time Operation Rescue was crumbling, Charles Kopp suffered a fatal heart attack. His children and grandchildren gathered for his funeral in Sherman, Texas, where he and Lynn lived. James Kopp showed up in his usual tattered attire.

Afterward, Lynn gathered the grandchildren and handed them balloons, telling them to say a prayer as they released them into the air. Jim, she said, turned his back in fury, incensed over what he evidently viewed as an act of sacrilege. After the funeral, he stayed for a while. Watching him walk around with his worn clothes and bent posture—he used a hoe from her garden as a walking cane—Lynn Kopp felt sorry for him, a grown man nearing forty with no shortage of potential who seemed to be drifting further and further into isolation. She remembered that he arranged to have money wired to him through one of her sons since he didn't want his whereabouts known. When Lynn Kopp drove him to the airport, she pleaded with him to make a change. "I asked him, please do something with your life," she told me. Facing the mounting fines and arrests, plenty of right-to-life activists would indeed refocus their energy around this time. Not Kopp. "He said, 'I am, I *am* [doing something],'" Lynn Kopp recalled. "He said he knew his father was proud of him. I said, 'Jim, how can you say that? Did he tell you that?' He said, 'No but I could see it in his eyes.'"

Lynn Kopp paused, then let out a sigh. "He saw what he wanted to see."

WHEN HE TRAVELED across America, James Kopp stayed on occasion at the home of James Gannon, a retired former security guard who lives in Whiting, New Jersey. Kopp would call roughly two hours in advance, asking whether he could drop in for a visit, to which Gannon would reply that his door was always open. The two had first met in 1989, shortly after Gannon started participating in rescues. Both were devout Catholics—Kopp had converted to the faith—and, during these visits, they would go to Mass and take Communion together every morning. Kopp would sleep on the couch, sometimes on the floor. Then, as suddenly as he'd arrived, he would leave, not mentioning where he was going next. His host rarely pried for details. "He was just as nice a person as you could want to be," said Gannon, "a God-loving, God-caring person."

Gannon never doubted the fervor of his friend's commitment to saving unborn babies. Just as surely, he found preposterous the charge that

Kopp would ever be capable of violence. When the FBI knocked on Gannon's door to question him about Dr. Slepian's murder and to search through his apartment for Kopp's possessions, some of which were stored in his attic, he told the investigators what he told me. "[For] him to be accused of that particular situation was totally beyond my comprehension," Gannon said. "It was totally beyond my belief." In all the years they'd known each other, Gannon said, Kopp "never once talked about justification for violence, nor did he ever talk about guns or having guns or being familiar with guns or anything else."

Kopp's silence does not surprise Kathleen Puckett. A former FBI agent with a Ph.D. in clinical psychology, Puckett spent much of the 1990s working in the bureau's behavioral analysis program, part of its national security division. Among her areas of expertise was "lone wolf" terrorists who dwelled on the fringes of social movements and ended up committing violence in the name of their beliefs. The individuals she examined include Timothy McVeigh, Theodore Kaczynski (the Unabomber), and several individuals involved in attacks on abortion clinic personnel.

All those whom Puckett studied were loners who had intense difficulty forming close bonds with other people and who not infrequently seemed harmless to those who knew them—or thought they did. It turned out that these seemingly nonthreatening men were leading secret lives as closet warriors whose grandiose acts of violence provided a frisson of excitement strikingly absent from their daily lives, which were often a source of torment and pain. In Puckett's view, the inability to sustain intimate relationships with other people accounts both for the fervor of their beliefs and for the lack of empathy such terrorists feel for their victims. "In psychological terms, they would attach, only instead of attaching to other people successfully what they attached to was the ideology," she told me. Ideology became their "shadow partner," which would never let them down and would fill their lives with meaning— provided their commitment was absolute. "If that's their primary attachment, it has to be important and pure enough to warrant their total attention," she said. "So you have to escalate the value of the ideology to match your dedication to it." A striking aspect of the lives of the men

Puckett examined was the frustration and powerlessness most felt in the presence of women (Timothy McVeigh, for example, apparently never consummated a physical relationship with a woman), something she believes contributed to their militancy. "The warrior persona was kind of a refuge for men who felt unmanned, literally, in the presence of women," she said.*

In his secretive meanderings, his obsessive focus, and the celibacy he maintained after the breakup of his one significant romantic relationship, James Kopp appears to fit the pattern Puckett discerned. He was not a lone wolf in the classic sense — Kopp stayed with various people in the pro-life movement, and counted numerous activists as friends — but the suspicion that even they might not understand what being a true believer entailed may explain why the meek persona he projected was a false front. It may explain why he was careful about what he disclosed even to people he seemingly trusted; for example, he never told his sister Anne where he lived, or told James Gannon about the scrap of paper stored among the possessions he left at his house, on which the notation "A to Z" was written. Next to the letter "Z" was a phone number, 883-9945. Kopp also left a hand-drawn map showing an address, 4990 Lebanon Road. In July 1997, investigators would discover, a place called the A to Z Pawnshop in Old Hickory, Tennessee, sold an SKS semi-automatic rifle to a slender man matching the description of James Kopp. The pawnshop was located at 4990 Lebanon Road. Its phone number was 615-883-9945. The rifle bore the serial number GYUT10251, which matched the number on the weapon that investigators found buried in the woods behind the Slepians' house. The man who bought the gun had presented a Virginia driver's license identifying him as B. James Milton. The FBI later found a computer disk, turned over by Kopp's brother-in-law, that contained sixteen fake driver's licenses with false names. A check of Virginia's Department of Motor Vehicles

---

*The most famous assassin to pass through Buffalo, Leon Czolgosz, turns out to fit the pattern. Czolgosz "never had anything to do with women and acted as though he was afraid of them," his father told investigators. Czolgosz himself claimed that he had been in love with a woman once, but that she had betrayed him, and that afterward he kept his distance from members of the opposite sex.

records would reveal that no driver's license had been issued to a B. James Milton in the state.

WHILE THE FBI continued searching for clues to James Kopp's whereabouts, Buffalo watched the Spring of Life reunion, officially dubbed Operation Save America, come and go. With Dr. Slepian's murder still fresh in people's minds, with the FACE law in effect and police on high alert, the reunion was bound to pale in comparison to the original seven years earlier. And it did. By a generous estimate, 200 demonstrators showed up from out of town. The few reporters who followed them around found it hard to tell whether the protesters' main goal was to stop abortion, remove books with racy images from the shelves of the local Barnes & Noble, or alert high school kids to the evils of promiscuity and homosexuality. Francis Schaeffer's vision of an army of Christians taking to the streets to reclaim America's rotted secular culture was briefly realized. But it was a minuscule, distracted army that almost completely failed in its effort to get Buffalo to enlist.

Having determined that the level of danger had dropped, the federal marshals left town, and with their departure my parents' brief experiment with living under round-the-clock police protection ended. My mother would have been happy to see the experiment prolonged. "They're so nice, so professional," she would say of the marshals whenever we spoke. I felt much the same way, although their presence did take some getting used to. Coming home to visit my parents meant getting acquainted with the cluster of armed guards who had set up surveillance cameras in a room upstairs. It meant walking through the front door and wondering for a moment whose house I was in. The person who found it strangest of all was, not surprisingly, my father. When he went to the office in the morning, the marshals drove him. When he ate dinner, they hovered nearby. They followed him through the supermarket aisles, even to the bathroom at a Bills game one time. It was an odd way for a man nearing sixty to live, and after a while it made my father, proudly independent spirit that he is, miss his freedom. He didn't say so at the time but I suspect the marshals' departure after several months left him quietly relieved.

I expected the tensions that had emerged within our family in the aftermath of Dr. Slepian's murder to crop up again: his murderer was still on the loose, after all. But they didn't. By this point, it was clear to all of us that my father was not going to stop performing abortions—that, if anything, the murder had made him more determined than ever *not* to quit. That same spring, he and my mother attended a ceremony at which the tombstone on Dr. Slepian's grave was unveiled. He was buried in the Jewish section of a cemetery off Ridge Road, in Cheektowaga. Afterward, my parents joined other friends and relatives of the Slepian family at a reception at 187 Roxbury Park. My father peered into the kitchen at one point, where, on a wall, investigators had placed a reproduction of a body with a circle marking the spot above the shoulder blade where Dr. Slepian had been shot. Seeing this was a visceral reminder of how easily he could have been the target of the attack, a thought that, in the presence of Lynne Slepian and her children, triggered not fear but discomfort and guilt. Why him and not me? he couldn't help but think. This feeling was not new—he'd experienced it on occasion in the past, as when, for example, he completed several weeks of reserve duty in northern Israel, near the border with Lebanon and Syria. On the day his duty ended, an ambush exactly where he'd been serving left two soldiers dead. The fact that other people paid with their lives for something he believed was important invariably elevated the significance of that thing in my father's eyes, and with it his sense of commitment and resolve.

Because the turmoil in the Middle East served as his point of comparison, my father did not consider serving as an abortion provider an especially courageous thing. It was what any physician who believed abortion should be legally available ought to do. On the other hand, he understood that more than a decade of increasingly violent protest—dozens of bombings, followed by several murders—gave many doctors pause. In the aftermath of Dr. Slepian's death, the other doctor who worked at Marilynn Buckham's clinic went into hiding. Others reacted the way a young obstetrician who'd recently started up a practice in Buffalo and who was friendly with my father did: by deciding that, as much as he believed in a woman's right to choose, the risk was simply too great.

One time, I asked my father what he would advise me to do if I were in that doctor's shoes—beginning a career, with a family to raise and no shortage of responsibilities to balance. He paused, looking at me with the protective eyes of a parent. "I guess," he said, "I would tell you to do whatever you feel comfortable with." It was a diplomatic answer, one somewhat at odds with the frustration I'd often heard him express over the way so many doctors who were pro-choice seemed happy to pass along the risks and burdens to someone else. While I can understand why the quiescence of other physicians grated on him, I can also understand why they wouldn't want to live the way he did. In 1998, the journalist Jack Hitt described flying in a six-seater plane over Minnesota with an abortion provider who single-handedly kept open the last remaining clinic in North Dakota. As Hitt observed, the doctor, who was old enough to remember the days when illegal abortions had cost women their lives, was living proof "that the practical reality of abortion is retreating into a half-lighted ghetto of pseudonyms, suspicion and fear." How many physicians wanted to deal with this? Evidently not many. After speaking with enough doctors who were too intimidated to provide abortions, and after noting that only 12 percent of ob-gyn hospital residency programs routinely taught abortion, Hitt posed a question: "Can people be said to possess a right if they're too afraid to exercise it?"

A YEAR PASSED and still there was no word of James Kopp. Then another year. As the search dragged on, it was hard not to wonder whether it might continue indefinitely. My mother was convinced Kopp would never be found.

Then, around noon in the middle of an otherwise ordinary day, she called me.

"Didn't you hear the news?" she asked, sounding unusually chipper. In the background I could hear the radio crackling.

"What news?" I asked.

"They caught Kopp, they caught him—in France."

It was March 29, 2001, and, though I was the journalist in the family, my mother had beaten me to a story that would land on the front pages of many of the nation's newspapers the next day: the exhaustive search for the fugitive known as Atomic Dog had culminated in Kopp's arrest in Dinan, a small village of cobbled streets nestled in northeast Brittany. Kopp had traveled there by ferry from Ireland, where he'd spent much of his time since becoming a fugitive, working odd jobs and staying at youth hostels under various false names until sensing, rightly, that the FBI was hot on his trail. In Dinan he'd checked into a place called the Moulin de Meen, a hostel located in a renovated water mill near the port. On the day he was caught, he went to the post office to pick up money that he had requested eight days earlier in an e-mail that hinted he was planning to return to the United States: "The sooner I get about 1,000, the sooner you see this smiling, cherubic face." The recipient was a Brooklyn woman, Loretta Marra; she and her husband, Dennis Malvasi, had been communicating regularly with Kopp. Malvasi had been convicted of firebombing abortion clinics; Marra had been arrested and spent time in jail with Kopp in the past. In an earlier letter, Kopp had written hopefully about returning "to the field" to pull a "Ronald Reagan"—code language that the FBI, which had obtained a warrant to intercept these communications, took to mean he was thinking about coming back to shoot some more physicians.

My mother had turned on the radio to hear the news conference about to begin. "I'm so excited!" she exclaimed.

I called my father after speaking with her, feeling pretty excited myself. "It's positive," he said of the development, although his tone was subdued. He said he was looking forward to seeing a trial take place so that the evidence could be presented, but he also admitted the arrest brought back memories of the murder. "You know," he said, "two weeks ago we were at a bar mitzvah for Dr. Slepian's third son."

That same morning, Lynne Slepian took her mother to a doctor's appointment. While she waited in the lobby, her cell phone rang. It was Bernard Tolbert, who had recently retired as head of the Buffalo office of the FBI. "Lynne, this is Bernie," Tolbert said. "Are you sitting down?"

"Why? What—have you got something to tell me?" she asked.

"We got him," he told her.

There was a long pause, Tolbert says, one of those pauses that "says everything."

Then, "there were some tears, some emotion."

"On both our parts," he admits.

Bernard Tolbert was not a man who spilled tears easily. A twenty-two-year law enforcement veteran and the first African-American to head the Buffalo office of the FBI, he had seen his share of crime and injustice. But for some reason the Slepian murder had gotten under his skin as no prior case had. On the morning after the shooting, he visited the scene of the crime. He looked at the photographs in the den of Dr. Slepian with his children. Tolbert lived not far from where the murder took place. He was a native Buffalonian with a proud sense of community, an affable man who was widely known and well liked. "I didn't know Lynne Slepian until that time," he says, "but after seeing those pictures in the house, and just seeing the impact of what Kopp did and how it shattered that family, it became personal to me. I thought, How dare somebody come into my hometown and my community and do this?"

When Tolbert had retired just a few weeks earlier, Lynne Slepian expressed fear the investigation might lose steam. He assured her it would not, although, privately, he must have wondered when the Bureau's streak of bad luck would run out. On several occasions, authorities were closing in on Kopp, only to see him slip away. As the search wore on, the police and FBI weathered harsh criticism. Most of it focused on the mystery of why it had taken five months to discover the murder weapon, which was found, wrapped in plastic inside a cardboard tube, roughly fifty yards from where the sniper had stood. Investigators claimed that ground conditions (leaves, snow) prevented earlier detection. Not a few neighbors found this explanation mystifying. I admit to harboring such thoughts myself.

Not surprisingly, the delay in finding the rifle fueled suspicion that the FBI had planted the gun and that James Kopp was being framed. The most detailed argument of this sort was put forward by Life Dynamics, a group in Texas that, shortly after Kopp's arrest, posted on its web site an article entitled "The United States of America vs. James

Charles Kopp: A Conclusion in Search of its Evidence." The man being fingered as a sniper by the FBI was known to have poor vision and to be gentle as a lamb, it noted. No witness had ever seen him with the murder weapon. Acquaintances from Pennsylvania, meanwhile, claimed Kopp had been staying with them during the month—July 1997—the rifle was purchased, in Tennessee. What of the map of the A to Z Pawnshop found among Kopp's possessions? This, too, could have been planted by the FBI. "I'm appalled by the persecution of Jim Kopp by the press," Mark Crutcher, the founder of Life Dynamics, declared.

James Kopp did nothing to dispel such thoughts. "I didn't do this," he would write in a letter to his brother, Walt. In another letter sent out to friends and supporters, he explained, "Preparing a defense means becoming familiar with the bizarre twists and turns of the fabricated evidence against me." It ended with the words "God bless you, please remember my chains." If the point was to muster sympathy—and donations—for his defense, it worked. Money poured in from pro-life activists convinced Kopp was the target of a witch hunt. "We all know that Jim is innocent," said Susan Brindle, a right-to-life activist. "Jim would not kill somebody." Denise O'Donnell, who at the time was head of the U.S. Attorney's Office for the Western District of New York, says that acquaintances of hers in Buffalo told her they believed Kopp was being framed. Joan Andrews Bell, a legendary figure in the right-to-life movement whose imprisonment in the 1980s had inspired countless activists, including James Kopp, went so far as to suggest that the real assailant was a pro-choice activist who had shot Dr. Slepian because he was about to change his mind about the morality of abortion. "It could have been a radical element in the pro-choice movement," she told *The Buffalo News*. "Slepian was starting to change."

· 14 ·

Brother, you better believe I'll get as good a lawyer as I can get and pull out all the stops on a technical defense."

These words are from the "Rescuers' Courtroom Handbook," a manual offering tips to pro-lifers on what to do when accused of a serious crime. Its author was Jim Kopp. Now the lawyer's son appeared to be taking his own advice to heart. The man representing him in Buffalo was Paul Cambria, Jr., one of the most successful criminal defense attorneys in the area. Cambria had won acquittals for several accused murderers in the past and had argued cases before the U.S. Supreme Court. A short, combative man, he owned a Harley-Davidson and did not lack for confidence, once telling *The Buffalo News*, in reference to Timothy McVeigh, "I would be afraid that my skills would get somebody like that off." Among Cambria's past clients were *Hustler* magazine's publisher, Larry Flynt, and the shock-rocker Marilyn Manson, making him something of an odd match for a devout Catholic who had once made his way to L'Abri, Francis Schaeffer's fundamentalist retreat in the Swiss Alps. On the other hand, if his aim was to poke holes in the prosecution's evidence, Kopp appeared to have chosen his lawyer well. When

I found out Cambria was representing him, I asked Glenn Murray, an attorney in Buffalo close to the Slepian family, what he thought. "He's a very good lawyer," Murray said, "one of the best around."

WHILE THE JUSTICE Department negotiated with France to extradite James Kopp, and while his friends visited him in jail in Rennes, I flew home to celebrate my thirty-first birthday. It was the first week in September, my favorite time of year in Buffalo, when the leaves turn bright gold and orange, the temperature hovers in the seventies, and football is in the air. I celebrated with my family over dinner at a restaurant in Canada. The next day, my father and I went to the Bills' home opener, our annual father-son ritual.

Two days later I flew back to New York City, on a plane that departed Buffalo at 8:55 A.M. It was ahead of schedule, circling above LaGuardia, when the pilot abruptly announced we were turning around due to an "incident" in New York, news that elicited an annoyed groan from my fellow passengers. When we landed in Buffalo, I rushed to the nearest gate to reserve a seat on the next available flight. "You won't be going anywhere today, honey," said the woman behind the check-in counter. At this point I looked over and saw the crowd gathered in front of the TV by the airport bar. On the screen was an image of the Pentagon, burning. I reached into my bag for my cell phone to call my mother. All circuits were busy. I had better luck reaching my father at his office from a pay phone. He told me he'd heard the news about planes crashing into the World Trade Center on his way to work that morning and instantly assumed it was an act of terrorism.

My parents and I ate dinner that night in a state of semi-shock. The next morning, my father came down for breakfast looking distraught. He told me he'd just seen a news segment in which a woman described her fruitless search for her fiancé, who had worked at the World Trade Center. They were planning to get married in December and had just had their first baby. Her story brought tears to his eyes, he confessed. I was stunned, not because his feelings had been stirred but because my father—a Sabra—*never* cried. Something my father instinctively associated with the Middle East (terrorism, hijacking) had taken place in a country that, despite everything he'd witnessed through the years, still seemed to him a refuge from the hatred and violence that racked so many other parts of the world: this was the land of freedom, the most open and tolerant nation on earth. Countless times through the years I had tried to convince him that this idealized view of America was missing certain details—slavery, racism, poverty. My father enjoyed talking— really, *arguing*—with me about this; a reenactment, my mother says, of the sparring matches she used to witness between him and my grandfather, one headstrong generation in the family following the last, each equally determined to change the other's mind—unsuccessfully, of course. Nothing I said remotely altered my father's view of the United States. "Impressive" was his favorite adjective for America, and the catalogue of reasons—its diversity, its vitality, its size, its values— seemed to grow annually. As it does for so many immigrants, the nation he'd once regarded with a mixture of fascination and awe had become a source of pride to him, never more so than after September 11. Later that day, my father came home with an American flag draped prominently across the dashboard of his car. It would remain there for months.

I spent the next few days in Buffalo, glued to the television as pundits talked about a new era in which terrorism would mark the lives of Americans as never before, courtesy of "sleeper cells" and shadowy networks of Islamic fundamentalists at war with modernity. (One such cell, consisting of six Yemeni-Americans who traveled to Afghanistan and spent time at an al-Qaeda training camp, would soon be discovered in nearby Lackawanna, though whether its members were guilty of any crimes would be hotly disputed.)*

Militants at war with modernity indeed seemed to be a growing presence in America, but not all of them drew their inspiration from the Koran. A month or so after 9/11, law enforcement agents intercepted a

---

*The six men never participated in or planned to commit an act of terrorism, the U.S. Justice Department has acknowledged. They were convicted of going to a training camp, prompting some in Lackawanna to view them as scapegoats rather than terrorists.

couple of packages sent to my father's office. More than 130 clinics and doctor's offices, including Buffalo GYN Womenservices, received letters filled with brown or white powder. Inside several of them a message was enclosed: "Army of God, you've been exposed to anthrax, you're dead."

IN EXCHANGE FOR assurances that Kopp would not face the death penalty, the French government agreed to extradite him, setting the stage for his trial. Its outcome was by no means a foregone conclusion, for there were no witnesses to Dr. Slepian's murder. The weapon used had turned up only after an oddly prolonged delay. DNA from hairs and fibers found on the tree against which the sniper stood and in a discarded baseball cap matched that on a toothbrush found among Kopp's possessions. But couldn't the FBI have planted these as well? Paul Cambria, for one, believed he had a "triable" case.

He would not get the opportunity to test his view. In October 2002, with the date of the trial approaching, Kopp abruptly announced he was switching attorneys. Cambria was dropping out. Bruce A. Barket, a pro-life lawyer from Long Island whose other clients included Kopp's friend Loretta Marra, was replacing him. Cambria had wanted to focus strictly on the facts in the case, while Barket announced a new strategy: "The issue that is going to be squarely presented in this case is the impropriety and the immorality of abortion."

A month later came a second, more surprising twist: a front-page story in *The Buffalo News* under the headline "Kopp Confesses." "James C. Kopp has admitted he shot and killed Dr. Barnett A. Slepian," wrote reporters Dan Herbeck and Lou Michel. Eight days earlier, Kopp had sat down with them and admitted to being the sniper. "To pick up a gun and aim it at another human being, and to fire, it's not a human thing to do," Kopp stated. "The only thing that would be worse, to me, would be to do nothing, and to allow abortions to continue."

Many of Kopp's friends and acquaintances were stunned. (Guilt over misleading them prompted him to come forward, Kopp claimed.) Those bringing him to justice were equally surprised. There would still be a trial, it was assumed, for in his interview with *The Buffalo News*

Kopp insisted he had intended to injure Dr. Slepian, not to kill him. A trial would offer Kopp what many assumed he still wanted: a stage on which to showcase his beliefs about abortion. But then came yet another twist: Kopp decided to forgo a jury trial and opt instead for a one-day stipulated-fact trial in which there would be no witnesses and no effort to contest the evidence amassed against him. As a legal strategy, the move seemed baffling. But perhaps there was an underlying rationale. A full trial might reveal facts about the murder, such as whether anyone else was involved, suspicions that centered on Loretta Marra and Dennis Malvasi. If Kopp's goal was to protect his comrades, his decision made sense.

THE TRIAL OF *The People of the State of New York v. James Charles Kopp* took place on March 17, 2003, in a wood-paneled room on the second floor of the Erie County Courthouse on Franklin Street, the same building where, a hundred years earlier, Leon Czolgosz had been tried. Four rows of chairs were laid out in the gallery for observers. Well before the judge, Michael L. D'Amico, entered the room, all those seats were filled. In front, on the left side, was Lynne Slepian. She was wearing a blue blouse and her hair was pulled back in a ponytail. I sat in the second row on the right side, next to a reporter from Canada. Vicki Saporta, head of the National Abortion Federation, was there. So was Marilynn Buckham. Later, I saw another familiar face: my father's. He was dressed in a gray sport coat, chinos, and soft leather shoes, and was leaning up against a wall in the back, quietly taking in the scene.

The night before, I'd tried to picture how James Kopp would look in person. I imagined him as a bearded figure with disheveled hair and intense, burning eyes. The man who entered the room in handcuffs looked nothing like this. Kopp was tall and slender, clean shaven, with slightly stooped shoulders and reddish-brown hair combed sideways. He wore glasses and was dressed in an oversized navy blazer that accentuated the slightness of his build. I watched him look around the room, his eyes darting about nervously. He looked like a lanky version of Richie Cunningham in *Happy Days. This* was Atomic Dog? Before the proceedings began, Kopp turned his head directly in my line of sight and flashed a wide, loopy grin. "Nice smile," quipped a woman behind me. For a minute, I thought he'd mistaken me for an old acquaintance. Then I noticed the man sitting in front of me, nodding in acknowledgment. His shirt had a clerical collar; his dark hair and handsome, square-jawed face struck me as vaguely familiar. The reason, I later realized, was that I'd seen him before, at a demonstration organized by the Army of God that I'd attended several months earlier, in Buffalo, on January 22, 2003, the thirtieth anniversary of *Roe v. Wade*. Roughly a dozen people had shown up, holding aloft signs that read, "Save a Baby, Call a Kopp." His name was Michael Bray and he was the author of a book called *A Time to Kill*, which laid out the rationale for using force to defend the unborn. Bray had been arrested during the 1980s for involvement in a series of abortion clinic bombings. He is a devotee of reconstruction theology, a strain of radical Christian fundamentalism that, in the words of one of its leading authors, Gary North, calls on Christians to "recapture every institution for Jesus Christ."* Each year, Bray hosted a meeting, the White Rose Banquet, where people who'd committed similar acts were honored as heroes.

Kopp sipped water and tapped his finger on the desk in front of him as Joseph Marusak, the district attorney, read out the stipulated facts in the case. While most of the reporters on hand looked bored, I was not. As Marusak recounted the details of the crime—the path of the bullet, the make of the gun, the scene in the kitchen afterward—the memories, as well as the feeling of having been arbitrarily spared experiencing it all myself, came flooding back. The person in the chair across from me, where Lynne Slepian was sitting, could have been my mother. At one point, Marusak described a witness who, prior to the shooting, had seen

---

*Paul Hill, who murdered Dr. John Britton, was a student of North's, but North himself strongly denounced Hill's action. In a September 29, 1994, letter to Hill, who was by then in jail, North assailed what he termed Hill's "vigilante theology," which he argued was a recipe for anarchy. "No one ordained you to this ecclesiastical position . . . no one anointed you," wrote North. "You ordained yourself, anointed yourself, to speak both as priest and civil magistrate in issuing your theological manifestoes. Then you gunned down a man, gunned down his escort, and wounded the escort's wife."

the defendant near the Amherst home of another local physician—"Dr. Press." Hearing my father's name instantly sent a chill down my spine, although it shouldn't have come as a surprise. In his *Buffalo News* interview months earlier, Kopp said he had scouted the homes of other physicians in the area "very, very carefully."

Since Kopp had admitted to the shooting, the issue before Judge D'Amico was not whether he was the sniper but what had been his intent: to murder Dr. Slepian, as the prosecution claimed, or to wound him, as Bruce Barket argued. A broad man with a shock of dark hair and a Long Island accent, Barket insisted that the bullet that struck Dr. Slepian had taken a "crazy ricochet" that accidentally cost him his life. He also stated, somewhat incongruously, that "Jim Kopp was justified in his view in using force, even deadly force, to save the lives of the unborn," and that he had acted in accordance with his Catholic faith. The latter claim drew a sharp retort from Marusak, himself a practicing Catholic: "That's an insult to Catholics. That is an insult of the highest magnitude," he snapped.

The following morning, Judge D'Amico issued the ruling that everyone expected in a trial without a jury and with no effort made to contest the basic facts as presented by the prosecutor: "I have concluded that, Mr. Kopp, you are guilty as charged under count one of this indictment. That is, the intentional murder of Barnett Slepian." As the verdict was delivered, I looked over at Lynne Slepian. Over both days, she had watched the proceedings impassively, offering no comments to the press. It was, I thought, a dignified way to handle an event that must have taxed her nerves and forbearance.

Outside the courtroom, I spoke to Elizabeth McDonald, a middle-aged woman from St. Louis who described herself as a "good friend" of James Kopp. She appeared disconsolate, explaining to me that she had traveled to France to visit Kopp after he was arrested, and had now come to Buffalo to offer him support. When asked what she made of the verdict, she said, "Very sad." She said of Kopp, "He should have been welcomed back to Buffalo with a ticker tape parade and keys to the city." I asked her why, in a predominantly Catholic city not lacking for people who were pro-life, he *hadn't* received such a welcome. "Well, I think people are really deceived. . . . The pro-lifers are not consistent."

Marilynn Buckham seemed only slightly more satisfied. We were standing on Franklin Street, beyond the area where many of the reporters and cameras were stationed to capture people's reactions to the verdict. She told me she was happy justice had been served, but disappointed that so many of the larger questions surrounding the case—Why Buffalo? Why Dr. Slepian? Who else might have been involved?—remained unanswered.

My father shared Buckham's disappointment. He told me that night that, nearly four years earlier, when he'd attended the reception following the unveiling of Dr. Slepian's tombstone, he had looked over the wooded area behind the house. He had carefully examined the window that the bullet pierced. The sniper had to have scoped out the area with exceptional care, he concluded, for it was no easy shot. He would have needed somewhere to stay while doing so and would have had to plan his getaway well in advance. It seemed inconceivable to my father that one person, an out-of-towner no less, could have done it all alone.

In my father's mind, though, the circle of responsibility was even wider. Like Marilynn Buckham, he viewed the murder not as an isolated event but as a product of the turmoil that had preceded it: the demonstrations that had taken place not only at physicians' offices but in front of their houses, the leaflets distributed to neighbors, and the radio ads aired during the Spring of Life, an event that placed Buffalo on the map in the mind of every militant abortion foe in the country. My father believed in free speech. But he also believed that incendiary speech—vitriol like that hurled at Yitzhak Rabin before his assassination—had the potential to inspire hate. And that those who used inflammatory words to advance their cause, no matter how just or urgent they believed it was, bore responsibility when those words ignited violence.

THE LINK BETWEEN the rhetoric of the pro-life movement and the actions of people like James Kopp weighed heavily on at least one former member of the Schenck brothers' church, a tall man with a mop of shaggy blond hair named Jerry Reiter. Reiter grew up in south Buffalo, in an Irish Catholic family. He became a born-again Christian as a teenager, after attending prayer groups affiliated with the charismatic renewal. He later joined New Covenant Tabernacle, where he took instantly to the lively services—the Schenck brothers were "excellent" preachers, he told me when we met for coffee one day in Buffalo—and the conservative political atmosphere. Reiter was a Republican who had an "Abortion Kills Children" bumper sticker on the back of his car. In 1992, he spent the Spring of Life holed up in the basement floor of a brown-brick building with tinted-glass windows on Holtz Drive, near the Buffalo airport. Pro-life activists called it the bunker. In reality, he says, it was the headquarters of the New York State Christian Coalition, in which Reiter was active at the time.

During the Spring of Life, Reiter served as Operation Rescue's media coordinator, a role he says he took up at the suggestion of Paul Schenck. He worked the phones, wrote press releases, and appeared on programs like CNN's *Sonya Live* to warn of possible violence—by the pro-choice side. "They have attacked my pastor," he declared, recounting an incident in which members of the National Women's Rights Organization Coalition, a small group of militant feminists, had knocked down Paul Schenck. "All the people on our side, the Pro Life side, have been very peaceful and calm. Right now you can hear them singing hymns."

Singing hymns and demonstrating peacefully is what Reiter thought pro-life activism was all about. He was an admirer of Martin Luther King, whose example he believed Operation Rescue was following. One day during the Spring of Life, however, he overheard a couple of activists casually debating the merits of blowing up abortion clinics. Then he was handed a copy of the Army of God Manual. When Reiter read it, he was stunned. Wasn't the whole point of being pro-life to promote respect for other human beings? Wasn't it the "deathscorts" and "pro-aborts" on the other side who supported violence?

A year and a half later, after Michael Griffin shot David Gunn, and after prominent pro-life activists started signing their names to statements praising the murder, Reiter traveled to Pensacola. There he struck up a conversation with a demonstrator standing outside the courthouse, a tall, bespectacled man who struck him as mild-mannered and harmless. But over lunch, the man told him he believed what Michael Griffin had done was justified. He insisted that if America were a true Christian nation, abortion providers throughout the country would be executed—and not only them but homosexuals, too, since they were likewise guilty of violating biblical law. The name of the demonstrator was Paul Hill. A few months later, he murdered John Britten.

Reiter continued traveling around and meeting people on the movement's fringe, including some who regarded Paul Hill and Michael Griffin as heroes. The more immersed in the subculture of the militants he got, the more he came to believe that the true goal of the radical anti-abortion movement was not merely to save babies but to impose a theocracy, one in which women would be returned to their traditionally subordinate role, and infidels—meaning anyone who did not endorse the militants' interpretation of the Bible—would be punished. Everywhere he went, he told me, people opened up to him once they found out he was on friendly terms with the Schenck brothers. It appalled Reiter that people could read the Bible and draw from it a justification for murdering people. And yet he understood where the militants had gotten their ideas: from people like himself. "When I was a leader in the Christian Coalition and later as a media coordinator for Operation Rescue," he would later write in a book, *Live from the Gates of Hell*, chronicling his experiences inside the antiabortion underground, "I was one of the pushers of political rhetoric that was red-hot enough to have created a climate where some men felt they must take up arms in the 'war' we told them about."

In Reiter's view, bombing clinics, even shooting physicians, though never openly endorsed, "were the logical next steps to the groups I had worked for, which called abortion the genocide of the unborn, the holocaust of the womb." At the end of his book, he lodged a more specific charge against his former pastors, Rob and Paul Schenck. "The Schencks and their allies had taunted the entire Slepian family for years," Reiter wrote. "Picketing and taunting . . . went on for a decade until Dr. Slepian was assassinated." By singling out and targeting Slepian, by calling him a murderer and a pig, he implied, the Schenck brothers shared responsibility for what had happened.*

SITTING WITH ROB Schenck at the headquarters of Faith and Action on the sunny afternoon when we met in Washington, I heard a rather different view. Schenck told me that he and his brother had "very superficial contact" with the militants in the movement who embraced violence, and "thunderously" denounced them.

"I did not think they were morally considered people," Schenck said of those who advocated shooting physicians. "I thought they were emotional. I thought that they were irresponsible. I didn't think they would ever carry out their threats, so I didn't find them credible. And then, sadly, one of them did."

I asked Schenck whether he ever grappled with the thought that his own rhetoric—that abortion was murder, that physicians were involved in genocide, that there was a higher law, which called for defying civil authority—might have fostered the impression that violence was justified. "No, never did," Schenck said. "I will tell you what we did wrestle with was the feeling that we failed to instill a strong enough understanding of the moral principles that drove the movement. In other words, we felt like where we did fail was in properly forming our people so that they did not draw those conclusions.

"Although," he went on, "you can't get to everybody, and some people who join up with a movement are there simply for the excitement of it, and they are morally flawed people from the start. And you can't fix them, no matter how hard you try—you can't fix them. . . . I think the average, normal person can discern the difference, and has a moral

---

*"[A] physician who kills instead of heals is as unclean as a pig," Paul Schenck said on one occasion. "You, Dr. Slepian—are a pig." In his 1993 book, *The Extermination of Christianity*, in which he argued that "a militant and secular coalition is using every means available to purge Christianity from the American landscape," Paul Schenck cited the incident as an example of how Christians were unfairly accused of "harassment." In a footnote, he wrote: "I confess it was not the most effective tactic, and if I had to do it over again, I would probably choose different terms."

governor within them that stops them, and you can't take responsibility for all of the psychologically and morally flawed people in the world— you just can't. So no, I never felt guilt or responsibility for that."

Schenck's remarks echoed Karen Swallow Prior's, shared during our very first interview, in her office at Liberty University. "I don't think that calling someone a murderer sends somebody else a message to kill that person," she said. "I think everybody should be more careful about language, but I don't think that makes someone responsible for someone [else] taking some illogical leap." As she spoke, I glanced up and spotted a plaque on the wall of Prior's office from the group Buffalo Feminists for Life honoring her for her "outstanding leadership." Next to it was a framed bulletin:

Harvard College Discussion Series
Pro-Life, Pro-Choice
Is There Common Ground?

The event at Harvard had taken place in 1998. Prior had participated in it, along with a woman named Marilyn Cohen, who at the time ran the Emma Goldman abortion clinic in Iowa City. The idea was to inject a note of civility—and to highlight areas of potential shared interest— into a conflict dominated by shouting and vitriol. It was not the first time that Prior, whose view of abortion has not changed since her days as the spokeswoman for Project Rescue in Buffalo, had participated in such a dialogue. In fact, she'd been taking part in such discussions from time to time since shortly after the Spring of Life, when the Buffalo Area Council of Churches first began organizing them in an effort to reduce the acrimony that had divided the community.

Not all pro-lifers agreed with the approach. Some quoted Prior an admonition from Second Corinthians: "Do not be unequally yoked together with unbelievers." But Prior was undeterred. Common ground, she emphasized, did not mean *middle* ground—she was still against abortion in all circumstances, and still believed Operation Rescue had served a worthy purpose. But she also saw the value of engaging people who held different views and treating them with the respect and consideration she hoped to receive in return. What's more, she told me, she had discovered that there actually *was* some common ground in the abortion conflict. Most people on both sides wanted to see the rate of teen pregnancy reduced (even if they might disagree on how to achieve that). And they generally believed in promoting male as well as female sexual responsibility. In 1999, partly in response to the announcement of the Spring of Life Reunion—an event in which Prior, believing the timing was inappropriate, chose not to participate—a group of religious leaders from western New York signed their name to a "Statement on a New Way." The statement emphasized seven concerns pro-choice and pro-life activists might share, among them reducing the number of teen pregnancies, improving prenatal and maternal care, fostering respect and equality for women, supporting and funding the choice of adoption, promoting sexual responsibility, and working to remove the conditions that lead to abortion. It is a list of objectives my father wholeheartedly supports, as I discovered upon reading them to him. The most surprising signatory was Paul Schenck.

While Prior's opposition to abortion had remained consistent, her view of the best means to make her beliefs known had evolved. In 1992, when she was profiled in *The Buffalo News*, she endorsed the picketing of doctors' homes. "I just realized the right to privacy ends once you infringe on someone's right to live," she told the reporter, David Montgomery. By the time I met with her, Prior had come to oppose such "house calls," both because they subjected members of a physician's family to intimidation and because, as she explained in a subsequent e-mail, they blurred the distinction between the objectionable act (abortion) and the person carrying it out. "It is the act of abortion I protest, not the life of the abortion provider," she explained.

Prior understood that my interest in these questions was more than abstract. Earlier, before I'd even begun recording our first interview, she had said she wanted to ask *me* some questions. Why was I writing a book about Buffalo? Because I grew up there, I told her. Was I any relation to Dr. Shalom Press?

"I'm his son."

There was silence, followed by a burst of awkward laughter. I feared she might ask me to leave and that there would be no opportunity for productive dialogue (which is why, I told her, I hadn't volunteered this information to begin with). But I was wrong. Instead of pointing me to the door, Prior opened up, as though knowing who I was made her more eager to share her perspective. It was at this point that she informed me she would gladly be pro-choice, if I or anyone else could persuade her. She told me the story of how she first became a pro-life activist. She defended the movement at every turn, without a hint of regret or contrition, until we got to the subject of Dr. Slepian's murder.

"I struggle with how much personal responsibility to take," she said all of a sudden. We had been talking for several hours by this point, mostly about Operation Rescue, the Spring of Life, and the events of the late eighties and early nineties.

"I just remember that Sunday, whatever Sunday it was," she said. She meant the Sunday following the murder. "That Sunday in church, just thinking about how [Dr. Slepian] had a wife and sons at home that were without their father and husband." She paused. I looked over at her. She had removed her glasses from her face, which was turned slightly away from mine. The tone of her voice had softened. I could just detect tears glistening in her eyes. "The idea that I might have anything even remotely to do with that just really . . . is . . . awful." She broke into sobs. "I don't—it's just the thought of it . . . just to even be tainted with that is pretty awful.

"I think about those boys a lot. Of course, they're young men now— just like you are."

I sat frozen, caught between two conflicting impulses. One was to reach over, clasp Prior's hand, and offer her the comfort anyone would think to extend at such a moment. Undoubtedly her regret stemmed partly from how the shooting had tarnished the legacy of a cause in which she believed fervently. But it was rooted as well in real sympathy for Barnett Slepian's family, for those who had known him as a loving husband and a father; rooted, too, I sensed, in a feeling of at least some responsibility. Maybe sitting there in my presence, putting a face to the memory (albeit the face of another abortion provider's son), elicited these feelings. If so, my meeting Prior served a purpose, evoking an expression of compassion—and of remorse—that transcended the barriers of a conflict that all too often prevented people from recognizing the humanity of their adversaries.

I told Prior that seeing her reaction moved me. But I did not reach across to comfort her. The reason, I realized afterward, is that a part of me didn't want her to feel comforted at that moment: the same part of me that thought about how I would have received her words had the victim of the shooting been my father. I imagined how Lynne Slepian and her children would have felt, sitting in that room. And I thought back to the house calls, the anonymous threats and other tactics—the private detective hired to dig up dirt about physicians like my father, for example—that Project Rescue had employed through the years. Had it really not occurred to anyone that these actions might precipitate violence? In fairness, in December 1994 Prior had announced the formation of a Pro-Life Alliance for Non-Violence. She felt it was necessary, she told me, to make explicit what to her was implicit: that no one who believed in the sanctity of life should shoot someone. By the time it was launched, however, several doctors had already been murdered, and Barnett Slepian's letter—warning nobody to be surprised if another one was—had already appeared in print.

· 15 ·

One morning in the middle of August, I drove to my father's office with a notebook and a tape recorder in my bag. I was visiting after he'd urged me to speak to a group of people whose voices have been oddly absent from the debate about abortion in recent years: women who have had them. "You can't write this book," he said one night, "until you talk to some of my patients." The thought hadn't occurred to me until then, perhaps because, like many people, I'd grown accustomed to reading stories about abortion that featured the views of advocates, politicians, legal scholars, medical experts—everyone but the more than one million women in America who elect to terminate their pregnancies every year. The latter's invisibility is not owed solely to the inherently private nature of the issue, nor is it simply the fault of the press. It is also a reflection of arguably the most striking achievement of the right-to-life movement in the years since *Roe v. Wade*: three decades after feminists held speakouts to remove the veil of shame and secrecy surrounding "illegal operations," the stigma surrounding abortion was very much back in place. It was no longer controversial for female characters on TV sitcoms to talk about divorce, desire, even being gay. But the experience of having an abortion was different.

You would never have guessed, from this silence, that abortion remained one of the most common forms of surgery in the United States, and that roughly four in ten women aged forty-five have had one.* The majority of these women are mothers—60 percent of women having abortions have also had one or more children. Fifty-four percent were using contraception during the month they got pregnant.

I pulled into the parking lot at my father's office at 9:30 A.M. It was hazy and humid outside. To the right of the building, as always on the days abortions were performed, a couple of protesters had gathered, the ring of faithful who, like Mickey van de Ven, kept at it long after the camera crews had departed and the crowds had thinned. "Excuse me, sir, can we talk to you?" one of them called out as I approached the front door. "You can't go in there. They're killing babies in there."

Inside, six women were waiting in the lobby, four white, two black; they ranged in age from about eighteen to about thirty. I arrived with a stack of consent forms explaining that I was a journalist working on a book and then waited in a corner office, thumbing through the morning papers and wondering whether anyone would be willing to speak to me. Half an hour later, there was a knock on the door. It was Diane, a nurse who works with my father. A cheerful, ebullient woman who has been on his staff for as long as I can remember, Diane has developed an intimate rapport with him, forged through years of working together, learning to communicate, and, not unlike a married couple (which patients sometimes take them to be, my father says), learning to be amused rather than exasperated by each other's foibles, faults, and tics.

Diane informed me that a couple of patients had signed the form. A short while later, one of them walked in. Jessica was nineteen years old.[†]

---

*This statistic was provided by Stanley Henshaw of the Alan Guttmacher Institute. According to Henshaw, if the recent decline in the abortion rate in America holds, the figure for women of childbearing age today will be one in three when they reach forty-five.
[†]This is not her real name. For reasons of privacy, none of the women I spoke to wanted their real names used.

She had shoulder-length brown hair, a pretty face, and a shy manner. She was there because she had gotten pregnant after having unprotected sex with a man she'd met who was in the armed services. They weren't married, a fact that might have prompted conservatives to shake their heads in disgust. In the real world, though, plenty of people didn't wait to get married before finding themselves in such situations, and not merely because they regarded getting pregnant and having an abortion as no big deal. I asked Jessica what it felt like to pass the protesters. "That used to be me," she said. A few years earlier, she told me, she had written a high school paper about abortion from a staunchly pro-life point of view. Jessica was Catholic. On one occasion, she had passed out pictures of aborted babies to her classmates. "I used to feel the same way they do," she said of the protesters. What had changed her mind? "This experience," she said after a pause. "I still think I'm a child. I'm just not ready to be a mom." She worked two jobs, she told me, and lived at home with her mother. I asked her whether, in light of her background, her decision had been accepted within the family. Jessica shook her head.

A few weeks later, in a follow-up phone conversation, I learned that, when she came home that day, Jessica found her belongings by the door—her mother, furious, had demanded she move out. After a week or two, the anger subsided, and she'd been invited back. I asked her what had prompted her mother's change of heart. "I'm not sure," she said, "just me telling her, her putting herself in my position." Did she have any regrets about her decision? "I still think about it a lot," she said. "I have friends who are having babies. But I feel it was the right decision for me. It has made me stronger. Now, before judging anyone else, I would want to put myself in their shoes."

The next patient I spoke to, Monica, was somewhat older. She was wearing a khaki skirt and an off-white blouse. With her blue eyes and her blond hair pulled back, she looked like a typical suburban soccer mom. Thirty-seven and married with two children, she was startled to be here. "This was not planned," she told me, "but, you know, I'm not sure I want to be changing diapers when I'm forty. Financially, we're in debt, and we have a lot of plans with our two girls. It was an accident and when it hits you in the face, it's a shock." Her in-laws were Catholic, she said, some of them extremely devout. She and her husband weren't planning on sharing the news with them. It had been hard walking past the protesters, Monica said: "They were screaming 'God loves you' at me. I was very uncomfortable." Then she lowered her voice. "Well, you know, between you and me, I see a lot of young girls in that lobby out there and it makes me very sad."

The tone of the comment wasn't judgmental, but it did suggest that Monica thought herself to be in a different position than the other women there, an attitude Melinda DuBois, the director of Marilynn Buckham's clinic, says is common. "We have lots of women who come to the clinic and say, 'Who are all those people in the waiting room? Are *they* all having abortions?'" says DuBois. "Some of them are appalled by the fact that we have a waiting room filled with women who need the same service they need. There are a lot of people who think, 'This is only happening to me, it's my issue, my case is different, I'm not like all those people out there.'"

Of course, not all women having abortions *are* in the same boat. After Monica left the room, Tracy, a soft-spoken woman with brown eyes, walked in. She had come to my father's office from Lockport, a forty-minute drive from Buffalo, where she lived in public housing. She was wearing jeans, sneakers, and a gray T-shirt. Twenty-four years old, Tracy was divorced and raising a five-year-old daughter while working as a waitress and putting herself through Niagara Community College so she could offer her daughter a better life. She'd fought for years to get child support from the father of her daughter. She had been on the pill but gotten pregnant after forgetting to take it just once. "I missed *one* pill," she said, shaking her head. The faintness of her voice and the meekness of her manner conveyed something rarely seen in women from more privileged backgrounds—a sense of shame, a feeling that she'd screwed up and had only herself to blame. Perhaps Tracy understood how little sympathy a woman in her circumstances could expect about the predicament she faced. Perhaps she knew the margin of error for women like herself was a lot thinner than for housewives in the suburbs with husbands and nice cars, just as it was thinner still if you were black or Hispanic and lived in an impoverished neighborhood of

Buffalo, which, in 2002, had the sixth-highest child poverty rate in the nation (38.7 percent), and the highest rate of all (a staggering 57 percent) for Hispanic children. For women in such circumstances, having children meant creating more problems for everyone else; or so states implied when they instituted family cap policies during the 1990s to deny welfare and other benefits to women on public assistance who had additional kids. Researchers in New Jersey would find that, by 1998, the state's family cap policy had resulted in 14,000 fewer births—and 1,429 more abortions. For the women targeted by such initiatives, *not* having kids could mean being stigmatized another way: as the kind of woman who slept around, got pregnant, and wound up having abortions for convenience's sake.

IN FAIRNESS, NONE of the pro-life activists I met portrayed women who had abortions in such terms. They referred to them, instead, as "victims" being pressured into the decision by others. "Somebody's intimidating them, somebody's bullying them," Rob Schenck told me. Leaving aside how little space such a view affords for the possibility that a woman might actually *want* to have an abortion, I couldn't help but find the terminology strange. Many of the same activists who described women as victims had no qualms about labeling physicians murderers. Was it not the case that, but for the women who went to see them, there would be no need to hound and harass those physicians? Shouldn't they be held accountable as well?

In 1996, Eric Zorn, a columnist for the *Chicago Tribune*, asked Al Salvi, a pro-life Republican running for U.S. Senate, why, if he believed abortion was the taking of an innocent life, he wasn't advocating that women who had them be charged with murder. "That's a very interesting philosophical question," Salvi replied. "I don't have an answer to it." Zorn then put the question to Joseph Scheidler. "It's kind of for political convenience," said Scheidler. "The general position of the pro-life movement has been that the woman is a victim along with the child because she is often pressured or coerced into abortion against her will." As Zorn pointed out, this was a peculiar attitude to find among conservatives, who tend to adopt a "no excuses" attitude toward crime. Scheidler admitted as much. "In reality, the gals usually know what they're doing and want to do it. . . . But if we started saying that women who have abortions should be sent to jail for life, we'd get into a real beehive. People would say we were hard and vindictive."

To suggest that more than a third of the women strolling down the aisles of your local supermarket are murderers who should be tossed in jail is, indeed, rather stark. It is evidently easier to pin the blame on the (far smaller) network of providers, or to suggest that women who have abortions do so against their will or better judgment, or that they don't really know what they're doing or are ignorant of the alternatives. Over the course of two days, I spoke to roughly a dozen women at my father's office. None claimed her decision was anybody's but her own. Nor did any seem ignorant of her options, not least because, before speaking to me, they sat through a counseling session during which the alternatives — having the baby; putting the child up for adoption — were spelled out. Sometimes, my father told me, patients left such sessions having changed their minds, which he viewed as a good thing, so long as the decision was considered and informed. Some women had second thoughts after seeing an ultrasound, which was standard procedure. Diane called me over to show me one. From a distance, it looked vaguely like the surface of the moon, swirling splotches of gray and black. Then I looked more closely and Diane pointed to what, upon closer examination, appeared to be the head of a human embryo. She pointed to a leg.

Seeing the ultrasound brought home the fact that, as pro-life activists often contended, terms like "uterine contents" obscure what is actually inside a pregnant woman's body: a human embryo that is alive and growing. This much is undeniable. It is also undeniable that an embryo's capacity to live and grow depends on someone else — the pregnant woman whose sonogram I was now standing before, sitting in the room next to me. To be there taking all this in was to be reminded why the debate about abortion is so volatile, and why it is unique. As Cynthia Gorney put it to me, "There simply is no other circumstance we have to confront in which an entity exists and we cannot agree as a society whether that entity is or is not a human being — *and* that entity is growing inside another person." To pro-lifers, the obvious priority is to protect the human embryo, which cannot defend itself, from harm. To feminists, the fact that this embryo cannot develop without a mother underscores why, to the contrary, the decision should be left to the woman, since in no other circumstance does society *require* one person to provide another with life support (the father of a child who needs a kidney to survive is not compelled to donate his, for example). Even if the fact that the fetus is a person could be agreed upon, why should women alone have to bear this burden? It is this imbalance, above and beyond the issue of privacy, that has led some legal scholars to argue that *Roe v. Wade* should have been decided on the basis of gender equality.

I didn't see anybody walk out of my father's office without having an abortion on the days I visited. I did hear several women talk about how difficult the decision had been for them. I saw several shed tears. Tracy, the woman from Lockport, was not among them, though she told me, "I'll probably cry later." Another woman—twenty-seven, blond, wearing cutoff jeans and a tank top—displayed no such ambivalence—at first. She told me she worked as a bartender, at a bar I later found out featured table dances. She had a confident, carefree manner and didn't seem terribly discomfited at being there. Afterward, she thanked my father and Diane and expressed relief—"Thank you, thank you very much," she said. After they left the room, her eyes suddenly filled. "I'm sad," she said, with an expression as heartrending as any I'd seen that day. Every so often, she told me, she saw women in the supermarket who looked "so happy" to be pregnant. Sometimes she saw them passing her on the streets. She said she wished she could be one of them.

At home later that night, I asked my father whether his patients' ambivalence and not infrequent grief ever weighed on him. It was at this point that he told me about the woman who had lashed out at him, demanding, "How can you do this?" Generally speaking, though, he said seeing patients register sadness did not disturb him—what else could be expected from a decision as weighty and personal as this? What did bother him was seeing a patient (and there were some) for her second, third, or fourth abortion, even after she had been counseled to use contraception, and finding that she still acted blasé about it. *"That* upsets me," he said.

"You know," he continued, "every doctor likes to deal with people who are in fortunate situations. But a lot of times in medicine, you don't. When you treat people who are sick or dying, you don't see a lot of smiles and happiness. Unplanned pregnancies are a reality. Nobody is thrilled about it. But I feel women in such situations deserve good care, and, if they consider the alternatives carefully and decide having an abortion is the best thing for them, I feel it is their right.

"And," he added, "I feel that I am helping them."

BY THE TIME my father said these words to me, the political landscape in America had shifted rather dramatically since 1973, the year he began his residency in Buffalo and the Supreme Court issued its decision in *Roe v. Wade.* The days were long gone when liberals believed a consensus was forming in favor of abortion rights. Congress was busy passing laws like the Unborn Victims of Violence Act, which made the murder of a pregnant woman a double homicide, and, in 2003, the Partial-Birth Abortion Ban Act. The latter bill prohibited a relatively rare method of late-term abortion that, as a series of pen-and-ink illustrations drawn by a pro-life activist would depict, required pulling the lower part of an unborn child out of a woman and then collapsing its skull. Pro-choice advocates pointed out that this method was used in less than 1 percent of abortions, often under dire circumstances or in cases where the pregnant woman's life or health was severely at risk, and that the procedure barred by the legislation was so vaguely defined as to potentially restrict other, more common methods. For the pro-life movement, however, the procedure and the accompanying illustrations—which were graphic, without being disgusting as blown-up photographs of aborted fetuses were—served not only as proof of the gruesomeness of abortion but also as a powerful organizing tool.

More striking than these legislative developments was the cultural shift. In the early 1970s, when elected officials spoke of the suffering associated with abortion, it was almost invariably in reference to women who had died or been injured following illegal ones. Three decades later, politicians on the floor of the House of Representatives decried "the dismemberment of living, distinct human beings" (House Majority Leader Tom DeLay, of Texas) and "the slaughter of human life" (Congresswoman Virginia Foxx, of North Carolina). They weren't even talking about abortion but about embryonic stem-cell research, which the religious right adamantly opposed on the grounds that destroying an embryo created through in vitro fertilization is no different from killing a person. In the corridors of power, it sometimes seemed the frozen embryo had assumed greater value than a person. In contrasting President George W. Bush's adamant opposition to stem cell research with his comparative silence about Darfur, a region of Sudan where at least 70,000 people had been murdered and more than two million driven from their homes, the *New York Times* columnist Nicholas Kristof observed, "Mr. Bush values a frozen embryo. But he . . . [is] continuing to avert his eyes from the first genocide of the 21st century."

While the fate of the unborn arguably commanded more attention in Washington than ever before, in Buffalo abortion at long last appeared to be fading from the headlines. In 2001, a Catholic group announced plans to build a 700-foot-tall pro-life arch on the Buffalo waterfront. The news came and went without too many people getting riled up. It was about time, I thought, not because abortion didn't matter but because so many other problems facing Buffalo had received far less attention through the years. The fact that the city ranked among the ten most racially segregated metropolitan areas in the country, for example. Or that many of its public schools were being forced to shed staff and cut extracurricular activities due to chronic budget shortfalls. Or that, as *The Buffalo News* found in an investigative report, the half billion dollars in federal aid poured into the city to combat poverty since the mid-1970s had largely been wasted on things (like subsidizing a bloated bureaucracy) that did nothing to help the poor. Addressing such problems would hardly be easy. But, as I walked through the streets of downtown Buffalo one day, past a bunch of vacant storefronts and the Lafayette Hotel, a beautiful French Renaissance–style building that was once among the fanciest in the country, but which is now a decrepit shadow of its former self, I couldn't help but think the city could benefit from focusing on other things.

That abortion had dropped out of the headlines did not mean people in western New York cared any less about it, of course. There were still plenty of local pro-life activists who picketed and demonstrated on occasions like the anniversary of *Roe v. Wade*. There were still people on the other side who showed up for events like the annual 5K Race for Non Violence in honor of Barnett Slepian. The year I attended, the race took place on an overcast day in the middle of June. Despite the less than perfect weather, several hundred people turned out, including Lynne Slepian and her sons. I bought a T-shirt afterward, on the front of which was a white dove. On the back was a list of sponsors and supporters, among them a couple of local businesses, New York State Attorney General Eliot Spitzer, various members of the Slepian family, and my father.

I drove home afterward happy that I'd gone, but wondering if the principle for which the race had been held was, in the context of the abortion conflict, a lost cause. There had been, it was true, a lull in attacks on abortion providers since Dr. Slepian's murder. But the violence appeared to have had a powerful chilling effect. Since 1992, more than 250 hospitals and 300 private practitioners had stopped performing abortions in the United States. By 2000, 87 percent of all U.S. counties had no abortion provider at all. As I watched my father grow more and more professionally isolated over the years, and as I read about states where the only abortion providers remaining were so-called circuit riders who flew in from elsewhere, the scenario articulated by some pro-choice advocates—that violence would scare away so many physicians as to make *Roe v. Wade* moot—seemed increasingly near at hand.

The murder of Dr. Slepian and the shootings of other physicians did, in fact, deter some doctors who might otherwise have considered performing abortions. I know this because I spoke to some in the Buffalo area who made this decision. What it did not do, most experts feel, is account for the steady drop in demand for abortion during the 1990s, a trend most analysts attribute to a host of other factors—laws curtailing access in many states; the increased use of birth control; improved sex education; wider access to emergency contraception, which one study credits with as much as 43 percent of the decline in the abortion rate between 1994 and 2000.*

Western New York fit the pattern. Between 1992 and 2002, the number of abortions performed in Erie County declined by 30 percent. Yet throughout this period, women who wanted to terminate their pregnancies still had their choice of places to go—Marilynn Buckham's clinic, my father's office, the offices of several physicians in Rochester (a one-hour drive away), and a branch of Planned Parenthood in Niagara Falls, twenty minutes from the city. That fewer women were having abortions owed less to a shortage of providers than to developments like the declining rate of teen pregnancy, which also fell by 30 percent in Erie County between 1992 and 2002. "Blunt Sex-Ed Effort Cuts Teen Pregnancy" announced the headline of a May 2002 front-page story in *The Buffalo News*, linking the decline to "beefed-up health curriculums and after-school programs that emphasize sexual abstinence but don't balk when teens ask about contraception and their bodies."†

EVEN IF HE believed it was morally justifiable, Rob Schenck told me he thought that shooting physicians would never succeed in putting an end to abortion. There was a time when I thought that was *exactly* what it was doing. Yet it appears, in retrospect, that Schenck was right—indeed, the violence may have backfired, not only because the shootings tarnished the pro-life movement's image but also because, although the violence deterred some physicians, it made others more committed than ever to preserving a woman's choice. "We have doubled our security

---

*Some pro-life activists view emergency contraception as *itself* a form of abortion, of course, on the grounds that it can prevent fertilized eggs from implanting in the womb.
†This may change if the religious right has its way and the only message teens receive about sex is abstinence. In 1999, just 14 percent of U.S. school districts taught abstinence as part of a comprehensive sex education program of the sort available in countries like Canada and France, where the teen abortion and pregnancy rates are notably lower than in the United States, even though the rate of sexual activity is similar. Studies suggest that three fourths of the decline in the teen pregnancy rate in America can be attributed to more effective contraceptive use, just one fourth to teenagers' abstaining from sex.

and our resolve," wrote Eric Schaff, a physician who until recently directed a reproductive health program in Rochester that trains doctors in family medicine to perform abortions, in a letter to *The Buffalo News* in 2002. "We do it for Slepian." At the University of Buffalo medical school, a branch of the national group Medical Students for Choice formed directly after Dr. Slepian's murder. Its goal was to train a new generation of abortion providers to replace the current one. Its founders aimed to send a message to supporters of violence that they were not going to be intimidated, and to communicate to medical school administrators that young physicians seeking to learn how to perform abortions should receive the proper training.

Carole Joffe, a sociologist at the University of California at Davis, says that while it is too soon to quantify the impact, the emergence of Medical Students for Choice, along with the growing number of physicians learning to perform abortions as part of their training in family medicine, may explain why she has noticed an influx of young physicians lately at the annual meetings of the National Abortion Federation. "You see people of your father's generation, but you also see a lot of young doctors, many of them women of color—Asian women, Indian women," says Joffe. My father attended an NAF conference in Montreal and noticed the same thing. He had gone to the meeting expecting to see a lot of gray-haired men. "I was really surprised," he told me afterward. "There were a lot of young people there."

ON MAY 9, 2003, I returned to the Erie County Courthouse once more. It was the day of James Kopp's sentencing, when I and the rest of Buffalo would get an opportunity to hear directly from the man who murdered Barnett Slepian.

I took a seat on the right side of the room, in the chamber where members of a jury would normally have been. Lynne Slepian was sitting where she had during the trial, alongside three of her sons, Philip, Michael, and Brian.

"Good morning, Judge," Kopp whispered, his voice so hushed it was barely audible at first. Reading from notes, he described the day after the shooting, when he peered up at a TV screen and learned that Dr. Slepian had died, as the "saddest" of his life. He then went on to describe the man he'd shot as a "mass murderer" responsible for the death of "25,000 children," the number of abortions Kopp estimated Dr. Slepian had performed over thirteen years. A man who, like all abortion providers, spent every waking moment "killing kids or rushing up from killing kids." A man guilty of "serial murdering racism and genocide." As the words spilled out, it was hard to see what about Dr. Slepian's death saddened Kopp. It was hard not to conclude he believed his victim had gotten exactly what he deserved.

Kopp's address was studded with references to America, but the nation that seemed to occupy the central place in his imagination was Germany, circa World War II. "This is a continuation of the Holocaust," he matter-of-factly declared, drawing a straight line from Hitler's plan to exterminate the Jews, to Margaret Sanger, to the legalization of abortion. "It didn't stop in 'forty-five. It went underground and resurfaced once again and started in New York State." The America he described was a forsaken land that sanctioned "anytime killing, everywhere killing, on-schedule killing for any reason." Kopp portrayed abortion as part of a eugenicist plot to eliminate minority babies. He depicted the clinics as death camps and himself as a resistance leader heroically trying to rescue the victims from their imminent deaths. At one point he declared, "You are morally obliged to refuse to punish me just as surely as you are required to refrain from participating in sending Jewish people, or those who protect them, to their death." As he said this, I looked over at Lynne Slepian, whose Jewish husband Kopp had murdered after he'd returned home from temple on a Friday night. Her expression was stony.

Kopp's sympathy for the unborn struck me as sincere, as was his contempt for the living. The FBI and police were "the enemies of children," to whom he owed straight answers no more than he would to "the Gestapo." The entire Town of Amherst, where Barnett Slepian lived, was guilty of cooperating "with evil." Kopp spoke of "forgiveness"—the forgiveness others should seek after they turned away from the murderous practice he alone had attempted to stop. "Even if I failed at my goal to preserve Dr. Slepian's life, nonetheless, I would be the only one I know of in this case who even had a plan whereby at the end of the day both Dr. Slepian and his victim will still be alive," he explained. As the speech wore on, the pace of Kopp's voice quickened, and the filament of rage beneath his diffident demeanor grew more pronounced. "Supreme Court, I will not kneel and worship before them," he declared. "I defy them, Judge. I defy anyone who carries out the murderous plans and to this defiance, resistance, I add half-truth to half-truth. I add nighttime operation to nighttime operation. I add no promise of safety to murderers to no promise of safety to murderers. I add no promise of sabotage to no promise of sabotage."

It was tempting, sitting there, to dismiss this as the raving of a lunatic. Yet, on the whole, Kopp did not come across as crazy. He struck me as an intelligent man possessed of a coherent—in some ways, strikingly coherent—worldview, the danger of which rested in the very quality that made it attractive and, paradoxically, mundane. Abortion was "not something to be voted on," Kopp explained to the court. Everything he knew about it was "proven." "You say this is a pluralistic society," he told Judge D'Amico. "You cannot take that position, not after this case, Judge, not with this case. Not when I am convicted." Kopp was speaking in the voice of extreme fundamentalism, a voice from which doubt— and with it, the willingness to tolerate multiple views—had been purged. The diamond-hard clarity of his beliefs might have made him sound unhinged to people who did not share them, yet its appeal was clear. To live in the modern world is to wrestle with temptation and choice. With impulses like the ones that led to the dissolution of the marriage of Charles and Nancy Kopp; with desire of the sort that might prompt a Catholic girl raised in an observant home to let a date go a bit farther than she'd planned; with the hunger and hope that causes risks to be taken and, on occasion, mistakes to be made. This is the world the women I'd met at my father's office inhabited—a place of hard decisions and uncertain consequences; of tremendous openness and freedom, which can be a frightening thing to those for whom an absence of fixed rules had led mostly to disappointment and pain.

"Jail, jail is not so bad," Kopp told the court as his statement wound down, "nowhere near as bad as being out of custody and constantly wondering what else could be done for the babies." These were the words of a man who seemed reconciled to serving out his days in prison, another step in the journey of suffering and self-abnegation to which he'd dedicated his life. He was now one step closer to sharing the fate of the unborn souls whose unblemished purity seemed to embody every-thing he found missing from the broken secular world: a victim-soul with a circle of admirers, who had God, if not the law, on his side; who had salvation to look forward to, if not freedom in this world. After Judge D'Amico announced that he was imposing a sentence of twenty-five years to life, I walked outside. I thought of Kopp being escorted to his cell in handcuffs, a soldier of God in chains, and found it hard to avoid concluding that, as much as he'd tried to evade their grasp, the FBI and Amherst police had unwittingly done him a favor. They had put a deeply tormented man—a would-be saint trapped in what he called "a culture of death," a devout Catholic whose quest for salvation had led him to the firing range—out of his misery.

A YEAR OR so after Kopp's sentencing, I took a bus to Washington, D.C., to attend what would turn out to be one of the largest political demonstrations in U.S. history. It was not an antiwar protest but the March for Women's Lives. It took place on a beautiful, sunny spring day. The Mall was packed with people. I stood on Pennsylvania Avenue after the speeches rang out and watched the demonstrators stream by with their placards and T-shirts, a sea of humanity that filled the streets for hours. Among those passing me were health care professionals, union members, students, mothers marching with their daughters, and an elderly woman walking with a cane. There was a dance troupe from Chicago, a group of Latino immigrants from Brooklyn, and contingents from organizations like the Black Women's Health Imperative and the National Latina Institute for Reproductive Health. I spoke to one vet-eran of the feminist movement who, picket in hand, told me she'd been marching for reproductive rights for thirty years—"I can't believe we're still out here fighting for this," she said—but also to plenty of young people attending a demonstration for the first time. Of the estimated one million marchers, one fourth were under the age of twenty-five.

Predictably, it hadn't occurred to my father to join the march, so I called him at one point to describe the scene. When I told him how many people were there, he sounded pleased, though his tone was measured. On the bus home afterward, it occurred to me that the reason for this might be something other than his even-keeled temperament. I had gone to the march to see whether the issue that had brought protesters to his door for so many years still mattered to people. My father already knew that it did. He'd seen the proof over and over again through the years, not at marches but with every new patient who arrived at his office on the days he performed abortions.

He would not be seeing too many more. Having entered the latter half of his sixties, he was nearing retirement and, finally, slowing down. He took more days off now than in the past. When he did work, he often started later and ended earlier, which meant more time for other things—fishing, his new favorite hobby; reading (each time I came home, there seemed to be a new book on the nightstand by his bed); traveling. As always, he tended to avoid reflecting too much on himself. When I called him one night and asked, out of the blue, what he considered the most satisfying aspect of his career, he paused in a manner that suggested he'd never really thought about it before. "Well," he said, "certainly delivering babies is the most satisfying thing," before his voice trailed off. I decided to change the subject, figuring he was too tired to engage in a serious conversation. Then he interrupted me to say something else. He told me he had seen a forty-one-year-old woman that day who had come in for an abortion. It had not been an easy decision for her—she had made a point of emphasizing this. She had also made a point of thanking him for doing what he did. If he thought of the part of his work that had made the greatest difference, he told me, it was helping women like her, not because having an abortion was an easy decision for anyone but because so many physicians who believed that it should be legally available opted to avoid the hassles and risks.

I can't say, given everything that has happened through the years, including what I witnessed firsthand, that I can entirely blame doctors who make decisions different from my father's. There have been times when, out of concern for his well-being as well as for my own peace of mind, I've wanted him to join their ranks. To steer clear of a controversy that divides our nation like no other, and that often seems to produce only an absence of reason and blind rage. But parents don't always do what their children want them to, and sometimes the lessons imparted as a consequence are among the most powerful and lasting ones. My father's decision to stay the course in the face of the most vociferous social movement of our time hasn't always been an easy or pleasant thing for me to watch. But it has taught me things I'm not sure I would otherwise know: about what it means to stand by one's principles; about the price that courage exacts; about the difference between saying you believe in something and committing your life to it. I don't know to what extent the qualities that account for his place in this story—his quiet determination, his fierce pride, his sense of duty, his refusal to compromise his beliefs in the face of a threat—mark my character as well. I do know that his example has shaped me profoundly, and that, as measured by integrity and courage, it is a standard I can only hope to match.

ON THE DAY my father does retire, the passions that swirl around abortion will not go away. They certainly won't disappear should the Supreme Court overturn *Roe v. Wade*, a possibility that may well be determined in the near future by the views of a man born in Buffalo, John G. Roberts, the federal judge whom George W. Bush appointed in 2005 to replace William H. Rehnquist as chief justice of the Supreme Court. Should a reversal come, the fierce convictions surrounding abortion—in America, at least—will remain. One can only hope that those who feel compelled to express their beliefs, no matter where they stand, do so in the only manner befitting a democracy—through words and principled action, not bullets or bombs—which is also the only method with the true power to persuade. "In the long run of history, immoral destructive means cannot bring about moral and constructive ends." The words are from a 1961 speech by Dr. Martin Luther King, Jr., "Love, Law, and Civil Disobedience." That their wisdom continues to elude us does not diminish their relevance and truth.

Notes

Note on Sources

All quotations in the book that are not attributed to sources in the notes below are drawn from interviews that I conducted. Some of the people I interviewed knew of my personal connection to the subject. Among those who did not, I neither went out of my way to hide my background nor to share it. Anyone who asked was of course told the truth. Otherwise, my aim was simply to talk to as many people as possible.

While every writer owes a debt to the scholars and journalists who have explored aspects of their subject beforehand, I would like to single out those who were especially helpful to me. On abortion, I have relied on Cynthia Gorney's *Articles of Faith*, an extremely balanced account that concentrates on events in Missouri but provides a valuable national overview as well, and James Risen and Judy L. Thomas's *Wrath of Angels*, the best single volume on the pro-life movement. I have also drawn on Kristen Luker's *Abortion and the Politics of Motherhood* and William Saletan's *Bearing Right*.

I owe a major debt to Mark Goldman, whose two books, *High Hopes* and *City on the Lake*, explore Buffalo's social history in depth. I am also grateful to Mark for the time he took to tour various neighborhoods of the city with me. On the abortion conflict in western New York, I am grateful to Gene Warner, a reporter at *The Buffalo News* who covered the subject for years and provided valuable tips on sources.

My understanding of religion in America draws on George M. Marsden's *Understanding Evangelicalism and Fundamentalism*, Garry Wills's *Under God*, Martin E. Marty and R. Scott Appleby's five-volume fundamentalism project, and the late William G. McLoughlin's *Revivals, Awakenings, and Reform*, the work of a brilliant scholar-activist who was also a mentor and a friend.

On Israel and the world of my father's past, I have relied on the numerous histories cited below by Tom Segev, Amos Oz's *A Tale of Love and Darkness*, and Yaron Ezrahi's *Rubber Bullets*, the book that best captures the mentality of my father's generation.

Finally, on the Slepian murder and James Kopp, in addition to the exhaustive coverage of the case in *The Buffalo News*, much of it by Dan Herbeck and Lou Michel, I have drawn on David Samuels's March 21, 1999, cover story in *The New York Times Magazine*, "The Making of a Fugitive," and Jon Wells's series for *The Hamilton Spectator*, "Sniper: The True Story of James Kopp."

Prologue

PAGE

2   keys, pager, and wallet: Transcript of stipulation of facts in trial, *The People of the State of New York v. James C. Kopp*, March 17, 2003, Indictment No. 98-2555-Sol. 25. Russian-made SKS rifle, 35. Full-metal jacketed bullet, 72. Path of the bullet and impact on Slepian, as observed by Erie County Associate Chief Medical Examiner Dr. Sung-ook Baik, 82–83. Just missing son Andrew, 26.

2   "Our cousins in the U.S.": Dan Herbeck, "Physician in Amherst Receives Protection," *The Buffalo News*, October 28, 1998.

5   a poll found: Gene Warner, "News Poll Finds Little Enthusiasm for Rescue Plans," *The Buffalo News*, April 5, 1992.

6   Since 1977: Statistics on clinic violence come from the National Abortion Federation, which keeps the most comprehensive data on the subject. Sent to author. The statistics are available at http://www.prochoice.org/pubs_research/publications/downloads/about_abor.

6   "our new wars of religion": Andrew Sullivan, "This Is a Religious War," *The New York Times Magazine*, October 7, 2001.

7   Between 1992 and 2005: Figures on number of hospitals and abortion providers come from Stanley Henshaw of the Alan Guttmacher Institute, which has compiled the most comprehensive data. Interview with author.

7   "We spend most": Phillip Lopate, *Portrait of My Body* (New York: Anchor Books, 1996), 169.

Chapter 1

13   "For a century": Tom Segev, *Elvis in Jerusalem: Post-Zionism and the Americanization of Israel* (New York: Metropolitan Books, 2001), 41.

14   "for people in the West": David Remnick, "The Spirit Level," *The New Yorker*, November 8, 2004.

15   Bialystok: My description draws on the entry in *Encyclopedia Judaica Jerusalem* (New York: MacMillan, 1971), volume 4.

16   "They love the land": Tom Segev, *One Palestine, Complete* (New York: Metropolitan Books, 1999), 258.

17   "In those days": Yaron Ezrahi, *Rubber Bullets* (Berkeley and Los Angeles: University of California Press, 1997), 153.

18   "almost a canon of existence": Amos Elon, *The Israelis: Founders and Sons* (New York: Holt, Rinehart & Winston, 1971), 224.

21   On that day: Mildred Spencer, "16 Abortions Performed Today in City Hospitals," *The Buffalo News*, July 1, 1970.

21   On George Michaels's vote, see Bill Kovach, "A Last-Minute Switch Rescues Bill After Bitter Debate," *The New York Times*, April 10, 1970.

21   12–4 *against*: "Eve and Hardt Stands Differ on Abortion Bill," *The Buffalo News*, April 10, 1970.

21   five of the area's six: "WNY Senators Vote 5–1 Against Abortion Bill," *The Buffalo News*, March 19, 1970.

21   "Today, my parents": Bill Kovach, "Final Approval of Abortion Bill Voted in Albany," *The New York Times*, April 11, 1970.

21   "I suppose I'm a square": "WNY Senators Vote 5–1 Against Abortion Bill."

21   a jarring spectacle: Mark Goldman, *High Hopes: The Rise and Decline of Buffalo, New York* (Albany: State University of New York Press, 1983), 260–63.

22   the Old First Ward . . . John Timon: Ibid., 78–80.

22   fallen by 30 percent: Neil Kraus, *Neighborhoods and Community Power: Buffalo Politics* (Albany: State University of New York Press, 2000), 29.

Chapter 2

25   "Nation Is Shocked": Robert D. McFadden, "Nation Is Shocked," *The New York Times*, January 23, 1973.

25   "a historic resolution": Warren Weaver, Jr., "High Court Rules Abortions Legal the First 3 Months," *The New York Times*, January 23, 1973.

25   "Shocking and appalling": "Catholic Physicians Condemn Ruling Allowing Abortions," *The Buffalo News*, January 26, 1973.

26   "Tragic": Dick Burke, "Press Meets Bishop Head and He Speaks His Mind," *The Buffalo News*, January 24, 1973.

26   "The present Supreme Court": Joseph Craft, " 'Conservative' on Abortion," *The Washington Post*, January 25, 1973.

26   "Supreme Court Allows": John P. MacKenzie, "Supreme Court Allows Early-Stage Abortions," *The Washington Post*, January 23, 1973.

26   Six weeks after: Richard L. Madden, "Mail to Javits and Buckley Dominated by Letters from the Foes of Abortion," *The New York Times*, March 10, 1973.

27   262,807 abortions: "8,923 Abortions Reported in County," *The Buffalo News*, September 1, 1972.

28   only to see Governor Nelson Rockefeller veto it: "Rocky's Vetoes," *The Washington Post*, Sunday May 14, 1972.

28   "The Court's verdict": "Respect for Privacy," *The New York Times*, January 24, 1973.

28   "to quiet a bitter moral controversy": "Closing Off Abortion Debate," *The Buffalo News*, January 23, 1973.

28   "painful tests of liberty ahead": Anthony Lewis, "Liberty, New and Old," *The New York Times*, February 3, 1973.

29   "Man Is Charged in Girl's Death," *The Buffalo News*, July 5, 1955. "Police Seek to Extradite Youth in Operation Case," *The Buffalo News*, December 4, 1941.

29   Among the trial transcripts: *The People of the State of New York v. Juanita Davis, Sophia Clara Nagi, and David F. Rose*, tried before the Hon. Lee L. O'Houry, November 15, 1950, in New York State Supreme Court. File date of trial is July 17, 1951.

30   In New York City: Leslie J. Regan, *When Abortion Was a Crime: Women, Medicine and Law in the United States, 1867–1973* (Berkeley and Los Angeles: University of California Press, 1997), 211.

30   Chicago's Cook County Hospital: Ibid., 209.

30   "An estimated three": Mildred Spencer, "What Guarantees of Life for Unborn Child?" *The Buffalo News*, April 8, 1967.

31   "I was determined": Mildred Spencer, "Divorcee's Visit to Abortionist: 'I'll Never Forget That Office,'" *The Buffalo News*, April 22, 1967.

31   Another woman described going to a hotel: Mildred Spencer, "A Tragic Toll—Up to 10,000 Deaths a Year," *The Buffalo News*, April 17, 1967.

31   "It was like the end of the world": Mildred Spencer, "A Mother's Torment Over Her Daughter: 'I Had No Choice,'" *The Buffalo News*, April 12, 1967.

31   A study performed: Mildred Spencer, "Negro Mother Tells of Deciding Factors in Difficult Decision," *The Buffalo News*, April 24, 1967.

31   "So many Negroes": "Negro Mother Tells of Deciding Factors in Difficult Decision."

31   In 1962: Details of the ALI model code and the Finkbine case appear in James Risen and Judy Thomas, *Wrath of Angels: The American Abortion War* (New York: Basic Books, 1998), 11–14. See also "Abortion: Mercy—or Murder?" *Newsweek*, August 13, 1962.

32   "Bill of Rights": Ruth Rosen, *The World Split Open: How the Modern Women's Movement Changed America* (New York: Viking, 2000), 82–83. Details on NOW's founding, 74.

32   "The only position": Ibid., 108.

33   "the hidden injuries": Ibid., chapter 5, passim.

34   "When we talk": Kristin Luker, *Abortion and the Politics of Motherhood* (Berkeley and Los Angeles: University of California Press, 1984), 97.

34   This network of ministers: For details of its formation, see Cynthia Gorney, *Articles of Faith: A Frontline History of the Abortion Wars* (New York: Simon & Schuster, 1998), 32–35.

35   A poll conducted: Jack Rosenthal, "Survey Finds 50% Back Liberalization of Abortion Law," *The New York Times*, October 28, 1971. 64 percent: Jack Rosenthal, "Survey Finds Majority, in Shift, Now Favors Liberalized Laws," *The New York Times*, August 25, 1972.

35   That same year: Rosen, *The World Split Open*, see timeline in front of the book.

36   "Every Jewish mother": Yael Yishai, "The Hidden Agenda: Abortion Politics in Israel," *Journal of Social Policy*, vol. 22, no. 2 (April 1993), 193–212. All details here drawn from Yishai.

36   "simply water": Elliott N. Dorff, *Matters of Life and Death: A Jewish Approach to Modern Medical Ethics* (Philadelphia: Jewish Publication Society, 1998), 128.

36   polls of Israelis: "The Hidden Agenda," 203.

37   a survey of 33,000: Jane E. Brody, "Doctors in Poll Favor Abortions," *The New York Times*, May 13, 1973.

37   "stretching, twisting": Jane E. Brody, "Abortion: Once a Whispered Problem, Now a Public Debate," *The New York Times*, May 8, 1967.

38   "Let us glance": "Criminal Abortions," *Buffalo Medical Journal and Monthly Review*, vol. 14, no. 4 (September 1858), 250.

38   physicians set about: James C. Mohr, *Abortion in America: The Origins and Evolution of National Policy, 1800–1900* (New York: Oxford University Press, 1978).

38   the birthrate among U.S.-born women: N. E. Hull and Peter Charles Hoffer, *Roe v. Wade: The Abortion Rights Controversy in American History* (Lawrence: University Press of Kansas, 2001), 25. Also see Mohr, *Abortion in America*, 82.

38   "Now we have ladies": "Criminal Abortions," 249.

39   ratio of abortions: Mohr, *Abortion in America*, 81 (citing a Michigan study esti-
      mating ratio of abortions to live births at 1 to 2), 78–79 (estimating ratio in New
      York as 1 to 4); Hull and Hoffer, *Roe v. Wade*, 27.

39   Bronx birth control clinic: Regan, *When Abortion Was a Crime*, 23.

39   In 1936: "25% of Maternal Deaths Laid to Illegal Operations," *The Buffalo News*,
      April 21, 1936.

39   "I don't like to admit it": Gene Warner, "Slepian Discusses Pressures Faced in
      Abortion Work," *The Buffalo News*, April 19, 1993.

39   "not a happy assignment": Linda Greenhouse, "Documents Reveal the Evolu-
      tion of a Justice," *The New York Times*, March 4, 2004.

40   "the right . . . to be let alone": Edward Lazarus, *Closed Chambers: The Rise,
      Fall and Future of the Modern Supreme Court* (New York: Penguin Books,
      1999), 368.

40   "For me, abortion": Quoted in William Saletan, *Bearing Right* (Berkeley: Uni-
      versity of California Press, 2003), 248. See also "'Abortion Is a Personal Choice,'"
      interview with Barbara Bush, *Newsweek*, August 24, 1992.

41   "Raw Judicial Power": John T. Noonan, Jr., "Raw Judicial Power," *National Re-
      view*, March 2, 1973.

41   the opinion's author: Linda Greenhouse, *Becoming Justice Blackmun: Harry
      Blackmun's Supreme Court Journey* (New York: Times Books, 2005), 5. For the
      approval by Rehnquist, see 46–47.

41   "Two out of three": George Gallup, "Abortion Seen Up to Woman, Doctor," *The
      Washington Post*, August 25, 1972. Greenhouse cites the article in *Becoming Jus-
      tice Blackmun*, 91.

42   how bitterly it divided: See, for example, "Pennsylvania: Bitter Abortion Battle,"
      Time, December 11, 1972.

42   "motel abortoriums": "Health Official Foresees Rise of Motel Abortoriums," *The
      Buffalo News*, June 25, 1970.

42   "massive recruiting call": *Articles of Faith*, 177.

Chapter 3

45   a privately sponsored poll: "Busing Rejected in Suburban Poll," *The Buffalo
      News*, May 25, 1970. Also Bob Buyer, "Keller's Report Chides Williamsville's
      Hostility to Voluntary Busing," *The Buffalo News*, December 11, 1970.

46   a local observer: *News of the Year: Buffalo's 150 Years of History* (Buffalo, N.Y.:
      University Press, 1982), entry for 1973.

48   no fewer than: "38 Major Plants Have Left Area in Last 5 Years," News Special,
      The Buffalo News, January 9, 1976.

48   "Down and Out": *The New York Times Magazine*, February 9, 1975.

48   In 1974: "Insight Buffalo, 1975," report prepared for Mayor Stanley Makowski by
      the Comprehensive Planning and Management Program, 53. This and other
      "Insight Buffalo" reports are located in special collections of the Buffalo and
      Erie County Public Library.

48   13.2 percent: "Insight Buffalo, 1976," 62.

48   "The most repetitive": Mike McKeating, "Dated Plants, High Costs, Changing
      Times Take Toll," *The Buffalo News*, January 28, 1976.

49   184,300 factory jobs: "The Frontier's Year: 1966," *Buffalo Magazine*, January
      1967.
49   "The Niagara Frontier": Ibid.
49   "roaring into 1968": Jim Reisch, "A Booming 1968 Forecast by 95% of Area Busi-
      nessmen," *The Buffalo News*, December 30, 1967.
49   "the highwater mark": David Halberstam, *The Reckoning* (New York: William
      Morrow, 1986), 362.
49   rice, and lard: Mark Goldman, *High Hopes: The Rise and Decline of Buffalo,
      New York* (Albany: State University of New York Press, 1983), 225.
50   "One huge Forest": William Chazanof, *Joseph Ellicott and The Holland Land
      Company* (Syracuse, N.Y.: Syracuse University Press, 1970), 100–01.
50   burned it to the ground: Goldman, *High Hopes*, 13.
50   "incredible": Ibid., 28.
50   "The whole river": André Jardin, *Tocqueville: A Biography* (New York: Farrar,
      Straus & Giroux, 1998), 133.
50   "What voices spoke": Charles Dickens, *American Notes* (New York: Fawcett,
      1961), 228–29.
50   Joseph Dart: *Buffalo Architecture: A Guide* (Boston: MIT Press, 1999), 29, and
      Goldman, *High Hopes*, 58.
50   By 1867: David Gerber, *The Making of an American Pluralism: Buffalo, New
      York, 1825–60* (Urbana: University of Illinois Press, 1989), 52.
51   three fourths of the nation's grain: Ibid., 6.
51   "I went down to the granaries": Goldman, *High Hopes*, 58.
51   eight of whom served as mayor: Gerber, *American Pluralism*, 11.
51   "dirty, mean-looking": Quoted in ibid., 26.
51   "the infected district": Ibid., 14. "work or bread": Ibid., 254–57.
51   "the best planned": *Buffalo Architecture: A Guide*, 19.
51   "noble city": Rollin Lynde Hartt, "The City at Night," *The Atlantic*, Septem-
      ber 1901.
52   He was in good spirits: Jeffrey W. Seibert, *"I Have Done My Duty": The Com-
      plete Story of the Assassination of President McKinley* (Bowie, Md.: Heritage
      Books, 2002), 46. Seibert is also the source for the detail that Czolgosz wielded
      an Iver Johnson pistol, on page 53 of his book.
52   "The Foulest Crime": Thomas Leary and Elizabeth Sholes, *Buffalo's Pan-
      American Exposition* (Charleston, S.C.: Arcadia Publishing, 1998), 114. Much of
      my description of the Pan-American Exposition comes from this book.
53   "This wonderful plant": Goldman, *High Hopes*, 135.
53   By 1914: Elwin H. Powell, *The Design of Discord: Studies of Anomie* (New
      Brunswick, N.J.: Transaction Books, 1988), 92. Chapter seven of Powell's book
      presents a detailed examination of class tensions in Buffalo between 1910 and
      1920.
53   "One never-ending factory": "Buffalo Hits Another Jackpot," *Business Week*, De-
      cember 3, 1955.
53   gleaming twelve-page photo spread: "Made in Buffalo," *Fortune*, July 1951.
53   "More than 200,000": Tom Dudleston, "Labor Optimistic About Future,"
      Courier Express, November 22, 1955. The same article reports that "manufactur-
      ing production workers led the state in average weekly earnings."
54   "Theoretically, if a union": "Our Jobless Speak of Their Problems," *The Buffalo
      News*, March 15, 1975.

54 "But the United Steel Workers": All quotes from workers come from "Our Job-less Speak of Their Problems."

55 steel strike of 1919: See Thomas E. Leary and Elizabeth C. Sholes, *From Fire to Rust* (Buffalo, N.Y.: Buffalo and Erie County Historical Society, 1987), 48, and Goldman, *High Hopes*, 206.

55 "CIO, CIO": James Richard McDonnell, *The Rise of the CIO in Buffalo, New York, 1936–1942*, unpublished Ph.D. thesis, University of Wisconsin, 1970. Can be found in special collections department of the Buffalo and Erie County Public Library. The description of workers being beaten up and bloodied appears on page 165.

56 only four unorganized plants: George Alexander Blair, *Struggling for a Union: Electrical Workers in Buffalo, New York, 1933–1956*, Ph.D. thesis, State University of New York at Buffalo, 1993, 33.

56 "Solid Unionism is": Goldman, *High Hopes*, 205.

56 58,956: Leary and Sholes, *From Fire to Rust*, 129.

57 Two decades later: Details on this wildcat strike in ibid., 107.

57 "When I joined": McDonnell, *The Rise of the CIO*, 151.

58 "We have millionaires": Quoted in Buffalo Labor Calendar, published by the New York State School of Industrial and Labor Relations, Cornell University, 1981.

58 A quarter century later: Powell, *The Design of Discord*, 84.

Chapter 4

62 "the only rational solution": Lawrence Lader, *Abortion II: Making the Revolution* (Boston: Beacon Press, 1973), 150.

62 "Raped by Medical": Cynthia Gorney, *Articles of Faith: A Frontline History of the Abortion Wars* (New York: Simon & Schuster, 1998), 203.

62 more than half of all abortions: Statistics from Richard Lacayo, "Abortion: The Future Is Already Here," *Time*, May 4, 1992.

62 In western New York: Rose Ciotta, "Abortion Decision *Roe v. Wade*: 25 Years Later—A Quarter-Century of Heart Rending Choices," *The Buffalo News*, January 18, 1998.

63 Jesse Ketchum: "Jesse Ketchum Is Expelled from Medical Society," *The Buffalo News*, April 3, 1972. Serving time in jail: Henry D. Locke, Jr., "Ketchum Paroled in Abortion Death," *Courier Express*, March 19, 1976.

65 "housewife": "Erie County Reports 1,064 Legal Abortions in First Three Months," *The Buffalo News*, November 11, 1970.

65 On August 2, 1975: James Risen and Judy Thomas, *Wrath of Angels: The American Abortion War* (New York: Basic Books, 1998), 62.

66 A year later: Ibid., 74. All details on O'Keefe are drawn from Risen and Thomas's account.

67 "the audience may change": Quoted in Gorney, *Articles of Faith*, 104.

67 "a referendum on": Kristin Luker, *Abortion and the Politics of Motherhood* (Berkeley: University of California Press, 1984), 193.

68 "a Democrat, Republican": Fred C. Shapiro, " 'Right to Life' Has a Message for New York State Legislators," *The New York Times Magazine*, August 20, 1972.

69 "I had supposed": Michelle McKeegan, *Abortion Politics: Mutiny in the Ranks of the Right* (New York: Free Press, 1992), 9.

69   one poll showed: Ibid., 30.

69   "forty-seven-year-old housewife": Richard M. Scammon and Ben J. Wattenberg, *The Real Majority* (New York: Donald I. Fine, 1970), 70.

69   "That the Democrats": Ibid., 63.

69   "Preempt the Social Issue": Bruce J. Schulman, *The Seventies: The Great Shift in American Culture, Society and Politics* (New York: Da Capo Press, 2002), 38.

70   In 1934: Harold P. Jarvis, "City Goes Democratic on Affiliation by 6,013," *Courier Express*, December 21, 1934.

70   For decades: Paul MacClennan, "WNY Governments Show Rising Democratic Power," *The Buffalo News*, November 9, 1971.

70   "neighborhood schools": Mark Goldman, *City on the Lake: The Challenge of Change in Buffalo, New York* (Buffalo, N.Y.: Prometheus Books, 1990), 119. Details on riots, 113.

71   "Most of these voters": David A. Gerber, "The Fate of the Righteous Style in Precinct 20: The 1972 McGovern Campaign in a Buffalo Neighborhood," *New York History*, October 1999, 464.

71   "Nixon Bungled": Rowland Evans and Robert Novak, "Nixon Bungled Abortion Issue," *The Washington Post*, May 14, 1972.

71   But Nixon was pioneering: See, for background, "In Center of Latest Dispute on Abortion: Nixon, Rockefellers," *U.S. News & World Report*, May 22, 1972; see also "New York: The Abortion Issue," *Time*, May 22, 1972, which points out that mail to Nixon in response to the recommendations of the U.S. Commission on Population Growth and the American Future, which had recommended loosening abortion laws and broadening access to contraception, was running 5–1 *against* these measures.

72   narrow margin of Nixon's defeat: Ray Herman, "Nixon Lost Buffalo by 21,500 Votes," *The Buffalo News*, November 11, 1972. "There are approximately 60,000 more Democrats than Republicans in Buffalo," Herman noted. "In the race four years ago, Humphrey's Buffalo plurality [over Nixon] was 71,574."

73   "This city is fighting": "What's It Like—Living in a City Drowning in Snow," *U.S. News & World Report*, February 14, 1977.

73    $300 million: "After the Thaw," *Newsweek*, July 25, 1977.

73   to more than 70,000: Neil Krauss, *Race, Neighborhoods and Community Power* (Albany: State University of New York Press, 2000), 44.

75   "hearts like caraway seeds": Paul Jayes, "City Hall's Feisty Boss," *Courier Express Sunday Magazine*, February 8, 1981.

76   "Buffalo Democrats Appall": Jerry Allan, "Buffalo Democrats Appall NYC Liberals," *The Buffalo News*, April 27, 1974. Other background articles on Griffin include George Borrelli, "Griffin Pledges Reforms to Deliver Basic Services: The Man . . . and the Issues," *The Buffalo News*, August 26, 1977; Ralph Dibble, "Griffin Gives Scoop on Days as Grain Worker in 1st War," *The Buffalo News*, February 10, 1979; George Gates, "Maverick Mayor-elect Wears Brand of Early Years in City's First Ward," *The Buffalo News*, November 12, 1977.

Chapter 5

78   "About 70,000": Tom Segev, *The Seventh Million: The Israelis and the Holocaust* (New York City: Hill & Wang, 1993), 90.

83   "I have deemed it": Selig Adler and Thomas E. Connolly, *From Ararat to Suburbia: The History of the Jewish Community of Buffalo* (Philadelphia: Jewish Publication Society, 1960), 8.

84   Even without: The information in this paragraph is drawn from Adler and Connolly, *From Ararat to Suburbia*. On the founding of the Western hotel, 46–47; on the eight synagogues and the William Street ghetto, 320; on the fraternal order of Labor Zionism, 302; on "Socialism as Messiah," 247.

84   "Russian Hebrews": Ibid., 257.

84   "Many of them": Ibid., 170.

85   "The pretended miracles": Mark Goldman, *High Hopes: The Rise and Decline of Buffalo, New York* (Albany: State University of New York Press, 1983), 114.

86   "To be a Protestant": Will Herberg, *Protestant, Catholic, Jew: An Essay in American Religious Sociology* (Garden City, N.Y.: Doubleday, 1955), 274.

86   "in a secularist framework": Ibid., 15; "secularized Puritanism," ibid., 94.

87   "the year of the evangelical": "Born Again!" *Newsweek*, October 25, 1976. Figures on the number of Americans saying religion was "increasing its influence" appear in "A Portrait of Religious America," *U.S. News & World Report*, April 11, 1977.

87   "What religious institutions": "Why Churches Are Worried," *U.S. News & World Report*, March 23, 1970.

87   the proportion that reported: David Frum, *How We Got Here: The '70s: The Decade That Brought You Modern Life—For Better or Worse* (New York: Basic Books, 1999), 149.

87   During this same period: "Protestants: Away from Activism and Back to the Basics," *U.S. News & World Report*, April 11, 1977.

88   fifty-two new prayer groups: Cindy Skrycki, "Praise the Lord," *The Buffalo News*, October 1, 1977.

88   Nearly one in five: George Marsden, *Understanding Fundamentalism and Evangelicalism* (Grand Rapids, Mich.: Eerdmans, 1991), 78.

88   "There can be no revival": Garry Wills, "What Religious Revival?" *Psychology Today*, April 1976, 80.

89   "I would find it": Marsden, *Understanding Fundamentalism*, 103.

89   "one of the major sins": William Martin, *With God On Our Side* (New York: Broadway Books, 1996), 201.

89   "evangelize and build up": Marsden, *Understanding Fundamentalism*, 61; "lingering aspirations," Ibid., 68.

90   "Your tax dollars": Michelle McKeegan, *Abortion Politics: Mutiny in the Ranks of the Right* (New York: Free Press, 1992), 9.

90   "We talk about": Cynthia Gorney, *Articles of Faith: A Frontline History of the Abortion Wars* (New York: Simon & Schuster, 1998), 343.

90   "Unfortunately, there are many": Ibid., 349.

91   "a beautifully accurate": Tim Stafford, "The Abortion Wars," *Christianity Today*, October 6, 1989.

91   "Listen, God used": Martin, *With God On Our Side*, 197. "Guru of Fundamentalism": Kenneth L. Woodward, "Guru of Fundamentalism," *Newsweek*, November 1, 1982.

91   *"The bottom line"*: Francis A. Schaeffer, *A Christian Manifesto* (Westchester, Ill.: Crossway Books, 1981), 93.

92   *"For a dissolute"*: Louis Menand, *The Metaphysical Club: A Story of Ideas in America* (New York: Farrar, Straus & Giroux, 2002), 81.

92   *"psychic highway"*: Whitney R. Cross, *The Burned Over District* (New York: Harper & Row, 1955), 3. All details in this paragraph come from Cross's book.

92   *"You have no idea"*: David Gerber, *The Making of an American Pluralism: Buffalo, New York, 1825–60* (Urbana: University of Illinois Press, 1989), 26.

Chapter 6

97   *"Let's don't give up"*: "150 Hear Call for Banning of Abortions," *The Buffalo News*, January 23, 1981. Also, "Events to Protest Abortion Ruling," *The Buffalo News*, January 21, 1981.

97   *"We want life"*: "Abortion Foes Meet with Reagan After March in Capital," *The New York Times*, January 23, 1981; Janet Cooke, "Abortion Foes Stage 8th Annual 'March for Life,'" *The Washington Post*, January 23, 1981; *"we want Reagan"*: Steven R. Weissman, "Reagan Orders Cut in Federal Travel and Consultant Use," *The New York Times*, January 23, 1981.

98   *"We're not, as some would have us believe"*: From the text of Reagan's first inaugural address, available at http://www.reaganfoundation.org/reagan/speeches/first .asp. All subsequent quotations in this paragraph are drawn from the same text.

99   *"Buffalo's got a spirit"*: "We're Talking Proud," *Western New York*, April 1981. All details of the campaign are drawn from this article.

99   A few days after Christmas: Ed Kelly, "Unemployment at 15.3% for Area," *The Buffalo News*, December 30, 1982.

100   the international distress signal: Incident described in Mark Goldman, *City on the Lake: The Challenge of Change in Buffalo, New York* (Buffalo, N.Y.: Prometheus Books, 1990), 177.

100   from 30 percent to 13 percent: Jerry Zremski and Susan Schulman, "Shift in Federal, State Policies Leaves City Bleeding," *The Buffalo News*, March 12, 1997.

100   The Village of Kenmore: John W. Percy, *Pioneer Suburb: A Comprehensive History of Kenmore, New York, 1899–1974* (Kenmore, N.Y.: Partner's Press, Abgott & Smith Print, 1974).

105   *"to dream heroic"*: From Reagan's first inaugural address, at http://www.reagan foundation.org/reagan/speeches/first.asp.

106   *"Outside the United States"*: Fred Barnes, "How a Cause Was Born," *The Wall Street Journal* (online editorial page, http://www_opinionjournal.com/ac/?id= 110004264), November 6, 2003.

106   *"like William Jennings Bryan"*: Frances Fitzgerald, "A Reporter at Large: A Disciplined Charging Army," *The New Yorker*, May 18, 1981.

107   *"Right-to-Life Day"*: "'Right-to-Life Day' in City Is Proclaimed by Griffin," *The Buffalo News*, January 22, 1982. Details on the march around city hall and Washington are in Agnes Palazzetti, "Right-to-Life Group Marches Here, in D.C., Against Abortion," *The Buffalo News*, January 23, 1982.

107   *"My finest hour"*: William Martin, *With God On Our Side* (New York: Broadway Books 1996), 220.

107   *"a constitutional entitlement"*: Supreme Court of the United States, *Harris v.*

McRae, 448 U.S. 297, April 21, 1980, June 30, 1980. The passage quoted appears in section 2b of the opinion. Brennan's comment appears in his dissent.

107   plummeted, from 350,000: Lesley Oelsner, "Strong Impact on Poor Reported from Cut in Medicaid Abortions," *The New York Times*, December 26, 1978.

108   "It's murder": "Abortion Foes from Erie County Join Lobbying Effort in Albany," *The Buffalo News*, March 14, 1978. On the Niagara County Legislature, see Agnes Palazzetti, "Niagara Legislature Defies Ruling by State on Abortion Payments," *The Buffalo News*, September 22, 1977.

108   "You can't endorse": Stryker McGuire, "The Battle of the Button," *Newsweek*, September 1, 1980.

108   On Reagan blaming doctors for the outcome of the permissive abortion law he signed in California, see Lou Cannon, *President Reagan: The Role of a Lifetime* (New York: Simon & Schuster, 1991), 812.

108   "to present a program": Michael Schaller and George Rising, *The Republican Ascendancy: American Politics, 1968–2001* (Wheeling, Ill.: Harlan Davidson, 2002), 81.

109   "victory for women's rights": quoted in Steven R. Weisman, "Reagan Nominating Woman, An Arizona Appeals Judge, To Serve On Supreme Court: Reaction Is Mixed," *The New York Times*, July 8, 1981. See also Fred Barbash, "Conservatives Feud in Wake of O'Connor Choice," *The Washington Post*, July 9, 1981.

109   That same year: "Griffin Seeks Action to Ban Abortion," *The Buffalo News*, February 5, 1976.

109   "It is no secret": Leslie Bennetts, "Antiabortion Forces in Disarray," *The New York Times*, September 22, 1981.

110   "We are a movement": Ibid.

110   "Do you favor": Poll cited in "Thousands March on Washington in Abortion Protest," *The Buffalo News*, January 23, 1982.

110   the GOP had risked: "Stands on Abortion, ERA Could Cost GOP Votes," *The Washington Post*, July 23, 1980; E. J. Dionne, Jr., "Even Carter's Successes May Be Helping Reagan," *The New York Times*, June 19, 1980.

110   "What do you want": Lou Cannon, *Reagan* (New York: G. P. Putnam's Sons, 1982), 316.

Chapter 7

112   "Some of the work": Karen Brady, "Abortion Foe Urges Allies to All-out Fight," *The Buffalo News*, May 18, 1985.

113   "the Green Beret": Linda Witt, "Man with a Mission," *Chicago Tribune Sunday Magazine*, August 11, 1985.

113   "Birch Bayh": James Risen and Judy Thomas, *Wrath of Angels: The American Abortion War* (New York: Basic Books, 1998), 109.

113   "disgusting": Witt, "Man with a Mission."

113   "If we don't start": Ibid.

113   "I can't get too excited": Ibid.

114   "Close your legs": Ibid.

114   "Conflict is always": Risen and Thomas, *Wrath of Angels*, 104.

114   "If you can't convert them": Ibid., 112.

114   "Know who your enemies are": Brady, "Abortion Foe Urges Allies to All-out Fight."

114   *"Murder!* Abortion is" through "Dear Friends" letter: Louise Continelli, "The Abortion Battle in Buffalo," *Buffalo Magazine,* October 27, 1985.

116   "suspicious and afraid": Mark Goldman, *High Hopes: The Rise and Decline of Buffalo* (Albany: State University of New York Press, 1983), 242.

116   "I very much resent": "Citizens Offer Comments on Recent Disorder at U.B.," *The Buffalo News,* March 20, 1970. For accounts of the general unrest, see "Police Move onto UB Campus," *Courier Express,* March 9, 1970; "Campus, City Police Battle UB Militants," *Courier Express,* January 26, 1970; "UB Official Quits Post, Protests Calling Police," *Courier Express,* March 10, 1970; and see Goldman, *High Hopes,* 260–63.

117   "anti-American activities": "Vets Cite Red Flags on Campus," *Courier Express,* March 17, 1970.

117   1,200 priests: Ed Kelly, "Prelate Named Buffalo Bishop," *The Buffalo News,* January 23, 1973.

117   "enclave mentality": Jay P. Dolan, *In Search of an American Catholicism: A History of Religion and Culture in Tension* (New York: Oxford University Press, 2002), 147.

117   "a nation apart": Quoted in ibid., 132.

118   Between 1959 and 1974: Timothy Richard Allan, "Roman Catholicism and Inner Urban Demographic Change in Buffalo, New York, 1960–1980: A Quantitative and Interpretive Overview," Ph.D thesis, State University of New York at Buffalo, 1992, 36 (in the special collections of the Buffalo and Eric County Public Library). The quotes in the following paragraph appear on these pages: "Neighborhood is going down," 46; "Much spiritual apathy breeding," 46; "They are mortally afraid of blacks," 47.

118   "The exodus of business": Quoted in Allan, "Roman Catholicism," 50.

119   "I feel it is tragic": Dick Burke, "Press Meets Bishop Head and He Speaks His Mind," *The Buffalo News,* January 24, 1973.

119   "We urge you": George Dugan, "State's 8 Catholic Bishops Ask Fight on Abortion Bill," *The New York Times,* February 13, 1967.

120   "tightly-knit . . . pro-life units": Risen and Thomas, *Wrath of Angels,* 153.

120   "willing to put": Ibid., 154.

120   "We must be ready": Paul Carroll, "Director of Abortion Fight Says Church Must Be Teacher, Healer," *The Buffalo News,* April 24, 1980.

121   "Prudence without fortitude": Risen and Thomas, *Wrath of Angels,* 155.

121   "Wimps for Life": Jerry Adler and John McCormick, "Chicago's Unsilent Scream," *Newsweek,* January 14, 1985.

121   "one mainstream and polite": Risen and Thomas, *Wrath of Angels,* 105.

123   44 percent of Catholics: Kenneth A. Briggs, "A Poll of Catholics Points Up Diversity," *The New York Times,* March 3, 1978.

123   45 percent agreed: Cited in Kenneth A. Briggs, "Catholic Prelates Organizing a Drive Against Abortions," *The New York Times,* August 17, 1977.

123   On *Humanae Vitae,* see John T. McGreevy, *Catholicism and American Freedom* (New York: W. W. Norton, 2003), 246.

123   Barbara Howe published: "Half of Women Seeking Abortion at Clinic Catholic," *The Buffalo News,* October 11, 1979.

123   "Despite the teaching": Governor Mario Cuomo, "Religious Belief and Public Morality: A Catholic Governor's Perspective," speech delivered at Notre Dame University, September 13, 1984. Available at http://pewforum.org/docs/[romt.php?DocID=14 (© The Pew Forum on Religion and Public Life).

124 "cannot be altered": Gene Warner, "Bishop Says Abortion Must Be Opposed as Much as Murder," *The Buffalo News*, September 18, 1984.
125 "We feel we're under siege": Quoted in Continelli, "The Abortion Battle in Buffalo."

Chapter 8

126 "to reintroduce the Word": "About Faith and Action," Web site, http://www.faith andaction.org/DDDAboutus.htm.
127 "We have been offended": Dave Robinson, "200 Abortion Foes in Kenmore Protest 'Dumping' of 4 Fetuses," *The Buffalo News*, September 25, 1987.
128 a group of pro-life activists: "41 from Area Held in Sit-in over Abortion," *The Buffalo News*, November 30, 1987.
128 Cherry Hill, New Jersey: Event described in James Risen and Judy Thomas, *Wrath of Angels: The American Abortion War* (New York: Basic Books, 1998), 262.
131 For Tom Wolfe's take on the Me Decade, see Tom Wolfe, *The Purple Decades* (New York: Farrar, Straus & Giroux, 1982), 282.
132 "*Our perspective is unashamedly*": Randall A. Terry, *To Rescue the Children: A Manual for Christ-Centered Pro-Life Activism*, Project Life, 3.
133 "liberal elite" and "rock music gods": Ibid., 22.
133 "The moral chaos": Ibid., 24.
133 "is a sword": Ibid., 6.
133 "Society, which is sick": David Briggs, "Evangelical Surge Stirring Ferment in WNY Religious Life," *Buffalo Evening News*, January 5, 1986.
135 "This is just outrageous": Michael Levy, "63 Seized as Abortion Protesters Block Kenmore Medical Offices," *The Buffalo News*, December 23, 1988.
138 "Death threats, obstruction": Richard Lacayo, "Abortion: The Future Is Already Here," *Time*, May 4, 1992.
139 "I respect people": Gene Warner, "3 Area Doctors Speak Out for Woman's Right to Choose," *The Buffalo News*, November 20, 1988.
139 "It's probably made me": Ibid.
139 Daren Dryzmala: For background on Dryzmala in Michael Beebe, "No Welcome Mat for 'House Call' Pastor," *The Buffalo News*, December 20, 1998.
140 "STOP THE KILLING": Michael Beebe, "With Project Jericho as Focal Point, Abortion Battle Sparks Violence," *The Buffalo News*, December 7, 1988.
140 "the one retreat": "Excerpts from Ruling in Picketing Ban Case," *Special to the New York Times*, June 28, 1988.
141 "The home is different" and "to intrude upon": "Excerpts from Ruling in Picketing Ban Case."

Chapter 9

147 "baloney": Dave Condren, "Degenhart Defends Police Response in Abortion Protests," *The Buffalo News*, November 1, 1988.
147 "We're not going": Tom Buckham, "Mayor Hints He Ordered Delay in Arrest of Abortion Protesters," *The Buffalo News*, November 3, 1988.

147 "My breakfast business": Charles Anzalone, "Police Slowness at Protest Assailed," *The Buffalo News*, October 29, 1988.

147 dismissed trespassing charges: Matt Gryta, "New Charges Filed for 125 in Abortion Protest," *The Buffalo News*, January 18, 1989; also see Matt Gryta, "Judge Refuses to Rescind Freeing of 83 Abortion Foes," *The Buffalo News*, January 21, 1989.

148 "Safe, legal abortion was not an option": Barbara O'Brien, "Forum on Personal Experiences Relates Abortion's Human Factor," *The Buffalo News*, March 23, 1989.

149 "best left up to a woman": William Saletan, *Bearing Right: How Conservatives Won the Abortion War* (Berkeley: University of California Press, 2003), 46–47.

151 highest rate of teenage abortion: Agnes Palazzetti, "Groups Target City Teen Pregnancies," *The Buffalo News*, February 9, 1986.

151 "contraceptive counseling": Agnes Palazzetti, "Youngsters Offer Insights into Why City Has Highest Teen Pregnancy Rate in State," *The Buffalo News*, April 11, 1993. Figures for 1989—on Buffalo having more teen abortions than anywhere except New York City—appear in Margaret Hammersley, "More Than Half of Pregnancies Among Young Here End in Abortions," *The Buffalo News*, January 22, 1992. The article discusses health statistics from 1989.

151 "mind-boggling": Quoted in Hammersley, "More Than Half of Pregnancies."

152 15.5 per 1,000 live births: Agnes Palazzetti, "Buffalo Infant Death Rate Tops All Cities in State," *The Buffalo News*, March 14, 1993. The article reports figures from 1991.

152 On Margaret Sanger: See Ellen Chesler, *Woman of Valor: Margaret Sanger and the Birth Control Movement in America* (New York: Simon & Schuster, 1992), 216–17. Chesler notes that while Sanger did pander on occasion to academics and scientists sympathetic to eugenics, most of the leading eugenicists in America were vocal *opponents* of birth control, in part because they recognized Sanger was a sincere proponent of women with "a deep sympathy and compassion toward the overburdened poor."

153 "In addition to abortion": From materials provided to the author by Laura Grube.

153 "a Nazi death camp": Margaret Hammersley, "Comerford Targets School Library Books," *The Buffalo News*, March 29, 1990.

153 "How they murdered the Jews": Ibid.

154 "No I don't": Kevin Collison, "Griffin Calls Arcara Ruling 'Stupid,'" *The Buffalo News*, October 5, 1990.

155 "The clinics are run for profit": Louise Continelli, "The Abortion Battle in Buffalo," *Buffalo Magazine*, October 27, 1985.

156 "It is hard to imagine": David L. Chappell, *A Stone of Hope: Prophetic Religion and the Death of Jim Crow* (Chapel Hill: University of North Carolina Press, 2004), 102.

157 "ministers of Satan": Henry Davis, "Coalition to Support Abortion Rights," *The Buffalo News*, January 18, 1989.

157 Nazi storm troopers: Susan Schulman, "Nazi Label by Abortion Foe Denounced by Buffalo Police," *The Buffalo News*, November 21, 1988.

157 "It is becoming quite a burden": Gene Warner and Susan Schulman, "Charges Filed in Anti-Abortion Protests," *The Buffalo News*, February 18, 1989.

Chapter 10

160 "Arcara is a Catholic": Gene Warner, "Arcara Defies the Image as Target of Pro-Life Anger," *The Buffalo News*, September 20, 1992. Details on Arcara's order in Charles Anzalone, "Abortion Foes Barred from Blocking Clinics," *The Buffalo News*, September 27, 1990.

161 "Ladies and gentlemen": Quoted in James Risen and Judy Thomas, *Wrath of Angels: The American Abortion War* (New York: Basic Books, 1998), 333. I largely follow their account of the demonstrations in Wichita, though I have supplemented it with news reports.

161 "Do you plan": Agnes Palazzetti, "Pro-Life Leader Vows Major Effort Here," *The Buffalo News*, October 4, 1991.

161 "Greetings in the name of Jesus!": Copy of January 7, 1992, letter from Randall Terry, obtained by author.

161 "welcome him with open arms": Kevin Collison, "Griffin Says He Welcomes Terry Visit," *The Buffalo News*, September 30, 1991.

162 "I want to see": Palazzetti, "Pro-Life Leader Vows Major Effort Here."

162 "I don't want Buffalo police officers": Kevin Collison, "Council Joins Operation Rescue Foes," *The Buffalo News*, January 8, 1992.

162 "During these tough times": Jane Kwiatkowski, "Gorski Warns Terry That He's Not Welcome," *The Buffalo News*, January 5, 1992.

163 "confusion for the patient": *Speak Out! The Pro-Choice Network Newsletter*, vol. IV, no. 3 (April/May 1992).

165 "constitutional law in this area": Linda Greenhouse, "Supreme Court, 5–4, Narrowing Roe v. Wade, Upholds Sharp State Limits on Abortion," *The New York Times*, July 4, 1989. Blackmun's quotes appear in same article.

166 "Is this real?": Robert J. McCarthy and Phil Fairbanks, "600 Demonstrate Outside Four Clinics," *The Buffalo News*, April 21, 1992.

168 "Some doctors deliver babies": Robert J. McCarthy and Phil Fairbanks, "600 Demonstrate Outside Four Clinics," *The Buffalo News*, April 21, 1992.

168 "Our intention in this neighborhood": Tom Ernst and Phil Fairbanks, "200 Seized in Abortion Protest," *The Buffalo News*, April 22, 1992.

169 "This place is where": Charles Anzalone and Michael Beebe, "100 Arrested Outside Office of Dr. Press," *The Buffalo News*, May 1, 1992.

169 "very strong pro-life city": Terry quoted in Palazzetti, "Pro-life Leader Vows Major Effort Here."

169 a poll commissioned: Gene Warner, "News Poll Finds Little Enthusiasm for Rescue Plans," *The Buffalo News*, April 5, 1992.

170 "I thought I was in Beirut": Jane Kwiatkowski, "City of Good Neighbors Tested by Demonstrators," *The Buffalo News*, April 28, 1992. All other quotes from same article.

171 "the vulgar Sodomite lifestyle": "Crowd Backs Activist Who Opposes Abortion," *St. Louis Post-Dispatch*, February 13, 1998.

172 "No clinics were closed": Gene Warner, "Spring of Life Fails to Live Up to Hype," *The Buffalo News*, May 3, 1992.

172 "Operation Fizzle": Priscilla Painton, "Operation Fizzle," *Time*, May 4, 1992.

173 "I think the services": Mary Tabor, "Under Attack, Doctor Still Defends Abortions," *The New York Times*, April 28, 1992.

174 "We conclude the central holding": Quoted in Edward Lazarus, *Closed Chambers* (New York: Penguin, 1998), 482.

174 "The destiny of the woman": Quoted in N. E. Hill and Peter Charles Hoffer, *Roe v. Wade* (Lawrence: University of Kansas Press, 2001), 254.

174 "Only the most convincing": Lazarus, *Closed Chambers*, 476.

174 "By foreclosing all democratic": From Scalia dissent, available online at http://www.dickinson.edu/~rudaleva/ppcasey.htm#Scalia.

Chapter 11

179 "Don't stop thinking": Donn Esmonde, "Savor the Glow, Masiello: The Tough Part Comes Next," *The Buffalo News*, November 3, 1993.

179 "the politics of inclusion": Gene Warner, "Masiello Meets with Gay Leaders," *The Buffalo News*, October 22, 1993.

179 "fruits and queers": See Michael Beebe, "Griffin's Years in Power: A Tale of Two Jimmy's," *The Buffalo News*, December 26, 1993.

180 "Savor the glow": Esmonde, "Savor the Glow, Masiello."

180 Buffalo's economy: David C. Perry and Beverly McLean, "The Aftermath of Deindustrialization: The Meaning of 'Economic Restructuring' in Buffalo, New York," *Buffalo Law Review*, vol. 39 (1991). On the growing income divide, see Susan Schulman, "Area Reflects Growing Gap Between Rich and Poor," *The Buffalo News*, February 14, 1993.

181 "We want to make": Quoted in Esmonde, "Savor the Glow."

181 the wood-paneled office: Thomas J. Dolan and Susan Schulman, "Office Sheds Remnants of Griffin; City Hall Prepared for Incoming Mayor," *The Buffalo News*, January 1, 1994.

181 "Abortion Kills Children" sign: Robert J. McCarthy, "Likelihood of Pro-Choice Mayor Points to New Era at City Hall," *The Buffalo News*, August 8, 1993.

181 "I've never been this afraid": Gene Warner, "Killing of Doctor at Abortion Clinic Spurs Drive for Tougher Laws," *The Buffalo News*, March 20, 1993.

181 "I've just shot": "Clinic Doctor Killed During Abortion Protest," *St. Petersburg (Fla.) Times*, March 11, 1993.

182 "great fits of violence": William Booth, "At Abortion Clinic, a Collision of Causes," *The Washington Post*, March 12, 1993.

182 claiming to have been inspired: Charles M. Sennott and Matthew Brelis, "Religious Fervor Fueled John Salvi's Rising Rage," *The Boston Globe*, January 8, 1995.

182 "I believe that abortion": Warner, "Killing of Doctor at Abortion Clinic."

183 "a birthday gift": Dallas A. Blanchard and Terry J. Prewitt, *Religious Violence and Abortion: The Gideon Project* (Gainesville: University Press of Florida, 1993), x. Statistics on bombing also in preface, x.

184 "solitary worldview" and other quotes: Blanchard and Prewitt, *Religious Violence and Abortion*, 210; "dualists," 208.

184 "This is a manual": All quoted material in this paragraph is from the Army of God Manual, 3rd edition.

185 In August 1993: Details in James Risen and Judy Thomas, *Wrath of Angels: The American Abortion War* (New York: Basic Books, 1998), 354–57.

186 "While we grieve": Quoted in ibid., 344.

187 "The members of the local": Barnett A. Slepian, "Free to Speak, Pro-Lifers Still Bear Responsibility," *The Buffalo News*, August 13, 1994.
188 It turns out that: Mark Juergensmeyer, *Terror in the Mind of God: The Global Rise of Religious Violence* (Berkeley: University of California Press, 2000), 47.
189 "According to Jewish law": John Kifner, "Zeal of Rabin's Assassin Linked to Rabbis of the Religious Right," *The New York Times*, November 12, 1995.
190 "minister of the Gospel": Christopher Martinez, "The Journey from Minister to Murderer," *The Tampa Tribune*, May 13, 1995.
190 In the mid-1980s: Robert Friedman, *Zealots for Zion: Inside Israel's West Bank Settlement Movement* (New York: Random House, 1992).
190 "I deliver to you": Quoted in Jessica Stern, *Terror in the Name of God: Why Religious Militants Kill* (New York: HarperCollins, 2003), 96, 102.
191 "The difference is between right and wrong": Quoted in Michael Beebe, "National Groups Rap City Action at Protests," *The Buffalo News*, November 5, 1998.
191 "Religious terrorism arises": Stern, *Terror in the Name of God*, on page before the introduction (it is not numbered).
193 "We have before us": Jerry Zremski, "High Court Voids Part of Order on Buffer Zones," *The Buffalo News*, February 19, 1997.
194 "It's like AIDS": Jodi Wolgren, "FBI Gets Tape of '93 Protest at Buffalo Abortion Clinic," *The Buffalo News*, November 17, 1998.

Chapter 12

196 "Safest Cities": "Off Main Street," *The Buffalo News*, December 8, 1996.
196 Amherst even had: Details can be found in Linda Levine, "A Waterfront University?" *Western New York Heritage*, winter 2002, 50–58. The architect Robert Coles, who was instrumental in pushing for an urban campus, provided me with other documents, including a proclamation from then-mayor Sedita supporting a waterfront campus and articles dating back to the 1960s in *The Spectrum*, UB's campus paper.
197 Between 1960 and 1990: Susan Schulman and Jerry Zremski, "Sprawl Causing Crisis in Buffalo Region, Urban Expert Says," *The Buffalo News*, June 4, 1997. The source for the statistics on sprawl is David Rusk, an urban policy expert.
198 "Wacky car": Transcript of stipulation of facts in trial, *The People of the State of New York v. James C. Kopp*, 41. The importance of Dorn's notation is dramatized in Jon Wells, "The Big Break: Sniper, the True Story of James Kopp," *The Hamilton Spectator*, May 8, 2004.
199 Eric Rudolph: Details in Tom Regan, "Eric Rudolph—'American Terrorist,'" *The Christian Science Monitor*, online edition, April 15, 2005.
199 one of more than fifty: Based on statistics provided to the author by the National Abortion Federation, listing every arson and bombing in the country.
200 James C. Kopp: My account of Kopp's background draws on David Samuels, "The Making of a Fugitive," *The New York Times Magazine*, March 21, 1999; John Kifner, "Religious Searching Leads to the Anti-Abortion Movement," *The New York Times*, March 30, 2001; and James Risen, "Tracing the Path of a Hard-Line Foe of Abortion," *The New York Times*, November 6, 1998.

200 The black Chevrolet: Details in this paragraph are drawn from the transcript of the stipulation of facts in *The People of the State of New York v. James C. Kopp*, 58, 39.

205 a series of packages: Janice L. Habuda and Gene Warner, "Abortion Package May Aid Police Hunt," *The Buffalo News*, February 5, 1999.

207 "Lynne, I think they've shot me": Gene Warner, "'Replaying the Nightmare': An Interview with Lynne Slepian," *The Buffalo News*, October 29, 1998.

208 people gathered for a vigil: Susan Schulman, "250 Gathered at Vigil for Slepian Vow to Fight to Keep Abortion Legal," *The Buffalo News*, October 25, 1998.

208 "No matter where": "Clinton Outraged by Slaying of Abortion Provider," *The Buffalo News*, October 25, 1998.

208 "I have no doubt": Jerry Zremski, "Anti-Abortion Fringe Considers Doctor's Coldblooded Killing Justifiable," October 26, 1998.

208 "I think God has chosen": Dan Herbeck, "'Spring of Life Reunion' Planned Here in April," *The Buffalo News*, November 1, 1998.

209 "My message to you": Gene Warner, "Slepian Widow Sends Flowers Back, Calls Rev. Schenck a 'Hypocrite,'" *The Buffalo News*, November 2, 1998.

209 "It'd be nice": Donn Esmonde, "Welcome Mat Gone for April Gathering of Pro-life Activists," *The Buffalo News*, November 13, 1998.

Chapter 13

210 "I know you're innocent": Matt Gryta, "Pro-Life Activist Says She Got Kopp Out of U.S.," *The Buffalo News*, February 8, 2003.

211 Shy, soft-spoken: See, for example, John F. Bonfatti, "Unassuming Youth Gave No Hint of Kopp Evolution into Pro-life Extremist," *The Buffalo News*, May 7, 1999.

215 "like a rag doll": Kopp described the incident in his statement at his May 19, 2003, sentencing, detailed in chapter 15. Also see his confession to *The Buffalo News*: Lou Michel and Dan Herbeck, "Kopp Confesses," *The Buffalo News*, November 20, 2002.

215 "My jury and/or judge": Quoted in David Samuels, "The Making of a Fugitive," *The New York Times Magazine*, March 21, 1999.

218 On Leon Czolgosz's problems with women, see Jeffrey W. Seibert, *"I Have Done MY Duty": The Complete Story of the Assassination of President McKinley* (Bowie, Md.: Heritage Books, 2002), 87.

218 In July 1997: Details about the gun and the false driver's license are drawn from the transcript of the stipulation of facts in *The People of the State of New York v. James C. Kopp*, 53, 44. Some of these details also appear in Michael Beebe, "Details Revealed in Slepian Killing," *The Buffalo News*, April 4, 2001.

219 a minuscule, distracted army: For a less than sympathetic take on the event, see Donn Esmonde, "Abortion Debate Has Moved Beyond Dueling Clinic Chants," *The Buffalo News*, April 22, 1999.

221 "a half-lighted ghetto": Jack Hitt, "Who Will Do Abortions Here?" *The New York Times Magazine*, January 18, 1998.

222 the exhaustive search: By far the most detailed reconstruction of Kopp's life as a fugitive and eventual capture appears in Jon Wells's series of articles in *The*

Hamilton (Ontario) *Spectator,* "Sniper: The True Story of James Kopp," in particular chapters 22–29, which ran from May 20 to May 29, 2004.

223   the murder weapon, which was found: Jerry Zremski, "Slepian Murder Weapon Confounds Many in Kopp Case," *The Buffalo News,* July 8, 2002.

224   "I'm appalled": Jerry Zremski, "Kopp Fights Extradition, Declares Innocence," *The Buffalo News,* June 7, 2001.

224   "I didn't do this": This and other quotations appear in the transcript of the sentence hearing, *The People of the State of New York v. James C. Kopp,* May 9, 2003, 28, 31–32.

224   "We all know that Jim": Dan Herbeck and Lou Michel, "Kopp Case Lacks Hard Evidence, but Both Sides Seem Confident," *The Buffalo News,* July 7, 2002.

224   "It could have been": Jerry Zremski, "Kopp Fights Extradition."

Chapter 14

225   "Brother, you better believe": Transcript of sentence hearing, *The People of the State of New York v. James C. Kopp,* May 9, 2003, 34.

225   "I would be afraid": Nicole Peradotto, "Larger Than Life: Why Paul Cambria, Lawyer to the Famous, Can't Stop Proving Himself," *The Buffalo News,* June 22, 1997.

227   One such cell: Jerry Zremski, "Security at What Price?" *The Buffalo News,* September 5, 2003. The case of the Lackawanna Six was the subject of a PBS *Frontline* episode, "Chasing the Sleeper Cell," October 16, 2003.

228   "Army of God": William Booth, "Bioterror Takes on Abortion Face," *The Washington Post,* October 21, 2001.

228   "The issue that is": Dan Herbeck, "'All About Abortion,'" *The Buffalo News,* November 4, 2002.

228   more surprising twist: Lou Michel and Dan Herbeck, "Kopp Confesses," *The Buffalo News,* November 20, 2002.

230   Michael Bray: Details of Bray's background, including the fact that he briefly dated a future talk-show hostess named Kathie Lee Gifford, appear in James Risen and Judy Thomas, *Wrath of Angels: The American Abortion War* (New York: Basic Books, 1998), 78–100.

230   "recapture every institution": Quoted in Mark Juergensmeyer, *Terror in the Mind of God: The Global Rise of Religious Violence* (Berkeley: University of California Press, 2000), 28.

230   For Gary North's letter to Paul Hill, see Gary North, "Letter to Paul Hill," September 29, 1994, at http://www.reformed.org/social/let_2_paul_hill.html.

231   "very, very carefully": Michel and Herbeck, "Kopp Confesses."

231   "crazy ricochet": This and all other quotes here taken from court transcript of trial, *The People of the State of New York v. James C. Kopp,* March 17, 2003.

231   "I have concluded": Verdict, County Court of the State of New York, County of Erie, Criminal Term, *The People of the State of New York v. James C. Kopp,* before Honorable Judge Michael L. D'Amico.

233   "They have attacked my pastor": *Sonya Live,* CNN, April 21, 1992, transcript #36–1.

234   "When I was a leader": Jerry Reiter, *Live from the Gates of Hell* (Buffalo, N.Y.: Prometheus Books, 2000), 116.

234 "were the logical next steps": Ibid.
234 "The Schencks and their allies": Ibid., 245.
235 "You, Dr. Slepian": See Paul Schenck, with Robert L. Schenck, *The Extermina-tion of Christianity* (Lafayette: Huntington House Publishers, 1993), 235.
237 The most surprising signatory: Gene Warner, "Rev. Schenck Joins Common-Ground Camp on Abortion," *The Buffalo News*, March 23, 1999.
237 "I just realized": David Montgomery, "The Unlikely Extremist," *The Buffalo News*, March 1, 1992.
239 a Pro-Life Alliance: See Gene Warner, "Local Activist Seeks to Forge Pro-Life Alliance for Non-Violence," *The Buffalo News*, December 31, 1994.

Chapter 15

241 abortion remained: The statistics in this paragraph are from "Induced Abortion in the United States," May 18, 2005, the Alan Guttmacher Institute. Available at http://wwww.agi-usa/pubs/fb_induced_abortion.html.
244 38.7 percent: Jay Rey, "City Ranks 6th-Highest Nationally in Child Poverty," *The Buffalo News*, June 7, 2002.
244 57 percent: Jay Rey, "City Leads in Poverty of Hispanic Children," *The Buffalo News*, May 24, 2003.
244 14,000 fewer births: William Saletan, *Bearing Right: How Conservatives Won the Abortion War* (Berkeley: University of California Press, 2003), 268.
244 "That's a very interesting": Eric Zorn, "Pro-Lifers Unwilling to Take Their Be-liefs to Logical Conclusion," *Chicago Tribune*, April 2, 1996.
247 For a superb discussion of the origins and impact of the Partial-Birth Abortion Ban Act, see Cynthia Gorney, "Gambling with Abortion," *Harpers* magazine, November 2004.
248 "the dismemberment": Quoted in William Saletan, "Leave No Embryo Behind: The Coming War Over In Vitro Fertilization," *Slate*, June 3, 2005, http://slate.msn.com/id/2120222/.
248 "Mr. Bush values": Nicholas D. Kristof, "Uncover Your Eyes," *The New York Times*, June 7, 2005.
248 racially segregated: On racial segregation in Buffalo, see Douglas S. Massey, "The Race Case," *The American Prospect*, March 2003, 22. Massey, a sociologist, is generally regarded as the foremost expert on racial segregation in America.
248 the half billion dollars: James Heaney, "The Half-Billion-Dollar Bust," *The Buffalo News*, November 14, 2004.
249 Since 1992: These figures are drawn from "Induced Abortion in the United States."
250 one study: R. K. Jones, J. E. Darroch, and S. K. Henshaw, "Contraceptive Use Among U.S. Women Having Abortions in 2000–2001," *Perspectives on Sexual and Reproductive Health*, vol. 34, no. 6 (2002), 294–303. It is cited in "Induced Abortion in the United States." See footnotes 11 and 15.
250 30 percent: The statistic on the decline in the abortion rate comes from the New York State Health Department, Bureau of Biometrics. It was provided to the au-thor by the Erie County Health Department. Statistics on the overall decline in the abortion rate in America come from "Induced Abortion in the United States."

250   "beefed-up health curriculums": Holly Auer, "Blunt Sex-Ed Effort Cuts Teen Pregnancy," *The Buffalo News*, May 20, 2002.

250   This may change: See "Sex Education: Needs, Programs and Policies," the Alan Guttmacher Institute, April 2004, prepared by Cynthia Dailard. A concurring view is presented in Jonathan D. Klein and the Committee on Adolescence, "Adolescent Pregnancy: Current Trends and Issues," *Pediatrics*, vol. 116, no. 1 (July 2005), 281–86.

250   "We have doubled our security": Eric Schaff, "Kopp Will Not Deter Abortion Doctors," *The Buffalo News*, December 3, 2002.

251   "Good morning, Judge": This and all other quotations in the section that follows are drawn from Kopp's statement in court on May 9, 2003: transcript of sentence, *The People of the State of New York v: James C. Kopp.*

257   "In the long run of history": James M. Washington, ed., *A Testament of Hope: The Essential Writings and Speeches of Martin Luther King, Jr.* (New York: HarperCollins, 1986), 45.

Acknowledgments

I would like to thank the many people who took time out of their busy schedules to share their recollections and insights with me. I am particularly grateful to those individuals who entrusted me to tell their personal stories on a subject that is by nature intensely private and highly charged. Many people also shared personal files containing news clips, fliers, and other materials that I would not otherwise have come across.

Thanks to David Valenzuela, library director at *The Buffalo News*, and Andy Bailey, news researcher, for helping me navigate my way through the paper's archives. Thanks also to the librarians and staff members at the Buffalo and Erie County Public Library, whose downtown branch has an excellent collection of materials on local history; to the Erie County Historical Society, where I found useful files on Buffalo's labor history; and to the University of Buffalo, which houses the archives of the Pro-Choice Network of western New York.

I am enormously grateful to my editor at Henry Holt, Vanessa Mobley, who saw this project through from start to finish and whose faith in its promise never wavered. In addition to being a brilliant editor, Vanessa served as a friend and ally throughout, providing encouragement, guidance, and critical feedback at exactly the right times. Her razor eye, enthusiasm for the subject, and attention to language, style, and narrative structure improved the book immeasurably and confirmed my initial hunch that she was the ideal editor for it. Thanks as well to Sadie Stein, who provided timely assistance at many stages, to Jolanta Benal for her excellent copyediting, to Kate Pruss, for her help with publicity, to David Lindrath for the map of Buffalo, and to the many people at Holt who put time and energy into turning my manuscript into a book. Special thanks also to John Sterling, Holt's publisher, who likewise saw promise in this idea and placed his faith in me to execute it.

Many thanks to my agent, Sarah Chalfant, at the Wylie Agency, for her generous assistance and support. Sarah's advice on how to steer the book to completion and her guidance at various junctures were invaluable. Thanks also to Edward Orloff at the Wylie Agency, who fielded many questions with aplomb and was always quick to answer an e-mail or a call. At the start of this project, I had a different agent, Susan Reed, who encouraged me to pursue this idea. I am extremely grateful to her and to Ellen Chesler, who answered a phone call many years ago from someone she had never met and put the two of us in touch. I also want to thank P. J. Mark, who provided much support and encouragement along the way.

Many thanks to a number of editors who have supported my work as a journalist through the years or encouraged me to write for their publications, in particular Katrina vanden Heuvel, Alex Star, Betsy Reed, Robert Kuttner, Monica Bauerlein, Daniel Zalewski, and Jack Beatty. I also want to thank two very special teachers who had a major impact on my life: the late William G. McLoughlin, who inspired my love of history, and Richard Stratton, who taught me how to write.

Many thanks to Kathryn Lewis, a superb research assistant who combed over every chapter of the book, saving me from many errors, and in addition offered numerous helpful editorial suggestions. Kathryn also provided a sympathetic ear whenever I called with a question, and was a calming presence as deadlines approached. Thanks, as well, to Jonathan Shainan, Liliana Segura, and Bianca Sepulveda, all of whom provided additional research assistance.

I want to thank Cynthia Gorney, who graciously agreed to read a draft of the manuscript and offered much helpful feedback. Valuable advice also came from Gene Warner, Mark Goldman, Carole Joffe, Kristin Luker, Max Blumenthal, and Jon Wells.

I am extremely grateful to the many friends and colleagues who offered advice and encouragement during the many years I was working on this book: Chase Madar, Johnny Temple, Kara Gilmour, Adam Haslett, Norman Kelley, Roane Carey, Scott Sherman, Eric Klinenberg, Ta-Nehisi Coates, Brendan Koerner, Nick Thompson, Bill Berkeley, Gara La Marche, Nathan Fox, Anne Feinsilber, Toby Beach, Jonathan Lipton, Gillian Lipton, Ruth Baldwin, Mireille Abelin, and Sarah Shatz. Thanks as well to the entire staff at the Nation Institute, which served as a second office for some time, and to Loretta Roome and Eric Feinstein, who provided a room in which to write.

I owe a special thanks to several dear friends who have served for years as an invaluable support network and with whom I have had the pleasure to share the joys (and occasional frustrations) of being a writer: Sasha Abramsky, Steve Dudley, David Gartner, Laura Secor, and Adam Shatz. You are comrades in the truest sense, as fine a circle of friends and colleagues as I could hope to have, and I am extremely lucky to know you all. I also want to thank three people who are part of my extended family and without whom growing up in Buffalo would have been incomparably less enriching and fun: Elizabeth Golan, Benjamin Yost, and Peter Yost, my best friend, surrogate brother, and fellow sufferer (along with Ben) in the fraternity of lifelong Bills fans.

My deepest thanks of all goes to Jennifer Washburn, without whose love and support this book could never have been written. Jennifer read the entire manuscript, several sections more than once. Her wise suggestions are reflected in every chapter. Beyond this, she kept me believing in the importance of this story, and in my ability to tell it, at times when I lost sight of these things myself.

Finally, I want to thank the members of my family, in particular my cousin Lior Eshdat, my aunt Talma, my cousin Sarit, my sister Sharon, and above all my parents, Carla and Shalom. As they know, I would not have gone forward without their collective encouragement, nor could I have told this story without their trust. They never stopped me from asking a question or pursuing a line of thought, even as I warned them that the final product would reflect my interpretation of events, not theirs. For their patience, their support, their generosity, and above all for their love, I am forever grateful.

Index

Entries in *italics* refer to illustrations.